MW00358983

CONTENTS

Air Fryer Guide

It's All Hot Air!

The big day has arrived! You finally have your hands on your shiny new Air Fryer. But you're probably wondering what it is and how to get set up. No worries, this chapter is designed with beginners in mind. First, let's begin by talking about the Air Fryer in general. Simply put, an Air Fryer is a countertop convection oven that cooks food with hot air. This is great because it means you can cook food affordably, quickly and easily! I personally think the term "air fryer" is misleading because people get confused by the old-fashioned air fryer that your grandma might have in her pantry. The big difference, however, between these two types of fryer is that the modern air fryer does not require huge amounts of oil because it cooks food with only hot air—nothing else is required! So, hopefully you have learned that the Air Fryer cooks food by circulating hot air around using a convection mechanism. Enough of the interesting science, for now.

Did you forget to prepare something for dinner? No problem—the Air Fryer can cook such lovely delicious food in just moments! Such scrumptious food includes sizzling burgers and dry crispy fries– super affordable, quick & easy too! What's more? When your fryer finishes cooking, the latent heat inside keeps your food warm. I can confidently say that my air fryer has changed the way I cook because I now spend less time in the kitchen and more time doing the things I enjoy, like spending precious time with family and walking my dogs. In fact, even my weekly shop at my local grocery store is super cheap and easy. I fill my grocery basket to the brim with all kinds of locally sourced, affordable and easy to find ingredients which I whack into my Air Fryer, allowing me to whip up amazing meals for my family to enjoy.

Every week, I love frying a batch of burgers for a quick 'on-the-go' lunch after I take my grandchildren to school. What's great is the temperature control on my Air Fryer dial because it means I can have it all cooked for when I return home. In fact, I whack all manner of things in the frying basket on a low temperature because my Fryer keeps it warm for hours. This appliance has revolutionized how I cook, and I have even retired my once beloved Instant Pot back to the pantry.

Air Fryer Safety

You, like most people, are probably wondering why I would want an Air Fryer? I mean, aren't they those machines that explode oil on the countertop? Well, that might have been the case for old-fashioned fryers, but this is not one of those! Rest assured, a modern Air Fryer comes equipped with loads of safety features. For example, it is physically impossible to to open the frying basket without pressing the lock button first, either naturally or manually—so burning hazards are minimized! This is great to know if you have small children around the house. Indeed, modern day Air Fryers are quiet, safe and easy to use. In fact, the US government recognizes their safety and so they even have 10 UL Certified proven safety mechanisms to prevent most issues. So, Air Fryers are a very safe appliance to have around your kitchen provided, of course, you use your common sense. Importantly, mop up any water spillages close to your fryer and keep it away from children, pets and vulnerable people at all times. For your safety, I have compiled a list of steps below that you should follow when using your Air Fryer.

1 Your Air Fryer gets hot. Do not touch any of its surfaces when its cooking. When cooking is done, use oven mitts or potholders to touch it and wait for it to cool down.

2 Avoid immersing the cord, plug or the Air Fryer unit in water or other liquid due to electric shocks.

3 Persons with reduced physical, sensory or mental capabilities, or lack of experience and knowledge, should not use your Air Fryer without supervision.

4 Always keep children away from your Air Fryer.

5 Avoid using your Air Fryer if it has a damaged plug or power cord.

6 Avoid using your Air Fryer outdoors due to adverse weather conditions.

7 Avoid letting the cord hang over the edge of the table or countertop, especially if you have pets around the house.

8 Avoid placing your Air Fryer near hot gas or electric burner.

9 Ensure that both the timer dial and temperature dial are OFF when disconnecting your Air Fryer from the power outlet.

10 Ensure that the frying basket is locked into position when turning on your Air Fryer.

11 Ensure that the frying basket drawer is fully closed, and the handle locked securely in the drawer when using your Air Fryer.

12 Carefully handle your Air Fryer after frying because the frying basket and the food inside of it are extremely hot.

Control Dials

Now that you've got to know more about your Air Fryer, I have included a picture below that shows you what a typical Air Fryer looks like and all its different parts. The Air Fryer in this picture is a standard model you might find online or in your department store. It is by no means typical of what your Air Fryer might look like. Rather, it is intended to give you a general idea of the different parts to your Air Fryer.

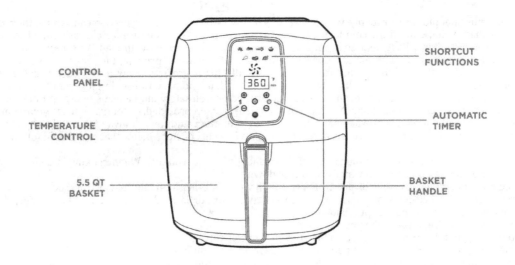

CONTROL PANEL

SHORTCUT FUNCTIONS

TEMPERATURE CONTROL

AUTOMATIC TIMER

5.5 QT BASKET

BASKET HANDLE

1 The Temperature Control Dial allows you to select frying temperatures from 175°F to 400°F. Temperatures can be adjusted at any time before or during the cooking period.

2 The Control Panel shows the HEAT ON light when cooking temperature is reached. It also shows the Red POWER light, which will turn on when you ise your Fryer. The shortcut functions are specifically designed for certain kinds of food, like poultry and fish, and you can select these if you think they are a better option than manually setting the frying temperature.

3 The Automatic Timer button allows you to select how long your food will cook for and will automatically count down during the cooking period. Typically, one beep sounds when frying time has reached 0 minutes. Most Air Fryers turn OFF automatically, but you should always check and turn both the temperature control dial and the timer dial to 0 (OFF).

Air Fryer Prep

So, now that you know a little more about your Air Fryer, it is time to get it prepped and ready for frying. I have complied a list of steps below which you should follow to avoid damaging your Air Fryer or causing yourself injury.

1 So, your Air Fryer is all boxed up in front of you. The first thing you should do is to assess the situation. What does your box look like? How big is it?

2 Your Air Fryer will come with warning cards and warning labels. Read these carefully.

3 Now carefully take your Air Fryer out of its box and remove all the warning stickers/cards on it.

4 Approach the front of your Air Fryer and firmly grip the frying basket handle to open the frying basket drawer. Remove the frying basket from your Air Fryer and place it on a flat, clean countertop.

5 Ensure that there is no packaging of any kind under and around the frying basket drawer.

6 Wash the frying basket and drawer in hot, soapy water. Dry all parts thoroughly with a kitchen towel.

7 **WARNING**: DO NOT immerse the main Air Fryer unit in water.

8 Lock frying basket into the drawer—you should hear a seal/click when it is locked securely in place.

Your First Meal

Are you feeling hungry? Well, I am! Now that you have prepped your Air Fryer, it is time to start cooking amazing recipes. The steps below will guide you to cook your first meal.

1 Place your Air Fryer on a kitchen countertop next to a power outlet.

2 Grip the frying basket handle and remove the frying basket. Carefully place it on a flat countertop.

3 Choose your recipe and toss in your food/ingredients into the frying basket. For proper cooking, do not overfill the basket.

4 Put the frying basket back into your Air Fryer, making sure you hear a nice audible click/lock sound.

5 Plug your Air Fryer into the nearest power outlet.

6 Following your recipe instructions, choose an air frying temperature between 175°F to 400°F.

7 Following your recipe instructions, choose a cooking time using the temperature control dial. Your Air Fryer may illuminate when this cooking temperature is reached. **Optional:** Halfway through cooking, you might want to open the frying basket and give it a good shake to ensure even, consistent cooking.

8 When cooking is done, you Air Fryer may make a beeping noise. Wait for it to cool down.

9 Using oven mitts, open the drawer and shake the frying basket vigorously to see if your food is cooked properly.

10 If satisfied, remove the frying basket from your Air Fryer and place it on a flat countertop.

11 Using kitchen utensils, scoop/take out the food from the frying basket and place it onto a plate.

12 Unplug your Air Fryer when finished. You can also cover it using a range of jazzy Air Fryer covers available online at Amazon.

Helpful Hints

Are you full up after that amazing first meal? I certainly am. I have put together some steps below which you can follow when cooking your other meals.

1 I have found over the years that a dash of olive oil or vegetable oil works well for air frying because it gives the food a tasty golden brown appearance. Of course, using oil is entirely optional as your Air Fryer is designed to cook without it. You should follow your recipe instructions for more information on this.

2 Never overfill the frying basket with food because doing so results in poorly and unevenly cooked food. As a rule, I never go over the 2/3 mark when I'm filling the basket.

3 For the best cooking results, certain types of foods (i.e. vegetables) need to be shaken vigorously or turned over halfway through cooking. See your recipe for more information on this.

4 Sometimes smoke might happen and set off your fire alarm when you're cooking high fat foods like chicken wings, sausages and other meats. To avoid this, you can empty your frying basket of oil halfway through the cooking period (it is the excess oil that causes the smoke!)

5 Spray your food with oil and pat it dry before cooking to ensure browning—works well with fish and chicken recipes.

6 Your Air Fryer can reheat previously cooked/refrigerated food. Set the temperature to 300ºF for up to 10 minutes. Ensure the food is piping hot all the way through to avoid food poisoning.

Air Fryer Cleaning

So, you've been cooking with your Air Fryer for some time now and have noticed that it needs a good cleaning. I have put together 10 steps you should follow to clean your Air Fryer.

1 The frying basket may be coasted in grease from repeated and frequent use. Smoking can occur when bits of burnt food get recooked many times. So, you should get into the habit of cleaning your frying basket after every use.

2 The pan, basket and the inside of the appliance have a non-stick coating, so you should avoid using abrasive materials to clean them.

3 Wipe the outside of the appliance with a damp kitchen towel.

4 Clean the frying basket with hot water, some washing-up liquid and a nonabrasive sponge. You can use a degreasing agent to remove grease and grime. Hint: The frying basket is dishwasher-proof.

5 Clean the inside of your Air Fryer (after you have taken out the frying basket) with warm water and a non-abrasive sponge.

6 Clean the heating element with a cleaning brush to remove any food residues.

7 Push the cord into the cord storage compartment. Fix the cord by inserting it into the cord fixing slot.

8 When not in use, cover your Fryer with a jazzy cover to avoid dust accumulation.

Air Fryer Fats

Fats are integral to Air Frying. In addition to consuming high proportions of fats, it is vital that you make sure you are consuming the right varieties. Let's cut through all the confusion surrounding the good and bad kinds of fat and discuss which fats you should be aiming to integrate into your frying.

Good Fats

We divide the 'good fats' into four distinct categories:

1 Saturated fats
2 Monounsaturated fatty acids (MUFAs)
3 Polyunsaturated fatty acids (PUFAs)
4 Trans fats (naturally occurring)

All fats constitute a combination of the above varieties but are named according to the kind that is most dominant in their makeup. We will now take a look at each type of fat and consider which ones you should be including as part of your frying recipes. This way, you will be able to make quick and informed decisions as to how best to fuel your mind and body.

Saturated Fats

Saturated fats get a bad rep – many of us have been advised to avoid them because of the potential harmful effects they can have on our heart health. However, recent research has shown that there is no strong correlation between saturated fats and heart disease. After all, saturated fats have been a major component of the human diet for millennia. There are in fact numerous ways in which saturated fats can be advantageous to us. Some foods with saturated fats in them contain medium-chain triglycerides (MCTs), particularly coconut oil, butter and palm oil. MCTs are easily digestible and are converted to energy in the liver. As a result, they are highly beneficial to those who want to lose weight or improve their performance during physical activity.

Here are some further benefits:

- Boosted immune system.
- Improved HDL-to-LDL cholesterol ratio.
- Improved bone density.
- Increased levels of HDL cholesterol to remove LDL from the arteries.
- Increased production of important hormones like cortisol and testosterone.

Foods which are rich in saturated fats include:

- Butter
- Cocoa butter
- Coconut oil
- Cream
- Eggs
- Lard
- Palm oil
- Red meat

Monounsaturated Fats

Monounsaturated fatty acids (MUFAs) differ from saturated fats in that they are pretty much universally embraced as a 'good' kind of fat. Numerous studies have revealed a link between MUFAs and certain positive outcomes like insulin resistance and good cholesterol. Other health benefits include:

- Lower blood pressure
- Decreased risk of developing heart disease
- Decrease in belly fat

The best sources of MUFAs are:

- Avocados and avocado oil
- Extra virgin olive oil
- Lard and bacon fat
- Macadamia nut oil

Polyunsaturated Fats

How you prepare foods containing polyunsaturated fatty acids (PUFAs) is critical. When PUFAs are subjected to heat, they can create free radicals (uncharged molecules) which cause inflammation and have even been linked to cancer and heart disease. This means that for the most part PUFAs should be eaten cold, and never cooked.

You can get PUFAs from processed oils and other heart-friendly sources. The right kinds of PUFAs have immense health benefits when adopted into a balanced diet. Some such fats are Omega 3 and Omega 6, which are the primary components of many superfoods such as salmon and flaxseed.

Integrating PUFAs into your diet is therefore crucial. An ideal ratio of Omega 3 to Omega 6 stands at around 1:1 – however, most Westerners consume a ratio of 1:30! A good balance between Omega 3 and Omega 6 greatly decreases the risk of developing the following:

- Autoimmune disorders and other inflammatory diseases
- Heart disease
- Stroke
- Depression and ADHD

PUFA-rich foods include:

- Avocado oil
- Chia seeds
- Extra virgin olive oil
- Flaxseeds and flaxseed oil
- Sesame oil
- Walnuts

Trans Fats

You might double-take at seeing trans fats listed as 'good' fats, but they do in fact have a right to be termed as such. Though most trans fats are indeed unhealthy, one particular naturally occurring variety is decidedly beneficial: vaccenic acid. Vaccenic acid can be absorbed from grass-fed meats and dairy products.

The potential health benefits of this type of trans fat include:

- Lower risk of developing diabetes and obesity
- Lower risk of developing heart disease
- Protection against cancer

The best sources of healthy and natural trans fats are:

- Butter
- Yogurt
- Grass-fed animal products

Bad Fats

Many people are drawn to the frying because it permits you to eat foods that, being high in fat, are satisfying and delicious. However, the idea that frying cooks can consume all the fat they want is a common misconception. On the contrary, there are several 'bad fats' which you should take the utmost care to avoid if you wish to achieve the best possible results. Remember, the quality of the food you eat should always be a number-one priority.

Processed Trans and Polyunsaturated Fats: You may be familiar with these kinds of fats, as they are present in many of the sweet and snack foods many of us enjoy. You may also already know that they are extremely damaging to your physical well-being. Artificial trans fats are the product of the processing of polyunsaturated fats. For this reason, you must try to consume only unprocessed PUFAs that have not been heated or modified in any way.

Trans fats are particularly harmful as they may lead to:

- An increased risk of cancer
- An increased risk of heart disease
- Inflammatory health issues
- A decrease in HDL cholesterol and an increase of LDL cholesterol

Here are some common sources of trans fats which you should aim to cut from your diet:

- Hydrogenated and partially hydrogenated oils that are in processed products like cookies, crackers, margarine, and fast food.
- Processed vegetable oils like cottonseed, sunflower, safflower, soybean, and canola oil.

Air Fryer Success

The Air Fryer doesn't come without its stumbling blocks, so here are some essential tips for staying on track as you progress further down the frying road..

- **Hydration:** As always, we should stress the importance of keeping yourself hydrated. Specifically, you should aim to drink at least 32 ounces of water within the first hour after waking up in the morning, and another 32-48 ounces before midday. Before the day ends, you should strive to drink at least half your body weight in water – ideally, close to your entire body weight.
- **Practice intermittent fasting:** Before jumping straight in, steadily reduce your carb intake in the days leading up to your fast days. Fast days should be divided into two phases:
- **Building phase**: The period of time between your first and last meal.

- **Cleaning phase:** The period of time between your last and first meal. To start, try a cleaning phase of between 12 and 16 hours and a building phase of between 8 and 12 hours. As your body adjusts to the change, you will find yourself in a position to tackle a 4-6-hour building time and an 18-20-hour cleaning phase.
- **Consume salt:** Too much sodium is generally deemed as unhealthy. However, a low-carb diet necessitates a high salt intake, as this type of regimen reduces your insulin levels and flushes out higher amounts of sodium from your kidneys. As a result, your sodium/potassium ratio is disrupted. Here are some tips to counteract this change:
- Add a quarter teaspoon of pink salt to every glass of water you drink.
- Incorporate kelp, nori or dulse into your meals.
- Season your food with generous helpings of pink salt.
- Snack on pumpkin seeds or macadamia nuts.
- Drink organic broth intermittently through the day.
- Eat cucumber and celery, both of which contain natural sodium.
- **Exercise regularly:** Daily rigorous exercise can help activate glucose molecules called GLUT-4 which are needed to return glucose to fat and muscle tissues. Additionally, it can double the amount of protein present in both the liver and the muscles.
- **Watch how much protein you eat:** Protein is integral to Air Fryer cooking but maintaining a proper balance is a must. If you eat too many protein-rich foods, you will end up converting the amino acids into glucose (through a process called gluconeogenesis). In the initial stages of your frying, vary the amounts of protein you consume in order to get a feel of how much is too much.
- **Pick your carbs wisely:** The few carb-rich foods you do consume should be selected very carefully. It is best to stick to starchy veggies and fruits like berries, apples, lemons, and oranges. For a quick morning hit, blend them into a healthy green smoothie.
- **Take MCT oil:** High-quality MCTs are extremely effective in replenishing the energy levels you deplete through the day. MCT oil can be used for cooking, as well as added to beverages like coffee, tea, smoothies, protein shakes, and so on.
- **Minimize your stress:** Stress is a major factor in decreased energy levels, so constant stress may serve as a threat to your cooking success. If you find yourself especially prone to stress at the moment, it may be wise to avoid dieting until you're in a better position to deal with the blow to your energy levels.
- **Improve the quality of your sleep:** Sleep is essential for managing stress, among other things. Make sure your bedroom is conducive to a good night's rest. This means sleeping in a comfortable bed, in a darkened room no warmer than 70 degrees. Most adults function best on 7 to 9 hours of sleep every night, though a particularly stressful lifestyle may require even longer.
- **Eat ghee:** Ghee works well as a butter substitute, as it can be used in more or less all the same ways and is exponentially healthier. Try frying meat or vegetables in it for a high-fat, healthy meal.
- **Seek out Omega 3s:** If you find it hard to integrate Omega-3-rich foods into your diet, then you might consider taking supplements. You should make sure your Omega 3 intake matches your Omega 6s. Omega 3 is an extremely beneficial kind of fat, which is crucial to healthy frying.
- **Avoid alcohol:** It may be hard to kiss the booze goodbye, but it is well-attested that alcohol impedes weight loss. Stay focused on your goals and order a glass of tonic water at the bar instead.
- **Drink lemon water:** Lemon water is a tasty and refreshing alternative to tap water that has the added benefit of balancing your pH levels.
- **Avoid 'sugar-free' products:** These labels may sound appealing but the vast majority of products advertised as 'sugar-free' or 'light' contain more carbs than the original!
- **Buy a food scale:** Food scales are a great utensil to keep handy in your kitchen as they help you to accurately monitor what you are putting into your body. They are indispensable in tracking your carb and overall caloric intake. Invest in your success – get a high-quality, durable scale with a conversion button, automatic shutdown, tare function, and a removable plate.
- **Stay carb-savvy:** To tackle the inevitable carb cravings, it is a good idea to make yourself aware of the many alternatives that exist. When the urge to order a bucket of fried chicken or a box of pad Thai arises, fight back with these tasty and healthy substitutes:
- **Shirataki noodles** are made from yams and make a great low-carb alternative to pasta.
- **Cauliflower rice**, basically shredded cauliflower, mimics the texture and neutral taste of white or brown rice.
- **Spaghetti squash** can be cut into the shape of noodles with the aid of a spiralizer or a fork. It tastes great and amounts to less than half the carbs and calories of conventional noodles.
- **Heavy whipping cream** or **milk** go great in your coffee instead of regular creamer, which is rich in calories.
- **Low-carb bread and tortillas** are available for those who just can't seem to kick the bread addiction.
- **Protein powder** can satisfy your sweet tooth in a shake or smoothie. It comes in a wide variety of flavors and is easily incorporated into practically any meal. Plus, needless to say, its high protein content is an added benefit, offering an easy boost to your health.

BREAKFASTS

English Egg Breakfast
Prep + Cook Time: 25 minutes | Servings: 2

Ingredients:
2 cups flour
1 cup pumpkin puree
1 tbsp. oil
2 tbsp. vinegar
2 tsp baking powder
½ cup milk
2 eggs
1 tsp. baking soda
1 tbsp. sugar
1 tsp. cinnamon powder

Instructions:
1. Set your Air Fryer at 300°F to pre-heat.
2. Crack the eggs into a bowl and beat with a whisk. Combine with the milk, flour, baking powder, sugar, pumpkin purée, cinnamon powder, and baking soda, mixing well and adding more milk if necessary.
3. Grease the baking tray with oil. Add in the mixture and transfer into the Air Fryer. Cook for 10 minutes.

Pancakes
Prep + Cook Time: 15 minutes | Servings: 2

Ingredients:
2 tbsp coconut oil
1 tsp maple extract
2 tbsp cashew milk
2 eggs
2/3 oz/20g pork rinds

Instructions
1. Grind up the pork rinds until fine and mix with the rest of the ingredients, except the oil.
2. Add the oil to a skillet. Add a quarter-cup of the batter and fry until golden on each side. Continue adding the remaining batter.

Breakfast Sandwich
Prep + Cook Time: 10 minutes | Servings: 1

Ingredients
2 oz/60g cheddar cheese
1/6 oz/30g smoked ham
2 tbsp butter
4 eggs

Instructions
1. Fry all the eggs and sprinkle the pepper and salt on them.
2. Place an egg down as the sandwich base. Top with the ham and cheese and a drop or two of Tabasco.
3. Place the other egg on top and enjoy.

Egg Muffins
Prep + Cook Time: 30 minutes | Servings: 1

Ingredients
1 tbsp green pesto
oz/75g shredded cheese
oz/150g cooked bacon
1 scallion, chopped
eggs

Instructions
1. You should set your fryer to 350°F/175°C.
2. Place liners in a regular cupcake tin. This will help with easy removal and storage.
3. Beat the eggs with pepper, salt, and the pesto. Mix in the cheese.
4. Pour the eggs into the cupcake tin and top with the bacon and scallion.
5. Cook for 15-20 minutes, or until the egg is set.

Bacon & Eggs
Prep + Cook Time: 5 minutes | Servings: 1

Ingredients
Parsley
Cherry tomatoes
1/3 oz/150g bacon
eggs

Instructions
1. Fry up the bacon and put it to the side.
2. Scramble the eggs in the bacon grease, with some pepper and salt. If you want, scramble in some cherry tomatoes. Sprinkle with some parsley and enjoy.

Eggs on the Go
Prep + Cook Time: 10 minutes | Servings: 1

Ingredients
oz/110g bacon, cooked
Pepper
Salt
eggs

Instructions
1. You should set your fryer to 400°F/200°C.
2. Place liners in a regular cupcake tin. This will help with easy removal and storage.
3. Crack an egg into each of the cups and sprinkle some bacon onto each of them. Season with some pepper and salt.
4. Bake for 15 minutes, or until the eggs are set.

Cream Cheese Pancakes
Prep + Cook Time: 10 minutes | Servings: 1

Ingredients
2 oz cream cheese
2 eggs
½ tsp cinnamon
1 tbsp coconut flour
½ to 1 packet of Sugar

Instructions
1. Mix together all the ingredients until smooth.
2. Heat up a non-stick pan or skillet with butter or coconut oil on medium-high.
3. Make them as you would normal pancakes.
4. Cook it on one side and then flip to cook the other side!
5. Top with some butter and/or sugar.

Breakfast Mix

Prep + Cook Time: 15 minutes | Servings: 1

Ingredients

tbsp coconut flakes, unsweetened
tbsp hemp seeds
tbsp flaxseed, ground
2 tbsp sesame, ground
2 tbsp cocoa, dark, unsweetened

Instructions

1. Grind the flaxseed and the sesame.
2. Make sure you only grind the sesame seeds for a very short period.
3. Mix all ingredients in a jar and shake it well.
4. Keep refrigerated until ready to eat.
5. Serve softened with black coffee or even with still water and add coconut oil if you want to increase the fat content. It also blends well with cream or with mascarpone cheese.

Breakfast Muffins

Prep + Cook Time: 30 minutes | Servings: 1

Ingredients

1 medium egg
¼ cup heavy cream
1 slice cooked bacon (cured, pan-fried, cooked)
1 oz cheddar cheese
Salt and black pepper (to taste)

Instructions

1. Preheat your fryer to 350°F/175°C.
2. In a bowl, mix the eggs with the cream, salt and pepper.
3. Spread into muffin tins and fill the cups half full.
4. Place 1 slice of bacon into each muffin hole and half ounce of cheese on top of each muffin.
5. Bake for around 15-20 minutes or until slightly browned.
6. Add another ½ oz of cheese onto each muffin and broil until the cheese is slightly browned. Serve!

Egg Porridge

Prep + Cook Time: 15 minutes | Servings: 1

Ingredients

2 organic free-range eggs
1/3 cup organic heavy cream without food additives
2 packages of your preferred sweetener
2 tbsp grass-fed butter ground organic cinnamon to taste

Instructions

1. In a bowl add the eggs, cream and sweetener, and mix together.
2. Melt the butter in a saucepan over a medium heat. Lower the heat once the butter is melted.
3. Combine together with the egg and cream mixture.
4. While Cooking, mix until it thickens and curdles.
5. When you see the first signs of curdling, remove the saucepan immediately from the heat.
6. Pour the porridge into a bowl. Sprinkle cinnamon on top and serve immediately.

Eggs Florentine

Prep + Cook Time: 20 minutes | Servings: 2

Ingredients

1 cup washed, fresh spinach leaves
2 tbsp freshly grated parmesan cheese
Sea salt and pepper
1 tbsp white vinegar
2 eggs

Instructions

1. Cook the spinach the microwave or steam until wilted.
2. Sprinkle with parmesan cheese and seasoning.
3. Slice into bite-size pieces and place on a plate.
4. Simmer a pan of water and add the vinegar. Stir quickly with a spoon.
5. Break an egg into the center. Turn off the heat and cover until set.
6. Repeat with the second egg.
7. Place the eggs on top of the spinach and serve.

Spanish Omelet

Prep + Cook Time: 15 minutes | Servings: 2

Ingredients

3 eggs
Cayenne or black pepper
½ cup finely chopped vegetables of your choosing.

Instructions

1. In a pan on high heat, stir-fry the vegetables in extra virgin olive oil until lightly crispy.
2. Cook the eggs with one tablespoon of water and a pinch of pepper.
3. When almost cooked, top with the vegetables and flip to cook briefly.
4. Serve

Cristy's Pancakes

Prep + Cook Time: 10 minutes | Servings: 1

Ingredients

1 scoop of genX Vanilla
1 tbsp or hazelnut meal
2 tbsp water
1 egg

Instructions

1. Add the ingredients together in a bowl and mix together.
2. Pour the mixture into a frying pan, cook on a medium heat for approximately 2 to 3 minutes on each side. (Watch carefully as it may burn quickly.)
3. Serve buttered with a handful of mixed berries.

Breakfast Tea

Prep + Cook Time: 5 minutes | Servings: 1

Ingredients

16 oz water
2 tea bags
1 tbsp ghee
1 tbsp coconut oil
½ tsp vanilla extract

Instructions

1. Make the tea and put it to one aside.
2. In a bowl, melt the ghee.
3. Add the coconut oil and vanilla to the melted ghee.
4. Pour the tea from a cup into a Nutribullet cup.
5. Screw on the lid and blend thoroughly.

Sausage Quiche

Prep + Cook Time: 35 minutes | Servings: 4

Ingredients

12 large eggs
1 cup heavy cream
1 tsp black pepper
12 oz sugar-free breakfast sausage
2 cups shredded cheddar cheese

Instructions

1. Preheat your fryer to 375°F/190°C.
2. In a large bowl, whisk the eggs, heavy cream, salad and pepper together.
3. Add the breakfast sausage and cheddar cheese.
4. Pour the mixture into a greased casserole dish.
5. Bake for 25 minutes.
6. Cut into 12 squares and serve hot.

Breakfast Sausage Casserole

Prep + Cook Time: 50 minutes | Servings: 4

Ingredients

8 eggs, beaten
1 head chopped cauliflower
1 lb sausage, cooked and crumbled
2 cups heavy whipping cream
1 cup sharp cheddar cheese, grated

Instructions

1. Cook the sausage as usual.
2. In a large bowl, mix the sausage, heavy whipping cream, chopped cauliflower, cheese and eggs.
3. Pour into a greased casserole dish.
4. Cook for 45 minutes at 350°F/175°C, or until firm.
5. Top with cheese and serve.

Scrambled Mug Eggs

Prep + Cook Time: 5 minutes | Servings: 1

Ingredients

1 mug
2 eggs
Salt and pepper
Shredded cheese
Your favorite buffalo wing sauce

Instructions

1. Crack the eggs into a mug and whisk until blended.
2. Put the mug into your microwave and cook for 1.5 – 2 minutes, depending on the power of your microwave.
3. Leave for a few minutes and remove from the microwave.
4. Sprinkle with salt and pepper. Add your desired amount of cheese on top.
5. Using a fork, mix everything together.
6. Then add your favorite buffalo or hot sauce and mix again.
7. Serve!

Banana Chia Seed Pudding

Prep + Cook Time: 1-2 days | Servings: 1

Ingredients

1 can full-fat coconut milk
1 medium- or small-sized banana, ripe
½ tsp cinnamon
1 tsp vanilla extract
¼ cup chia seeds

Instructions

1. In a bowl, mash the banana until soft.
2. Add the remaining ingredients and mix until incorporated.
3. Cover and place in your refrigerator overnight.
4. Serve!

Strawberry Rhubarb Parfait

Prep + Cook Time: 1-2 days | Servings: 1

Ingredients

1 package crème fraiche or plain full-fat yogurt (8.5 oz)
2 tbsp toasted flakes
2 tbsp toasted coconut flakes
6 tbsp homemade strawberry and rhubarb jam (4.25 oz)

Instructions

1. Add the jam into a dessert bowl (3 tbsp per serving).
2. Add the crème fraîche and garnish with the toasted and coconut flakes.
3. Serve!

Sausage Egg Muffins

Prep + Cook Time: 30 minutes | Servings: 4

Ingredients

6 oz Italian sausage
6 eggs
1/8 cup heavy cream
3 oz cheese

Instructions

1. Preheat the fryer to 350°F/175°C.
2. Grease a muffin pan.
3. Slice the sausage links and place them two to a tin.
4. Beat the eggs with the cream and season with salt and pepper.
5. Pour over the sausages in the tin.
6. Sprinkle with cheese and the remaining egg mixture.
7. Cook for 20 minutes or until the eggs are done and serve!

Salmon Omelet

Prep + Cook Time: 15 minutes | Servings: 2

Ingredients

3 eggs
1 smoked salmon
3 links pork sausage
¼ cup onions
¼ cup provolone cheese

Instructions

1. Whisk the eggs and pour them into a skillet.
2. Follow the standard method for making an omelette.
3. Add the onions, salmon and cheese before turning the omelet over.
4. Sprinkle the omelet with cheese and serve with the sausages on the side.
5. Serve!

Black's Bangin' Casserole

Prep + Cook Time: 40 minutes | Servings: 4

Ingredients

5 eggs
3 tbsp chunky tomato sauce
2 tbsp heavy cream
2 tbsp grated parmesan cheese

Instructions

1. Preheat your fryer to 350°F/175°C.
2. Combine the eggs and cream in a bowl.
3. Mix in the tomato sauce and add the cheese.
4. Spread into a glass baking dish and bake for 25-35 minutes.
5. Top with extra cheese.
6. Enjoy!

Hash Brown

Prep + Cook Time: 20 minutes | Servings: 2

Ingredients

12 oz grated fresh cauliflower (about ½ a medium-sized head)
4 slices bacon, chopped
3 oz onion, chopped
1 tbsp butter, softened

Instructions

1. In a skillet, sauté the bacon and onion until brown.
2. Add in the cauliflower and stir until tender and browned.
3. Add the butter steadily as it cooks.
4. Season to taste with salt and pepper.
5. Enjoy!

Bacon Cups

Prep + Cook Time: 40 minutes | Servings: 2

Ingredients

2 eggs
1 slice tomato
3 slices bacon
2 slices ham
2 tsp grated parmesan cheese

Instructions

1. Preheat your fryer to 375°F/190°C.
2. Cook the bacon for half of the directed time.
3. Slice the bacon strips in half and line 2 greased muffin tins with 3 half-strips of bacon
4. Put one slice of ham and half slice of tomato in each muffin tin on top of the bacon
5. Crack one egg on top of the tomato in each muffin tin and sprinkle each with half a teaspoon of grated parmesan cheese.
6. Bake for 20 minutes.
7. Remove and let cool.
8. Serve!

Spinach Eggs and Cheese

Prep + Cook Time: 40 minutes | Servings: 2

Ingredients

3 whole eggs
3 oz cottage cheese
3-4 oz chopped spinach
¼ cup parmesan cheese
¼ cup of milk

Instructions

1. Preheat your fryer to 375°F/190°C.
2. In a large bowl, whisk the eggs, cottage cheese, the parmesan and the milk.
3. Mix in the spinach.

4. Transfer to a small, greased, fryer dish.
5. Sprinkle the cheese on top.
6. Bake for 25-30 minutes.
7. Let cool for 5 minutes and serve.

Fried Eggs

Prep + Cook Time: 7 minutes | Servings: 2

Ingredients

2 eggs
3 slices bacon

Instructions

1. Heat some oil in a deep fryer at 375°F/190°C.
2. Fry the bacon.
3. In a small bowl, add the 2 eggs.
4. Quickly add the eggs into the center of the fryer.
5. Using two spatulas, form the egg into a ball while frying.
6. Fry for 2-3 minutes, until it stops bubbling.
7. Place on a paper towel and allow to drain.
8. Enjoy!

Scotch Eggs

Prep + Cook Time: 40 minutes | Servings: 4

Ingredients

4 large eggs
1 package Jimmy Dean's Pork Sausage (12 oz)
8 slices thick-cut bacon
4 toothpicks

Instructions

1. Hard-boil the eggs, peel the shells and let them cool.
2. Slice the sausage into four parts and place each part into a large circle.
3. Put an egg into each circle and wrap it in the sausage.
4. Place inside your refrigerator for 1 hour.
5. Make a cross with two pieces of thick-cut bacon.
6. Place a wrapped egg in the center, fold the bacon over top of the egg and secure with a toothpick.
7. Cook inside your fryer at 450°F/230°C for 25 minutes.
8. Enjoy!

Toasties

Prep + Cook Time: 30 minutes | Servings: 2

Ingredients

¼ cup milk or cream
2 sausages, boiled
3 eggs
1 slice bread, sliced lengthwise
4 tbsp. cheese, grated
Sea salt to taste
Chopped fresh herbs and steamed broccoli [optional]

Instructions

1. Pre-heat your Air Fryer at 360°F and set the timer for 5 minutes.
2. In the meantime, scramble the eggs in a bowl and add in the milk.
3. Grease three muffin cups with a cooking spray. Divide the egg mixture in three and pour equal amounts into each cup.
4. Slice the sausages and drop them, along with the slices of bread, into the egg mixture. Add the cheese on top and a little salt as desired.Transfer the cups to the Fryer and cook for 15-20 minutes, depending on how firm you would like them. When ready, remove them from the fryer and serve with fresh herbs and steam broccoli if you prefer.

Egg Baked Omelet

Prep + Cook Time: 15 minutes | Servings: 1

Ingredients
tbsp. ricotta cheese
1 tbsp. chopped parsley
1 tsp. olive oil
3 eggs
¼ cup chopped spinach
Salt and pepper to taste

Instructions
1.　Set your Air Fryer at 330°F and allow to warm with the olive oil inside.
2.　In a bowl, beat the eggs with a fork and sprinkle some salt and pepper as desired.
3.　Add in the ricotta, spinach, and parsley and then transfer to the Air Fryer. Cook for 10 minutes before serving.

Breakfast Omelet

Prep + Cook Time: 30 minutes | Servings: 2

Ingredients
1 large onion, chopped
2 tbsp. cheddar cheese, grated
3 eggs
½ tsp. soy sauce
Salt
Pepper powder
Cooking spray

Instructions
1.　In a bowl, mix the salt, pepper powder, soy sauce and eggs with a whisk.
2.　Take a small pan small enough to fit inside the Air Fryer and spritz with cooking spray. Spread the chopped onion across the bottom of the pan, then transfer the pan to the Fryer. Cook at 355°F for 6-7 minutes, ensuring the onions turn translucent.
3.　Add the egg mixture on top of the onions, coating everything well. Add the cheese on top, then resume cooking for another 5 or 6 minutes.
4.　Take care when taking the pan out of the fryer. Enjoy with some toasted bread.

Ranch Risotto

Prep + Cook Time: 40 minutes | Servings: 2

Ingredients
1 onion, diced
2 cups chicken stock, boiling
½ cup parmesan OR cheddar cheese, grated
1 clove garlic, minced
¾ cup Arborio rice
1 tbsp. olive oil
1 tbsp. unsalted butter

Instructions
1.　Set the Air Fryer at 390°F for 5 minutes to heat up.
2.　With oil, grease a round baking tin, small enough to fit inside the fryer, and stir in the garlic, butter, and onion.
3.　Transfer the tin to the Air Fryer and allow to cook for 4 minutes. Add in the rice and cook for a further 4 minutes, giving it a stir three times throughout the cooking time.
4.　Turn the fryer down to 320°F and add in the chicken stock, before gently mixing it. Leave to cook for 22 minutes with the fryer uncovered. Before serving, throw in the cheese and give it one more stir. Enjoy!

Coffee Donuts

Prep + Cook Time: 20 minutes | Servings: 6

Ingredients
1 cup flour
¼ cup sugar
½ tsp. salt
1 tsp. baking powder
1 tbsp. aquafaba
1 tbsp. sunflower oil
¼ cup coffee

Instructions
1.　In a large bowl, combine the sugar, salt, flour, and baking powder.
2.　Add in the coffee, aquafaba, and sunflower oil and mix until a dough is formed. Leave the dough to rest in and the refrigerator.
3.　Set your Air Fryer at 400°F to heat up.
4.　Remove the dough from the fridge and divide up, kneading each section into a doughnut.
5.　Put the doughnuts inside the Air Fryer, ensuring not to overlap any. Fry for 6 minutes. Do not shake the basket, to make sure the doughnuts hold their shape.

Taco Wraps

Prep + Cook Time: 30 minutes | Servings: 4

Ingredients
1 tbsp. water
4 pc commercial vegan nuggets, chopped
1 small yellow onion, diced
1 small red bell pepper, chopped
2 cobs grilled corn kernels
4 large corn tortillas
Mixed greens for garnish

Instructions
1.　Pre-heat your Air Fryer at 400°F.
2.　Over a medium heat, water-sauté the nuggets with the onions, corn kernels and bell peppers in a skillet, then remove from the heat.
3.　Fill the tortillas with the nuggets and vegetables and fold them up. Transfer to the inside of the fryer and cook for 15 minutes. Once crispy, serve immediately, garnished with the mixed greens.

Bistro Wedges

Prep + Cook Time: 20 minutes | Servings: 4

Ingredients
1 lb. fingerling potatoes, cut into wedges
1 tsp. extra virgin olive oil
½ tsp. garlic powder
Salt and pepper to taste
½ cup raw cashews, soaked in water overnight
½ tsp. ground turmeric
½ tsp. paprika
1 tbsp. nutritional yeast
1 tsp. fresh lemon juice
2 tbsp. to ¼ cup water

Instructions
1.　Pre-heat your Air Fryer at 400°F.
2.　In a bowl, toss together the potato wedges, olive oil, garlic powder, and salt and pepper, making sure to coat the potatoes well.
3.　Transfer the potatoes to the basket of your fryer and fry for 10 minutes.

4. In the meantime, prepare the cheese sauce. Pulse the cashews, turmeric, paprika, nutritional yeast, lemon juice, and water together in a food processor. Add more water to achieve your desired consistency.
5. When the potatoes are finished cooking, move them to a bowl that is small enough to fit inside the fryer and add the cheese sauce on top. Cook for an additional 3 minutes.

Spinach Balls

Prep + Cook Time: 20 minutes | Servings: 4

Ingredients

1 carrot, peeled and grated
1 package fresh spinach, blanched and chopped
½ onion, chopped
1 egg, beaten
½ tsp. garlic powder
1 tsp. garlic, minced
1 tsp. salt
½ tsp. black pepper
1 tbsp. nutritional yeast
1 tbsp. flour
2 slices bread, toasted

Instructions

1. In a food processor, pulse the toasted bread to form breadcrumbs. Transfer into a shallow dish or bowl.
2. In a bowl, mix together all the other ingredients.
3. Use your hands to shape the mixture into small-sized balls. Roll the balls in the breadcrumbs, ensuring to cover them well.
4. Put in the Air Fryer and cook at 390°F for 10 minutes.

Cheese & Chicken Sandwich

Prep + Cook Time: 15 minutes | Servings: 1

Ingredients

⅓ cup chicken, cooked and shredded
2 mozzarella slices
1 hamburger bun
¼ cup cabbage, shredded
1 tsp. mayonnaise
2 tsp. butter
1 tsp. olive oil
½ tsp. balsamic vinegar
1/4 tsp. smoked paprika
¼ tsp. black pepper
¼ tsp. garlic powder
Pinch of salt

Instructions

1. Pre-heat your Air Fryer at 370°F.
2. Apply some butter to the outside of the hamburger bun with a brush.
3. In a bowl, coat the chicken with the garlic powder, salt, pepper, and paprika.
4. In a separate bowl, stir together the mayonnaise, olive oil, cabbage, and balsamic vinegar to make coleslaw.
5. Slice the bun in two. Start building the sandwich, starting with the chicken, followed by the mozzarella, the coleslaw, and finally the top bun.
6. Transfer the sandwich to the fryer and cook for 5 – 7 minutes.

Bacon & Horseradish Cream

Prep + Cook Time: 1 hour 40 minutes | Servings: 4

Ingredients

½ lb. thick cut bacon, diced
2 tbsp. butter
2 shallots, sliced
½ cup milk
1 ½ lb. Brussels sprouts, halved
2 tbsp. flour
1 cup heavy cream
2 tbsp. prepared horseradish
½ tbsp. fresh thyme leaves
1/8 tsp. ground nutmeg
1 tbsp. olive oil
½ tsp. sea salt
Ground black pepper to taste
½ cup water

Instructions

1. Pre-heat your Air Fryer at 400°F.
2. Coat the Brussels sprouts with olive oil and sprinkle some salt and pepper on top. Transfer to the fryer and cook for a half hour. At the halfway point, give them a good stir, then take them out of the fryer and set to the side.
3. Put the bacon in the basket of the fryer and pour the water into the drawer underneath to catch the fat. Cook for 10 minutes, stirring 2 or 3 times throughout the cooking time.
4. When 10 minutes are up, add in the shallots. Cook for a further 10 – 15 minutes, making sure the shallots soften up and the bacon turns brown. Add some more pepper and remove. Leave to drain on some paper towels.
5. Melt the butter over the stove or in the microwave, before adding in the flour and mixing with a whisk. Slowly add in the heavy cream and milk, and continue to whisk for another 3 – 5 minutes, making sure the mixture thickens.
6. Add the horseradish, thyme, salt, and nutmeg and stirring well once more.
7. Take a 9" x 13" baking dish and grease it with oil. Pre-heat your fryer to 350°F.
8. Put the Brussels sprouts in the baking dish and spread them across the base. Pour over the cream sauce and then top with a layer of bacon and shallots.
9. Cook in the fryer for a half hour and enjoy.

Vegetable Toast

Prep + Cook Time: 25 minutes | Servings: 4

Ingredients

4 slices bread
1 red bell pepper, cut into strips
1 cup sliced button or cremini mushrooms
1 small yellow squash, sliced
2 green onions, sliced
1 tbsp. olive oil
2 tbsp. softened butter
½ cup soft goat cheese

Instructions

1. Drizzle the Air Fryer with the olive oil and pre-heat to 350°F.
2. Put the red pepper, green onions, mushrooms, and squash inside the fryer, give them a stir and cook for 7 minutes, shaking the basket once throughout the cooking time. Ensure the vegetables become tender.
3. Remove the vegetables and set them aside.
4. Spread some butter on the slices of bread and transfer to the Air Fryer, butter side-up. Brown for 2 to 4 minutes.
5. Remove the toast from the fryer and top with goat cheese and vegetables. Serve warm.

Cinnamon Toasts

Prep + Cook Time: 15 minutes | Servings: 4

Ingredients

10 bread slices
1 pack salted butter
4 tbsp. sugar
2 tsp. ground cinnamon
½ tsp. vanilla extract

Instructions

1. In a bowl, combine the butter, cinnamon, sugar, and vanilla extract. Spread onto the slices of bread.
2. Set your Air Fryer to 380°F. When warmed up, put the bread inside the fryer and cook for 4 – 5 minutes.

Toasted Cheese

Prep + Cook Time: 20 minutes | Servings: 2

Ingredients

2 slices bread
4 oz cheese, grated
Small amount of butter

Instructions

1. Grill the bread in the toaster.
2. Butter the toast and top with the grated cheese.
3. Set your Air Fryer to 350°F and allow to warm.
4. Put the toast slices inside the fryer and cook for 4 - 6 minutes.
5. Serve and enjoy!

Peanut Butter Bread

Prep + Cook Time: 15 minutes | Servings: 3

Ingredients

1 tbsp. oil
2 tbsp. peanut butter
4 slices bread
1 banana, sliced

Instructions

1. Spread the peanut butter on top of each slice of bread, then arrange the banana slices on top. Sandwich two slices together, then the other two.
2. Oil the inside of the Air Fryer and cook the bread for 5 minutes at 300°F.

English Builder's Breakfast

Prep + Cook Time: 35 minutes | Servings: 2

Ingredients

1 cup potatoes, sliced and diced
2 cups beans in tomato sauce
2 eggs
1 tbsp. olive oil
1 sausage
Salt to taste

Instructions

1. Set your Air Fryer at 390°F and allow to warm.
2. Break the eggs onto an fryer-safe dish and sprinkle on some salt.
3. Lay the beans on the dish, next to the eggs.
4. In a bowl small enough to fit inside your fryer, coat the potatoes with the olive oil. Sprinkle on the salt, as desired.
5. Transfer the bowl of potato slices to the fryer and cook for 10 minutes.
6. Swap out the bowl of potatoes for the dish containing the eggs and beans. Leave to cook for another 10 minutes. Cover the potatoes with parchment paper.

7. Slice up the sausage and throw the slices in on top of the beans and eggs. Resume cooking for another 5 minutes. Serve with the potatoes, as well as toast and coffee if desired.

Avocado Eggs

Prep + Cook Time: 15 minutes | Servings: 4

Ingredients

2 large avocados, sliced
1 cup breadcrumbs
½ cup flour 2 eggs, beaten
¼ tsp. paprika
Salt and pepper to taste

Instructions

1. Pre-heat your Air Fryer at 400°F for 5 minutes.
2. Sprinkle some salt and pepper on the slices of avocado. Optionally, you can enhance the flavor with a half-tsp. of dried oregano.
3. Lightly coat the avocados with flour. Dredge them in the eggs, before covering with breadcrumbs. Transfer to the fryer and cook for 6 minutes.

Avocado Tempura

Prep + Cook Time: 20 minutes | Servings: 4

Ingredients

½ cup breadcrumbs
½ tsp. salt
1 Haas avocado, pitted, peeled and sliced
Liquid from 1 can white beans or aquafaba

Instructions

1. Set your Air Fryer to 350°F and allow to warm.
2. Mix the breadcrumbs and salt in a shallow bowl until well-incorporated.
3. Dip the avocado slices in the bean/aquafaba juice, then into the breadcrumbs. Put the avocados in the fryer, taking care not to overlap any slices, and fry for 10 minutes, giving the basket a good shake at the halfway point.

Potato & Kale Nuggets

Prep + Cook Time: 25 minutes | Servings: 4

Ingredients

1 tsp. extra virgin olive oil
1 clove of garlic, minced
4 cups kale, rinsed and chopped
2 cups potatoes, boiled and mashed
1/8 cup milk
Salt and pepper to taste
Vegetable oil

Instructions

1. Pre-heat your Air Fryer at 390°F.
2. In a skillet over medium heat, fry the garlic in the olive oil, until it turns golden brown. Cook with the kale for an additional 3 minutes and remove from the heat.
3. Mix the mashed potatoes, kale and garlic in a bowl. Throw in the milk and sprinkle with some salt and pepper as desired.
4. Shape the mixture into nuggets and spritz each one with a little vegetable oil. Put in the basket of your fryer and leave to cook for 15 minutes, shaking the basket halfway through cooking to make sure the nuggets fry evenly.

Bread Rolls

Prep + Cook Time: 30 minutes | Servings: 5

Ingredients

5 large potatoes, boiled and mashed
Salt and pepper to taste
1 tbsp. olive oil
½ tsp. mustard seeds
2 small onions, chopped
½ tsp. turmeric
2 sprigs curry leaves
8 slices of bread, brown sides discarded
2 green chilis, seeded and chopped
1 bunch coriander, chopped

Instructions

1. Pre-heat your Air Fryer at 400°F.
2. Put the mashed potatoes in a bowl and sprinkle on salt and pepper. Set to one side.
3. Fry the mustard seeds in a little olive oil over a medium-low heat, stirring continuously, until they sputter.
4. Add in the onions and cook until they turn translucent. Add the curry leaves and turmeric powder and stir. Cook for a further 2 minutes until fragrant.
5. Remove the pan from the heat and combine the contents with the potatoes. Remove from heat and add to the potatoes. Mix in the green chilies and coriander.
6. Wet the bread slightly and drain of any excess liquid.
7. Spoon a small amount of the potato mixture into the center of the bread and enclose the bread around the filling, sealing it entirely. Continue until the rest of the bread and filling is used up. Brush each bread roll with some oil and transfer to the basket of your fryer.
8. Cook for 15 minutes, gently shaking the fryer basket at the halfway point to ensure each roll is cooked evenly.

Veg Frittata

Prep + Cook Time: 35 minutes | Servings: 2

Ingredients

¼ cup milk
1 zucchini
½ bunch asparagus
½ cup mushrooms
½ cup spinach or baby spinach
½ cup red onion, sliced
4 eggs
½ tbsp. olive oil
5 tbsp. feta cheese, crumbled
4 tbsp. cheddar, grated
¼ bunch chives, minced
Sea salt and pepper to taste

Instructions

1. In a bowl, mix together the eggs, milk, salt and pepper.
2. Cut up the zucchini, asparagus, mushrooms and red onion into slices. Shred the spinach using your hands.
3. Over a medium heat, stir-fry the vegetables for 5 – 7 minutes with the olive oil in a non-stick pan.
4. Place some parchment paper in the base of a baking tin. Pour in the vegetables, followed by the egg mixture. Top with the feta and grated cheddar.
5. Set the Air Fryer at 320°F and allow to warm for five minutes.
6. Transfer the baking tin to the fryer and allow to cook for 15 minutes. Take care when removing the frittata from the Air Fryer and leave to cool for 5 minutes.

7. Top with the minced chives and serve.

Maple Cinnamon Buns

Prep + Cook Time: 1 hour 55 minutes | Servings: 9

Ingredients

3/4 cup unsweetened milk
4 tbsp. maple syrup
1 ½ tbsp. active yeast
1 tbsp. ground flaxseed
1 tbsp. coconut oil, melted
1 cup flour
1 ½ cup flour
2 tsp. cinnamon powder
½ cup pecan nuts, toasted
2 ripe bananas, sliced
4 Medjool dates, pitted
¼ cup sugar

Instructions

1. Over a low heat, warm the milk until it is tepid. Combine with the yeast and maple syrup, waiting 5 – 10 minutes to allow the yeast to activate.
2. In the meantime, put 3 tbsp. of water and the flaxseed in a bowl and stir together. This is your egg substitute. Let the flaxseed absorb the water for about 2 minutes.
3. Pour the coconut oil into the bowl, then combine the flaxseed mixture with the yeast mixture.
4. In a separate bowl, mix together one tbsp. of the cinnamon powder and the white and flour. Add the yeast-flaxseed mixture and mix to create a dough.
5. Dust a flat surface with flour. On this surface, knead the dough with your hands for a minimum of 10 minutes.
6. Grease a large bowl and transfer the dough inside. Cover with a kitchen towel or saran wrap. Let sit in a warm, dark place for an hour so that the dough may rise.
7. In the meantime, prepare the filling. Mix the banana slices, dates, and pecans together before throwing in a tbsp. of cinnamon powder.
8. Set the Air Fryer to 390°F and allow to warm. On your floured surface, flatten the dough with a rolling pin, making it thin. Spoon the pecan mixture onto the dough and spread out evenly.
9. Roll up the dough and then slice it in nine. Transfer the slices to a dish small enough to fit in the fryer, set the dish inside, and cook for 30 minutes.
10. Top with a thin layer of sugar before serving.

Taj Tofu

Prep + Cook Time: 40 minutes | Servings: 4

Ingredients

1 block firm tofu, pressed and cut into 1-inch thick cubes
2 tbsp. soy sauce
2 tsp. sesame seeds, toasted
1 tsp. rice vinegar
1 tbsp. cornstarch

Instructions

1. Set your Air Fryer at 400°F to warm.
2. Add the tofu, soy sauce, sesame seeds and rice vinegar in a bowl together and mix well to coat the tofu cubes. Then cover the tofu in cornstarch and put it in the basket of your fryer.
3. Cook for 25 minutes, giving the basket a shake at five-minute intervals to ensure the tofu cooks evenly.

Rice Paper Bacon

Prep + Cook Time: 30 minutes | Servings: 4

Ingredients

3 tbsp. soy sauce or tamari
2 tbsp. cashew butter
2 tbsp. liquid smoke
2 tbsp. water
4 pc white rice paper, cut into 1-inch thick strips

Instructions

1. Pre-heat your Air Fryer at 350°F.
2. Mix together the soy sauce/tamari, liquid smoke, water, and cashew butter in a large bowl.
3. Take the strips of rice paper and soak them for 5 minutes. Arrange in one layer in the bottom of your fryer.
4. Cook for 15 minutes, ensuring they become crispy, before serving with some vegetables.

Posh Soufflé

Prep + Cook Time: 25 minutes | Servings: 4

Ingredients

¼ cup flour
⅓ cup butter
1 cup milk
4 egg yolks
1 tsp. vanilla extract
6 egg whites
1 oz. sugar
1 tsp. cream of tartar

Instructions

1. Set your Air Fryer at 320°F and allow to warm.
2. In a bowl, mix together the butter and flour until a smooth consistency is achieved.
3. Pour the milk into a saucepan over a low-to-medium heat. Add in the and allow to dissolve before raising the heat to boil the milk.
4. Pour in the flour and butter mixture and stir rigorously for 7 minutes to eliminate any lumps. Make sure the mixture thickens. Take off the heat and allow to cool for 15 minutes.
5. Spritz 6 soufflé dishes with oil spray.
6. Place the egg yolks and vanilla extract in a separate bowl and beat them together with a fork. Pour in the milk and combine well to incorporate everything.
7. In a smaller bowl mix together the egg whites and cream of tartar with a fork. Fold into the egg yolks-milk mixture before adding in the flour mixture. Transfer equal amounts to the 6 soufflé dishes.
8. Put the dishes in the fryer and cook for 15 minutes.

Egg Muffin Sandwich

Prep + Cook Time: 15 minutes | Servings: 1

Ingredients

1 egg
2 slices bacon
1 English muffin

Instructions

1. Pre-heat your Air Fryer at 395°F
2. Take a ramekin and spritz it with cooking spray. Break an egg into the ramekin before transferring it to the basket of your fryer, along with the English muffin and bacon slices, keeping each component separate.
3. Allow to cook for 6 minutes. After removing from the fryer, allow to cool for around two minutes. Halve the muffin.
4. Create your sandwich by arranging the egg and bacon slices on the base and topping with the other half of the muffin.

Pea Delight

Prep + Cook Time: 25 minutes | Servings: 2 – 4

Ingredients

1 cup flour
1 tsp. baking powder
3 eggs
1 cup coconut milk
1 cup cream cheese
3 tbsp. pea protein
½ cup chicken/turkey strips
1 pinch sea salt
1 cup mozzarella cheese

Instructions

1. Set your Air Fryer at 390°F and allow to warm.
2. In a large bowl, mix all ingredients together using a large wooden spoon.
3. Spoon equal amounts of the mixture into muffin cups and allow to cook for 15 minutes.

Choco Bars

Prep + Cook Time: 30 minutes | Servings: 8

Ingredients

2 cups old-fashioned oats
½ cup quinoa, cooked
½ cup chia seeds
½ cup s, sliced
½ cup dried cherries, chopped
½ cup dark chocolate, chopped
¾ cup butter
⅓ cup honey
2 tbsp. coconut oil
¼ tsp. salt
½ cup prunes, pureed

Instructions

1. Pre-heat your Air Fryer at 375°F.
2. Put the oats, quinoa, s, cherries, chia seeds, and chocolate in a bowl and mix well.
3. Heat the butter, honey, and coconut oil in a saucepan, gently stirring together. Pour this over the oats mixture.
4. Mix in the salt and pureed prunes and combine well.
5. Transfer this to a baking dish small enough to fit inside the fryer and cook for 15 minutes. Remove from the fryer and allow to cool completely. Cut into bars and enjoy.

French Toast

Prep + Cook Time: 25 minutes | Servings: 2

Ingredients

4 slices bread of your choosing
2 tbsp. soft butter
2 eggs, lightly beaten
Pinch of salt
Pinch of cinnamon
Pinch of ground nutmeg
Pinch of ground cloves
Nonstick cooking spray
Sugar for serving

Instructions

1.   In a shallow bowl, mix together the salt, spices and eggs.
2.   Butter each side of the slices of bread and slice into strips. You may also use cookie cutters for this step.
3.   Set your Air Fryer to 350°F and allow to warm up briefly.
4.   Dredge each strip of bread in the egg and transfer to the fryer. Cook for two minutes, ensuring the toast turns golden brown.
5.   At this point, spritz the tops of the bread strips with cooking spray, flip, and cook for another 4 minutes on the other side. Top with a light dusting of sugar before serving.

Cheddar & Bacon Quiche

Prep + Cook Time: 30 minutes | Servings: 4

Ingredients

3 tbsp. Greek yogurt
½ cup grated cheddar cheese
3 oz. chopped bacon
4 eggs, beaten
¼ tsp. garlic powder
Pinch of black pepper
1 shortcrust pastry
¼ tsp. onion powder
¼ tsp. sea salt
Some flour for sprinkling

Instructions

1.   Pre-heat your Air Fryer at 330°F.
2.   Take 8 ramekins and grease with a little oil. Coat with a sprinkling of flour, tapping to remove any excess.
3.   Cut the shortcrust pastry in 8 and place each piece at the bottom of each ramekin.
4.   Put all of the other ingredients in a bowl and combine well. Spoon equal amounts of the filling into each piece of pastry.
5.   Cook the ramekins in the Air Fryer for 20 minutes.

Chorizo Risotto

Prep + Cook Time: 1 hour 20 minutes | Servings: 4

Ingredients

¼ cup milk
½ cup flour
4 oz. breadcrumbs
4 oz. chorizo, finely sliced
1 serving mushroom risotto rice
1 egg
Sea salt to taste

Instructions

1.   In a bowl, combine the mushroom risotto rice with the risotto and salt before refrigerating to cool.
2.   Set your Air Fryer at 390°F and leave to warm for 5 minutes.
3.   Use your hands to form 2 tablespoonfuls of risotto into a rice ball. Repeat until you have used up all the risotto. Roll each ball in the flour.
4.   Crack the egg into a bowl and mix with the milk using a whisk. Coat each rice ball in the egg-milk mixture, and then in breadcrumbs.
5.   Space the rice balls out in the baking dish of the Air Fryer. Bake for 20 minutes, ensuring they develop a crispy golden-brown crust.
6.   Serve warm with a side of fresh vegetables and salad if desired.

Choco Bread

Prep + Cook Time: 30 minutes | Servings: 12

Ingredients

1 tbsp. flax egg [1 tbsp. flax meal + 3 tbsp. water]
1 cup zucchini, shredded and squeezed
½ cup sunflower oil
½ cup maple syrup
1 tsp. vanilla extract
1 tsp. apple cider vinegar
½ cup milk
1 cup flour
1 tsp. baking soda
½ cup unsweetened cocoa powder
¼ tsp. salt
⅓ cup chocolate chips

Instructions

1.   Pre-heat your Air Fryer to 350°F.
2.   Take a baking dish small enough to fit inside the fryer and line it with parchment paper.
3.   Mix together the flax meal, zucchini, sunflower oil, maple, vanilla, apple cider vinegar and milk in a bowl.
4.   Incorporate the flour, cocoa powder, salt and baking soda, stirring all the time to combine everything well.
5.   Finally, throw in the chocolate chips.
6.   Transfer the batter to the baking dish and cook in the fryer for 15 minutes. Make sure to test with a toothpick before serving by sticking it in the center. The bread is ready when the toothpick comes out clean.

Red Rolls

Prep + Cook Time: 45 minutes | Servings: 6

Ingredients
7 cups minced meat
1 small onion, diced
1 packet spring roll sheets
2 oz. Asian noodles
3 cloves garlic, crushed
1 cup mixed vegetables
1 tbsp. sesame oil
2 tbsp. water
1 tsp. soy sauce

Instructions
1. Cook the noodles in hot water until they turn soft. Drain and cut to your desired length.
2. Grease the wok with sesame oil. Put it over a medium-high heat and fry the minced meat, mixed vegetables, garlic, and onion, stirring regularly to ensure the minced meat cooks through. The cooking time will vary depending on the pan you are using – allow 3-5 minutes if using a wok, and 7-10 if using a standard frying pan.
3. Drizzle in the soy sauce and add to the noodles, tossing well to allow the juices to spread and absorb evenly.
4. Spoon the stir-fry diagonally across a spring roll sheet and fold back the top point over the filling. Fold over the sides. Before folding back the bottom point, brush it with cold water, which will act as an adhesive.
5. Repeat until all the filling and sheets are used.
6. Pre-heat your Air Fryer at 360°F.
7. If desired, drizzle a small amount of oil over the top of the spring rolls to enhance the taste and ensure crispiness.
8. Cook the spring rolls in the fryer for 8 minutes, in multiple batches if necessary. Serve and enjoy.

Chia & Oat Porridge

Prep + Cook Time: 15 minutes | Servings: 4

Ingredients
4 cups milk
2 tbsp. peanut butter
2 cups oats
1 cup chia seeds
4 tbsp. honey
1 tbsp. butter, melted

Instructions
1. Pre-heat the Air Fryer to 390°F.
2. Put the peanut butter, honey, butter, and milk in a bowl and mix together using a whisk. Add in the oats and chia seeds and stir.
3. Transfer the mixture to an fryer-proof bowl that is small enough to fit inside the fryer and cook for 5 minutes. Give another stir before serving.

American Donuts

Prep + Cook Time: 1 hour 20 minutes | Servings: 6

Ingredients
1 cup flour
¼ cup sugar
1 tsp. baking powder
½ tsp. salt
¼ tsp. cinnamon
1 tbsp. coconut oil, melted
2 tbsp. aquafaba or liquid from canned chickpeas
¼ cup milk

Instructions
1. Put the sugar, flour and baking powder in a bowl and combine. Mix in the salt and cinnamon.
2. In a separate bowl, combine the aquafaba, milk and coconut oil.

3. Slowly pour the dry ingredients into the wet ingredients and combine well to create a sticky dough.
4. Refrigerate for at least an hour.
5. Pre-heat your Air Fryer at 370°F.
6. Using your hands, shape the dough into several small balls and place each one inside the fryer. Cook for 10 minutes, refraining from shaking the basket as they cook.
7. Lightly dust the balls with sugar and cinnamon and serve with a hot cup of coffee.

Tofu Scramble

Prep + Cook Time: 40 minutes | Servings: 3

Ingredients
2 ½ cups red potato, chopped
1 tbsp. olive oil
1 block tofu, chopped finely
1tbsp. olive oil
2 tbsp. tamari
1 tsp. turmeric powder
½ tsp. onion powder
½ tsp. garlic powder
½ cup onion, chopped
4 cups broccoli florets

Instructions
1. Pre-heat the Air Fryer at 400°F.
2. Toss together the potatoes and olive oil.
3. Cook the potatoes in a baking dish for 15 minutes, shaking once during the cooking time to ensure they fry evenly.
4. Combine the tofu, olive oil, turmeric, onion powder, tamari, and garlic powder together, before stirring in the onions, followed by the broccoli.
5. Top the potatoes with the tofu mixture and allow to cook for an additional 15 minutes. Serve warm.

Spinach Quiche

Prep + Cook Time: 1 hour 15 minutes | Servings: 4

Ingredients
¾ cup flour
Pinch of salt
½ cup cold coconut oil
2 tbsp. cold water
2 tbsp. olive oil
1 onion, chopped
4 oz. mushrooms, sliced
1 package firm tofu, pressed to remove excess water, then crumbled
1 lb. spinach, washed and chopped
½ tbsp. dried dill
2 tbsp. nutritional yeast
Salt and pepper
Sprig of fresh parsley, chopped

Instructions
1. Pre-heat the Air Fryer at 375°F.
2. Firstly, prepare the pastry. Use a sieve to sift together the salt and flour into a bowl. Combine with the coconut oil to make the flour crumbly. Slowly pour in the water until a stiff dough is formed.
3. Wrap the dough in saran wrap and refrigerate for a half hour.
4. Sauté the onion in a skillet over medium heat for a minute. Add in the tofu and mushroom, followed by the spinach, yeast, and dill.
5. Sprinkle in salt and pepper as desired. Finally add in the parsley. Take the skillet off the heat.
6. Dust a flat surface with flour and roll out the dough until it is thin.
7. Grease a baking dish that is small enough to fit inside the fryer. Place the dough in the tin and pour in the tofu mixture. Transfer the dish to the fryer and cook for 30 minutes, ensuring the pastry crisps up.

LUNCH & DINNER

Monkey Salad

Prep + Cook Time: 10 minutes | Servings: 1

Ingredients
2 tbsp butter
1 cup unsweetened coconut flakes
1 cup raw, unsalted cashews
1 cup raw, unsalted s
1 cup 90% dark chocolate shavings

Instructions
1. In a skillet, melt the butter on a medium heat.
2. Add the coconut flakes and sauté until lightly browned for 4 minutes.
3. Add the cashews and s and sauté for 3 minutes. Remove from the heat and sprinkle with dark chocolate shavings.
4. Serve!

Jarlsberg Lunch Omelet

Prep + Cook Time: 10 minutes | Servings: 2

Ingredients
4 medium mushrooms, sliced, 2 oz
1 green onion, sliced
2 eggs, beaten
1 oz Jarlsberg or Swiss cheese, shredded
1 oz ham, diced

Instructions
1. In a skillet, cook the mushrooms and green onion until tender.
2. Add the eggs and mix well.
3. Sprinkle with salt and top with the mushroom mixture, cheese and the ham.
4. When the egg is set, fold the plain side of the omelet on the filled side.
5. Turn off the heat and let it stand until the cheese has melted.
6. Serve!

Mu Shu Lunch Pork

Prep + Cook Time: 10 minutes | Servings: 2

Ingredients
4 cups coleslaw mix, with carrots
1 small onion, sliced thin
1 lb cooked roast pork, cut into ½" cubes
2 tbsp hoisin sauce
2 tbsp soy sauce

Instructions
1. In a large skillet, heat the oil on a high heat.
2. Stir-fry the cabbage and onion for 4 minutes until tender.
3. Add the pork, hoisin and soy sauce.
4. Cook until browned.
5. Enjoy!

Fiery Jalapeno Poppers

Prep + Cook Time: 40 minutes | Servings: 4

Ingredients
5 oz cream cheese
¼ cup mozzarella cheese
8 medium jalapeno peppers
½ tsp Mrs. Dash Table Blend
8 slices bacon

Instructions
1. Preheat your fryer to 400°F/200°C.
2. Cut the jalapenos in half.
3. Use a spoon to scrape out the insides of the peppers.
4. In a bowl, add together the cream cheese, mozzarella cheese and spices of your choice.
5. Pack the cream cheese mixture into the jalapenos and place the peppers on top.
6. Wrap each pepper in 1 slice of bacon, starting from the bottom and working up.
7. Bake for 30 minutes. Broil for an additional 3 minutes.
8. Serve!

Bacon & Chicken Patties

Prep + Cook Time: 15 minutes | Servings: 2

Ingredients
1 ½ oz can chicken breast
4 slices bacon
¼ cup parmesan cheese
1 large egg
3 tbsp flour

Instructions
1. Cook the bacon until crispy.
2. Chop the chicken and bacon together in a food processor until fine.
3. Add in the parmesan, egg, flour and mix.
4. Make the patties by hand and fry on a medium heat in a pan with some oil.
5. Once browned, flip over, continue cooking, and lie them to drain.
6. Serve!

Cheddar Bacon Burst

Prep + Cook Time: 90 minutes | Servings: 8

Ingredients
30 slices bacon
2 ½ cups cheddar cheese
4-5 cups raw spinach
1-2 tbsp Tones Southwest Chipotle Seasoning
2 tsp Mrs. Dash Table Seasoning

Instructions
1. Preheat your fryer to 375°F/190°C.
2. Weave the bacon into 15 vertical pieces & 12 horizontal pieces. Cut the extra 3 in half to fill in the rest, horizontally.
3. Season the bacon.
4. Add the cheese to the bacon.
5. Add the spinach and press down to compress.
6. Tightly roll up the woven bacon.
7. Line a baking sheet with kitchen foil and add plenty of salt to it.
8. Put the bacon on top of a cooling rack and put that on top of your baking sheet.
9. Bake for 60-70 minutes.
10. Let cool for 10-15 minutes before
11. Slice and enjoy!

Grilled Ham & Cheese

Prep + Cook Time: 30 minutes | Servings: 2

Ingredients
3 low-carb buns
4 slices medium-cut deli ham
1 tbsp salted butter
1 oz. flour
3 slices cheddar cheese
3 slices muenster cheese

Instructions
Bread:
1. Preheat your fryer to 350°F/175°C.
2. Mix the flour, salt and baking powder in a bowl. Put to the side.
3. Add in the butter and coconut oil to a skillet.
4. Melt for 20 seconds and pour into another bowl.
5. In this bowl, mix in the dough.
6. Scramble two eggs. Add to the dough.
7. Add ½ tablespoon of coconut flour to thicken, and place evenly into a cupcake tray. Fill about ¾ inch.
8. Bake for 20 minutes until browned.
9. Allow to cool for 15 minutes and cut each in half for the buns.
Sandwich:
1. Fry the deli meat in a skillet on a high heat.
2. Put the ham and cheese between the buns.
3. Heat the butter on medium high.
4. When brown, turn to low and add the dough to pan.
5. Press down with a weight until you smell burning, then flip to crisp both sides.
6. Enjoy!

Prosciutto Spinach Salad

Prep + Cook Time: 5 minutes | Servings: 2

Ingredients
2 cups baby spinach
1/3 lb prosciutto
1 cantaloupe
1 avocado
¼ cup diced red onion handful of raw, unsalted walnuts

Instructions
1. Put a cup of spinach on each plate.
2. Top with the diced prosciutto, cubes of balls of melon, slices of avocado, a handful of red onion and a few walnuts.
3. Add some freshly ground pepper, if you like.
4. Serve!

Riced Cauliflower & Curry Chicken

Prep + Cook Time: 30 minutes | Servings: 6

Ingredients
2 lbs chicken (4 breasts)
1 packet curry paste
3 tbsp ghee (can substitute with butter)
½ cup heavy cream
1 head cauliflower (around 1 kg)

Instructions
1. In a large skillet, melt the ghee.
2. Add the curry paste and mix.
3. Once combined, add a cup of water and simmer for 5 minutes.
4. Add the chicken, cover the skillet and simmer for 18 minutes.

5. Cut a cauliflower head into florets and blend in a food processor to make the riced cauliflower.
6. When the chicken is cooked, uncover, add the cream and cook for an additional 7 minutes.
7. Serve!

Mashed Garlic Turnips

Prep + Cook Time: 10 minutes | Servings: 2

Ingredients
3 cups diced turnip
2 cloves garlic, minced
¼ cup heavy cream
3 tbsp melted butter
Salt and pepper to season

Instructions
1. Boil the turnips until tender.
2. Drain and mash the turnips.
3. Add the cream, butter, salt, pepper and garlic. Combine well.
4. Serve!

Lasagna Spaghetti Squash

Prep + Cook Time: 90 minutes | Servings: 6

Ingredients
25 slices mozzarella cheese
1 large jar (40 oz) Rao's Marinara sauce
30 oz whole-milk ricotta cheese
2 large spaghetti squash, cooked (44 oz)
4 lbs ground beef

Instructions
1. Preheat your fryer to 375°F/190°C.
2. Slice the spaghetti squash and place it face down inside a fryerproof dish. Fill with water until covered.
3. Bake for 45 minutes until skin is soft.
4. Sear the meat until browned.
5. In a large skillet, heat the browned meat and marinara sauce. Set aside when warm.
6. Scrape the flesh off the cooked squash to resemble strands of spaghetti.
7. Layer the lasagna in a large greased pan in alternating layers of spaghetti squash, meat sauce, mozzarella, ricotta. Repeat until all increased have been used.
8. Bake for 30 minutes and serve!

Blue Cheese Chicken Wedges

Prep + Cook Time: 45 minutes | Servings: 4

Ingredients
Blue cheese dressing
2 tbsp crumbled blue cheese
4 strips of bacon
2 chicken breasts (boneless)
3/4 cup of your favorite buffalo sauce

Instructions
1. Boil a large pot of salted water.
2. Add in two chicken breasts to pot and cook for 28 minutes.
3. Turn off the heat and let the chicken rest for 10 minutes. Using a fork, pull the chicken apart into strips.
4. Cook and cool the bacon strips and put to the side.
5. On a medium heat, combine the chicken and buffalo sauce. Stir until hot.
6. Add the blue cheese and buffalo pulled chicken. Top with the cooked bacon crumble.
7. Serve and enjoy.

'Oh so good' Salad

Prep + Cook Time: 10 minutes | Servings: 2

Ingredients

6 brussels sprouts
½ tsp apple cider vinegar
1 tsp olive/grapeseed oil
1 grind of salt
1 tbsp freshly grated parmesan

Instructions

1. Slice the clean brussels sprouts in half.
2. Cut thin slices in the opposite direction.
3. Once sliced, cut the roots off and discard.
4. Toss together with the apple cider, oil and salt.
5. Sprinkle with the parmesan cheese, combine and enjoy!

'I Love Bacon'

Prep + Cook Time: 90 minutes | Servings: 4

Ingredients

30 slices thick-cut bacon
12 oz steak
10 oz pork sausage
4 oz cheddar cheese, shredded

Instructions

1. Lay out 5 x 6 slices of bacon in a woven pattern and bake at 400°F/200°C for 20 minutes until crisp.
2. Combine the steak, bacon and sausage to form a meaty mixture.
3. Lay out the meat in a rectangle of similar size to the bacon strips. Season with salt/peppe.
4. Place the bacon weave on top of the meat mixture.
5. Place the cheese in the center of the bacon.
6. Roll the meat into a tight roll and refrigerate.
7. Make a 7 x 7 bacon weave and roll the bacon weave over the meat, diagonally.
8. Bake at 400°F/200°C for 60 minutes or 165°F/75°C internally.
9. Let rest for 5 minutes before serving.

Lemon Dill Trout

Prep + Cook Time: 10 minutes | Servings: 1

Ingredients

2 lb pan-dressed trout (or other small fish), fresh or frozen
1 ½ tsp salt
½ cup butter or margarine
2 tbsp dill weed
3 tbsp lemon juice

Instructions

1. Cut the fish lengthwise and season the with pepper.
2. Prepare a skillet by melting the butter and dill weed.
3. Fry the fish on a high heat, flesh side down, for 2-3 minutes per side.

4. Remove the fish. Add the lemon juice to the butter and dill to create a sauce.
5. Serve the fish with the sauce.

'No Potato' Shepherd's Pie

Prep + Cook Time: 70 minutes | Servings: 6

Ingredients

1 lb lean ground beef
8 oz low-carb mushroom sauce mix
¼ cup ketchup
1 lb package frozen mixed vegetables
1 lb Aitkin's low-carb bake mix or equivalent

Instructions

1. Preheat your fryer to 375°F/190°C.
2. Prepare the bake mix according to package instructions. Layer into the skillet base.
3. Cut the dough into triangles and roll them from base to tip. Set to the side.
4. Brown the ground beef with the salt. Stir in the mushroom sauce, ketchup and mixed vegetables.
5. Bring the mixture to the boil and reduce the heat to medium, cover and simmer until tender.
6. Put the dough triangles on top of the mixture, tips pointing towards the center.
7. Bake for 60 minutes until piping hot and serve!

Easy Slider

Prep + Cook Time: 70 minutes | Servings: 6

Ingredients

1 lb Ground Beef
1 Egg
Garlic/salt/pepper/onion powder to taste
Several dashes of Worcestershire sauce
8 oz cheddar cheese (½ oz per patty)

Instructions

1. Mix the beef, eggs and spices together.
2. Divide the meat into 1.5 oz patties.
3. Add a half-ounce of cheese to each patty and combine two patties to make one burger, like a sandwich. Heat the oil on high and fry the burgers until cooked as desired. Serve.

Dijon Halibut Steak

Prep + Cook Time: 20 minutes | Servings: 1

Ingredients

1 6-oz fresh or thawed halibut steak
1 tbsp butter
1 tbsp lemon juice
½ tbsp Dijon mustard
1 tsp fresh basil

Instructions

1. Heat the butter, basil, lemon juice and mustard in a small saucepan to make a glaze.
2. Brush both sides of the halibut steak with the mixture.
3. Grill the fish for 10 minutes over a medium heat until tender and flakey.

Cast-Iron Cheesy Chicken

Prep + Cook Time: 10 minutes | Servings: 4

Ingredients
4 chicken breasts
4 bacon strips
4 oz ranch dressing
2 green onions
4 oz cheddar cheese

Instructions
1.   Pour the oil into a skillet and heat on high. Add the chicken breasts and fry both sides until piping hot.
2.   Fry the bacon and crumble it into bits.
3.   Dice the green onions.
4.   Put the chicken in a baking dish and top with soy sauce.
5.   Toss in the ranch, bacon, green onions and top with cheese.
6.   Cook until the cheese is browned, for around 4 minutes.
7.   Serve.

Cauliflower Rice Chicken Curry

Prep + Cook Time: 40 minutes | Servings: 4

Ingredients
2 lb chicken (4 breasts)
1 packet curry paste
3 tbsp ghee (can substitute with butter)
½ cup heavy cream
1 head cauliflower (around 1 kg/2.2 lb)

Instructions
1.   Melt the ghee in a pot. Mix in the curry paste.
2.   Add the water and simmer for 5 minutes.
3.   Add the chicken, cover, and simmer on a medium heat for 20 minutes or until the chicken is cooked.
4.   Shred the cauliflower florets in a food processor to resemble rice.
5.   Once the chicken is cooked, uncover, and incorporate the cream.
6.   Cook for 7 minutes and serve over the cauliflower.

Bacon Chops

Prep + Cook Time: 20 minutes | Servings: 2

Ingredients
2 pork chops (I prefer bone-in, but boneless chops work great as well)
1 bag shredded brussels sprouts
4 slices of bacon
Worcestershire sauce
Lemon juice (optional)

Instructions
1.   Place the pork chops on a baking sheet with the Worcestershire sauce inside a preheated grill for 5 minutes.
2.   Turnover and cook for another 5 minutes. Put to the side when done.
3.   Cook the chopped bacon in a large pan until browned. Add the shredded brussels sprouts and cook together.
4.   Stir the brussels sprouts with the bacon and grease and cook for 5 minutes until the bacon is crisp.

Chicken in a Blanket

Prep + Cook Time: 60 minutes | Servings: 3

Ingredients
3 boneless chicken breasts
1 package bacon
1 8-oz package cream cheese
3 jalapeno peppers
Salt, pepper, garlic powder or other seasonings

Instructions
1.   Cut the chicken breast in half lengthwise to create two pieces.
2.   Cut the jalapenos in half lengthwise and remove the seeds.
3.   Dress each breast with a half-inch slice of cream cheese and half a slice of jalapeno. Sprinkle with garlic powder, salt and pepper.
4.   Roll the chicken and wrap 2 to 3 pieces of bacon around it—secure with toothpicks.
5.   Bake in a preheated 375°F/190°C fryer for 50 minutes.
6.   Serve!

Stuffed Chicken Rolls

Prep + Cook Time: 45 minutes | Servings: 4

Ingredients
4 boneless, skinless chicken breasts
7 oz cream cheese
¼ cup green onions, chopped
4 slices bacon, partially cooked

Instructions
1.   Partially cook your strips of bacon, about 5 minutes for each side and set aside.
2.   Pound the chicken breasts to a quarter-inch thick.
3.   Mix the cream cheese and green onions together. Spread 2 tablespoons of the mixture onto each breast. Roll and wrap them with the strip of bacon, then secure with a toothpick.
4.   Place the chicken on a baking sheet and bake in a preheated fryer at 375°F/190°C for 30 minutes.
5.   Broil for 5 minutes to crisp the bacon.
6.   Serve.

Duck Fat Ribeye

Prep + Cook Time: 20 minutes | Servings: 1

Ingredients
One 16-oz ribeye steak (1 - 1 ¼ inch thick)
1 tbsp duck fat (or other high smoke point oil like peanut oil)
½ tbsp butter
½ tsp thyme, chopped
Salt and pepper to taste

Instructions
1.   Preheat a skillet in your fryer at 400°F/200°C.
2.   Season the steaks with the oil, salt and pepper. Remove the skillet from the fryer once pre-heated.
3.   Put the skillet on your stove top burner on a medium heat and drizzle in the oil.
4.   Sear the steak for 1-4 minutes, depending on if you like it rare, medium or well done.
5.   Turn over the steak and place in your fryer for 6 minutes.
6.   Take out the steak from your fryer and place it back on the stove top on low heat.
7.   Toss in the butter and thyme and cook for 3 minutes, basting as you go along.
8.   Rest for 5 minutes and serve.

Easy Zoodles & Turkey Balls

Prep + Cook Time: 35 minutes | Servings: 2

Ingredients

1 zucchini, cut into spirals
1 can vodka pasta sauce
1 package frozen Armour Turkey meatballs

Instructions

1. Cook the meatballs and sauce on a high heat for 25 minutes, stirring occasionally.
2. Wash the zucchini and put through a vegetable spiral maker.
3. Boil the water and blanch the raw zoodles for 60 seconds. Remove and drain.
4. Combine the zoodles and prepared saucy meatballs.
5. Serve!

Sausage Balls

Prep + Cook Time: 25 minutes | Servings: 6

Ingredients

12 oz Jimmy Dean's Sausage
6 oz. shredded cheddar cheese
10 cubes cheddar (optional)

Instructions

1. Mix the shredded cheese and sausage.
2. Divide the mixture into 12 equal parts to be stuffed.
3. Add a cube of cheese to the center of the sausage and roll into balls.
4. Fry at 375°F/190°C for 15 minutes until crisp.
5. Serve!

Bacon Scallops

Prep + Cook Time: 10 minutes | Servings: 6

Ingredients

12 scallops
12 thin bacon slices
12 toothpicks
Salt and pepper to taste
½ tbsp oil

Instructions

1. Heat a skillet on a high heat while drizzling in the oil.
2. Wrap each scallop with a piece of thinly cut bacon—secure with a toothpick.
3. Season to taste.
4. Cook for 3 minutes per side.
5. Serve!

Buffalo Chicken Salad

Prep + Cook Time: 40 minutes | Servings: 1

Ingredients

3 cups salad of your choice
1 chicken breast
1/2 cup shredded cheese of your choice
Buffalo wing sauce of your choice
Ranch or blue cheese dressing

Instructions

1. Preheat your fryer to 400°F/200°C.
2. Douse the chicken breast in the buffalo wing sauce and bake for 25 minutes. In the last 5 minutes, throw the cheese on the wings until it melts.
3. When cooked, remove from the fryer and slice into pieces.

4. Place on a bed of lettuce.
5. Pour the salad dressing of your choice on top.
6. Serve!

Meatballs

Prep + Cook Time: 30 minutes | Servings: 6

Ingredients

1 lb ground beef (or ½ lb beef, ½ lb pork)
½ cup grated parmesan cheese
1 tbsp minced garlic (or paste)
½ cup mozzarella cheese
1 tsp freshly ground pepper

Instructions

1. Preheat your fryer to 400°F/200°C.
2. In a bowl, mix all the ingredients together.
3. Roll the meat mixture into 5 generous meatballs.
4. Bake inside your fryer at 170°F/80°C for about 18 minutes.
5. Serve with sauce!

Fat Bombs

Prep + Cook Time: 100 minutes | Servings: 2

Ingredients

1 cup coconut butter
1 cup coconut milk (full fat, canned)
1 tsp vanilla extract (gluten free)
½ tsp nutmeg
½ cup coconut shreds

Instructions

1. Pour some water into pot and put a glass bowl on top.
2. Add all the ingredients except the shredded coconut into the glass bowl and cook on a medium heat.
3. Stir and melt until they start melting.
4. Then, take them off of the heat.
5. Put the glass bowl into your refrigerator until the mix can be rolled into doughy balls. Usually this happens after around 30 minutes.
6. Roll the dough into 1-inch balls through the coconut shreds.
7. Place the balls on a plate and refrigerate for one hour.
8. Serve!

Cabbage & Beef Casserole

Prep + Cook Time: 40 minutes | Servings: 6

Ingredients

½ lb ground beef
½ cup chopped onion
½ bag coleslaw mix
1-1/2 cups tomato sauce
1 tbsp lemon juice

Instructions

1. In a skillet, cook the ground beef until browned and to the side.
2. Mix in the onion and cabbage to the skillet and sauté until soft.
3. Add the ground beef back in along with the tomato sauce and lemon juice.
4. Bring the mixture to a boil, then cover and simmer for 30 minutes.
5. Enjoy!

Roast Beef Lettuce Wraps

Prep + Cook Time: 10 minutes | Servings: 4

Ingredients

8 large iceberg lettuce leaves
8 oz (8 slices) rare roast beef
½ cup homemade mayonnaise
8 slices provolone cheese
1 cup baby spinach

Instructions

1. Wash the lettuce leaves and sake them dry. Try not to rip them.
2. Place 1 slice of roast beef inside each wrap.
3. Smother 1 tablespoon of mayonnaise on top of each piece of roast beef.
4. Top the mayonnaise with 1 slice of provolone cheese and 1 cup of baby spinach.
5. Roll the lettuce up around the toppings.
6. Serve & enjoy!

Turkey Avocado Rolls

Prep + Cook Time: 10 minutes | Servings: 6

Ingredients

12 slices (12 oz) turkey breast
12 slices Swiss cheese
2 cups baby spinach
1 large avocado, cut into 12 slices
1 cup homemade mayonnaise (see recipe in Chapter 9)

Instructions

1. Lay out the slices of turkey breast flat and place a slice of Swiss cheese on top of each one.
2. Top each slice with 1 cup baby spinach and 3 slices of avocado.
3. Drizzle the mayonnaise on top.
4. Sprinkle each "sandwich" with lemon pepper.
5. Roll up the sandwiches and secure with toothpicks.
6. Serve immediately or refrigerate until ready to serve.

Nearly Pizza

Prep + Cook Time: 30 minutes | Servings: 4

Ingredients

4 large portobello mushrooms
4 tsp olive oil
1 cup marinara sauce
1 cup shredded mozzarella cheese
10 slices sugar-free pepperoni

Instructions

1. Preheat your fryer to 375°F/190°C.
2. De-steam the 4 mushrooms and brush each cap with the olive oil, one spoon for each cap.
3. Place on a baking sheet and bake stem side down for 8 minutes.
4. Take out of the fryer and fill each cap with 1 cup marinara sauce, 1 cup mozzarella cheese and 3 slices of pepperoni.
5. Cook for another 10 minutes until browned.
6. Serve hot.

Taco Stuffed Peppers

Prep + Cook Time: 30 minutes | Servings: 4

Ingredients

1 lb. ground beef
1 tbsp. taco seasoning mix
1 can diced tomatoes and green chilis
4 green bell peppers
1 cup shredded Monterey jack cheese, divided

Instructions

1. Set a skillet over a high heat and cook the ground beef for seven to ten minutes. Make sure it is cooked through and brown all over. Drain the fat.
2. Stir in the taco seasoning mix, as well as the diced tomatoes and green chilis. Allow the mixture to cook for a further three to five minutes.
3. In the meantime, slice the tops off the green peppers and remove the seeds and membranes.
4. When the meat mixture is fully cooked, spoon equal amounts of it into the peppers and top with the Monterey jack cheese. Then place the peppers into your fryer.
5. Cook at 350°F for fifteen minutes.
6. The peppers are ready when they are soft, and the cheese is bubbling and brown. Serve warm and enjoy!

Beef Tenderloin & Peppercorn Crust

Prep + Cook Time: 45 minutes | Servings: 6

Ingredients

2 lb. beef tenderloin
2 tsp. roasted garlic, minced
2 tbsp. salted butter, melted
3 tbsp. ground 4-peppercorn blender

Instructions

1. Remove any surplus fat from the beef tenderloin.
2. Combine the roasted garlic and melted butter to apply to your tenderloin with a brush.
3. On a plate, spread out the peppercorns and roll the tenderloin in them, making sure they are covering and clinging to the meat.
4. Cook the tenderloin in your fryer for twenty-five minutes at 400°F, turning halfway through cooking.
5. Let the tenderloin rest for ten minutes before slicing and serving.

Bratwursts

Prep + Cook Time: 18 minutes | Servings: 4

Ingredients

4 x 3-oz. beef bratwursts

Instructions

1. Place the beef bratwursts in the basket of your fryer and cook for fifteen minutes at 375°F, turning once halfway through.
2. Enjoy with the low-carb toppings and sides of your choice.

Bacon-Wrapped Hot Dog

Prep + Cook Time: 25 minutes | Servings: 4

Ingredients

4 slices sugar-free bacon
4 beef hot dogs

Instructions

1.   Take a slice of bacon and wrap it around the hot dog, securing it with a toothpick. Repeat with the other pieces of bacon and hot dogs, placing each wrapped dog in the basket of your fryer.
2.   Cook at 370°F for ten minutes, turning halfway through to fry the other side.
3.   Once hot and crispy, the hot dogs are ready to serve. Enjoy!

Herb Shredded Beef

Prep + Cook Time: 25 minutes | Servings: 6

Ingredients

1 tsp. dried dill
1 tsp. dried thyme
1 tsp. garlic powder
2 lbs. beefsteak
3 tbsp. butter

Instructions

1.   Pre-heat your fryer at 360°F.
2.   Combine the dill, thyme, and garlic powder together, and massage into the steak.
3.   Cook the steak in the fryer for twenty minutes, then remove, shred, and return to the fryer. Add the butter and cook for a further two minutes at 365°F. Make sure the beef is coated in the butter before serving.

Herbed Butter Rib Eye Steak

Prep + Cook Time: 60 minutes | Servings: 4

Ingredients

4 ribeye steaks
Olive oil
¾ tsp. dry rub
½ cup butter
1 tsp. dried basil
3 tbsp. lemon garlic seasoning

Instructions

1.   Massage the olive oil into the steaks and your favorite dry rub. Leave aside to sit for thirty minutes.
2.   In a bowl, combine the button, dried basil, and lemon garlic seasoning, then refrigerate.
3.   Pre-heat the fryer at 450°F and set a rack inside. Place the steaks on top of the rack and allow to cook for fifteen minutes.
4.   Remove the steaks from the fryer when cooked and serve with the herbed butter.

Flank Steak & Avocado Butter

Prep + Cook Time: 40 minutes | Servings: 1

Ingredients

1 flank steak
Salt and pepper
2 avocados
2 tbsp. butter, melted
½ cup chimichurri sauce

Instructions

1.   Rub the flank steak with salt and pepper to taste and leave to sit for twenty minutes.
2.   Pre-heat the fryer at 400°F and place a rack inside.
3.   Halve the avocados and take out the pits. Spoon the flesh into a bowl and mash with a fork. Mix in the melted butter and chimichurri sauce, making sure everything is well combined.
4.   Put the steak in the fryer and cook for six minutes. Flip over and allow to cook for another six minutes.
5.   Serve the steak with the avocado butter and enjoy!

Mozzarella Beef

Prep + Cook Time: 30 minutes | Servings: 6

Ingredients

12 oz. beef brisket
2 tsp. Italian herbs
2 tsp. butter
1 onion, sliced
7 oz. mozzarella cheese, sliced

Instructions

1.   Pre-heat the fryer at 365°F.
2.   Cut up the brisket into four equal slices and season with the Italian herbs.
3.   Allow the butter to melt in the fryer. Place the slices of beef inside along with the onion. Put a piece of mozzarella on top of each piece of brisket and cook for twenty-five minutes.
4.   Enjoy!

Rosemary Rib Eye Steaks

Prep + Cook Time: 40 minutes | Servings: 2

Ingredients

¼ cup butter
1 clove minced garlic
Salt and pepper
1 ½ tbsp. balsamic vinegar
¼ cup rosemary, chopped
2 ribeye steaks

Instructions

1.   Melt the butter in a skillet over medium heat. Add the garlic and fry until fragrant.
2.   Remove the skillet from the heat and add in the salt, pepper, and vinegar. Allow it to cool.
3.   Add the rosemary, then pour the whole mixture into a Ziploc bag.
4.   Put the ribeye steaks in the bag and shake well, making sure to coat the meat well. Refrigerate for an hour, then allow to sit for a further twenty minutes.
5.   Pre-heat the fryer at 400°F and set the rack inside. Cook the ribeyes for fifteen minutes.
6.   Take care when removing the steaks from the fryer and plate up. Enjoy!

Herbed Butter Beef Loin

Prep + Cook Time: 25 minutes | Servings: 4

Ingredients

1 tbsp. butter, melted
¼ dried thyme
1 tsp. garlic salt
¼ tsp. dried parsley
1 lb. beef loin

Instructions

1. In a bowl, combine the melted butter, thyme, garlic salt, and parsley.
2. Cut the beef loin into slices and generously apply the seasoned butter using a brush.
3. Pre-heat your fryer at 400°F and place a rack inside.
4. Cook the beef for fifteen minutes.
5. Take care when removing it and serve hot.

Lamb Ribs

Prep + Cook Time: 25 minutes | Servings: 4

Ingredients

1 lb. lamb ribs
2 tbsp. mustard
1 tsp. rosemary, chopped
Salt and pepper
¼ cup mint leaves, chopped
1 cup Green yogurt

Instructions

1. Pre-heat the fryer at 350°F.
2. Use a brush to apply the mustard to the lamb ribs, and season with rosemary, as well as salt and pepper as desired.
3. Cook the ribs in the fryer for eighteen minutes.
4. Meanwhile, combine together the mint leaves and yogurt in a bowl.
5. Remove the lamb ribs from the fryer when cooked and serve with the mint yogurt. Enjoy!

Lamb Satay

Prep + Cook Time: 25 minutes | Servings: 2

Ingredients

¼ tsp. cumin
1 tsp ginger
½ tsp. nutmeg
Salt and pepper
2 boneless lamb steaks
Olive oil cooking spray

Instructions

1. Combine the cumin, ginger, nutmeg, salt and pepper in a bowl.
2. Cube the lamb steaks and massage the spice mixture into each one.
3. Leave to marinate for ten minutes, then transfer onto metal skewers.
4. Pre-heat the fryer at 400°F.
5. Spritz the skewers with the olive oil cooking spray, then cook them in the fryer for eight minutes.
6. Take care when removing them from the fryer and serve with the low-carb sauce of your choice.

Italian Lamb Chops

Prep + Cook Time: 20 minutes | Servings: 2

Ingredients

2 lamp chops
2 tsp. Italian herbs
2 avocados
½ cup mayonnaise
1 tbsp. lemon juice

Instructions

1. Season the lamb chops with the Italian herbs, then set aside for five minutes.
2. Pre-heat the fryer at 400°F and place the rack inside.
3. Put the chops on the rack and allow to cook for twelve minutes.
4. In the meantime, halve the avocados and open to remove the pits. Spoon the flesh into a blender.
5. Add in the mayonnaise and lemon juice and pulse until a smooth consistency is achieved.
6. Take care when removing the chops from the fryer, then plate up and serve with the avocado mayo.

Breaded Pork Chops

Prep + Cook Time: 25 minutes | Servings: 4

Ingredients

1 tsp. chili powder
½ tsp. garlic powder
1 ½ oz. pork rinds, finely ground
4 x 4-oz. pork chops
1 tbsp. coconut oil, melted

Instructions

1. Combine the chili powder, garlic powder, and ground pork rinds.
2. Coat the pork chops with the coconut oil, followed by the pork rind mixture, taking care to cover them completely. Then place the chops in the basket of the fryer.
3. Cook the chops for fifteen minutes at 400°F, turning halfway through.
4. Once they are browned, check the temperature has reached 145°F before serving with the sides of your choice.

Juicy Mexican Pork Chops

Prep + Cook Time: 25 minutes | Servings: 2

Ingredients

¼ tsp. dried oregano
1 ½ tsp. taco seasoning mix
2 x 4-oz. boneless pork chops
2 tbsp. unsalted butter, divided

Instructions

1. Combine the dried oregano and taco seasoning to rub into the pork chops.
2. In your fryer, cook the chops at 400°F for fifteen minutes, turning them over halfway through to cook on the other side.
3. When the chops are a brown color, check the internal temperature has reached 145°F and remove from the fryer. Serve with a garnish of butter.

Baby Back Ribs

Prep + Cook Time: 45 minutes | Servings: 2

Ingredients

2 tsp. red pepper flakes
¾ ground ginger
3 cloves minced garlic
Salt and pepper
2 baby back ribs

Instructions

1. Pre-heat your fryer at 350°F.
2. Combine the red pepper flakes, ginger, garlic, salt and pepper in a bowl, making sure to mix well. Massage the mixture into the baby back ribs.
3. Cook the ribs in the fryer for thirty minutes.
4. Take care when taking the rubs out of the fryer. Place them on a serving dish and enjoy with a low-carb barbecue sauce of your choosing.

Pulled Pork

Prep + Cook Time: 30 minutes | Servings: 1

Ingredients

1 lb. pork tenderloin
2 tbsp. barbecue dry rub
1/3 cup heavy cream
1 tsp. butter

Instructions

1. Pre-heat your fryer at 370°F.
2. Massage the dry rub of your choice into the tenderloin, coating it well.
3. Cook the tenderloin in the fryer for twenty minutes. When cooked, shred with two forks.
4. Add the heavy cream and butter into the fryer along with the shredded pork and stir well. Cook for a further four minutes.
5. Allow to cool a little, then serve and enjoy.

Ribs

Prep + Cook Time: 60 minutes | Servings: 4

Ingredients

1 lb. pork ribs
1 tbsp. barbecue dry rub
1 tsp. mustard
1 tbsp. apple cider vinegar
1 tsp. sesame oil

Instructions

1. Chop up the pork ribs.
2. Combine the dry rub, mustard, apple cider vinegar, and sesame oil, then coat the ribs with this mixture. Refrigerate the ribs for twenty minutes.
3. Preheat the fryer at 360°F.
4. When the ribs are ready, place them in the fryer and cook for 15 minutes. Flip them and cook on the other side for a further fifteen minutes. Then serve and enjoy!

Pork Chops

Prep + Cook Time: 15 minutes | Servings: 3

Ingredients

3 pork chops
½ tsp. dried rosemary
1 tsp. garlic salt
1 tsp. peppercorns
1 tbsp. butter

Instructions

1. Pre-heat your fryer to 365°F.
2. Combine the dried rosemary and garlic salt and rub into the pork chops.
3. Place the peppercorns and butter into the fryer and allow the butter to melt.
4. Add in the pork chops and cook for six minutes. Flip them and cook for an additional five minutes before serving.

Sriracha Cauliflower

Prep + Cook Time: 25 minutes | Servings: 4

Ingredients

¼ cup vegan butter, melted
¼ cup sriracha sauce
4 cups cauliflower florets
1 cup bread crumbs
1 tsp. salt

Instructions

1. Mix together the sriracha and vegan butter in a bowl and pour this mixture over the cauliflower, taking care to cover each floret entirely.
2. In a separate bowl, combine the bread crumbs and salt.
3. Dip the cauliflower florets in the bread crumbs, coating each one well. Cook in the Air Fryer for 17 minutes in a 375°F pre-heated Air Fryer.

Ratatouille

Prep + Cook Time: 30 minutes | Servings: 4

Ingredients

1 sprig basil
1 sprig flat-leaf parsley
1 sprig mint
1 tbsp. coriander powder
1 tsp. capers
½ lemon, juiced
Salt and pepper to taste
2 eggplants, sliced crosswise
2 red onions, chopped
4 cloves garlic, minced
2 red peppers, sliced crosswise
1 fennel bulb, sliced crosswise
3 large zucchinis, sliced crosswise
5 tbsp. olive oil
4 large tomatoes, chopped
2 tsp. herbs de Provence

Instructions

1. Blend together the basil, parsley, coriander, mint, lemon juice and capers, with a little salt and pepper. Make sure all ingredients are well-incorporated.
2. Pre-heat the Air Fryer at 400°F.
3. Coat the eggplant, onions, garlic, peppers, fennel, and zucchini with olive oil.
4. Take a baking dish small enough to fit inside the fryer. Transfer the vegetables into the dish and top with the tomatoes and herb puree. Sprinkle on some more salt and pepper if desired, as well as the herbs de Provence.
5. Fry for 25 minutes.

Pesto Stuffed Bella Mushrooms

Prep + Cook Time: 25 minutes | Servings: 6

Ingredients

1 cup basil
½ cup cashew nuts, soaked overnight
½ cup nutritional yeast
1 tbsp. lemon juice
2 cloves of garlic
1 tbsp. olive oil
Salt to taste
1 lb. baby Bella mushroom, stems removed

Instructions

1. Pre-heat the Air Fryer at 400°F.
2. Prepare your pesto. In a food processor, blend together the basil, cashew nuts, nutritional yeast, lemon juice, garlic and olive oil to combine well. Sprinkle on salt as desired.
3. Turn the mushrooms cap-side down and spread the pesto on the underside of each cap.
4. Transfer to the fryer and cook for 15 minutes.

Veg Burger

Prep + Cook Time: 25 minutes | Servings: 8

Ingredients

½ lb. cauliflower, steamed and diced
2 tsp. coconut oil melted
2 tsp. garlic, minced
¼ cup desiccated coconut
½ cup oats
3 tbsp. flour
1 flax egg [1 tbsp. flaxseed + 3 tbsp. water]
1 tsp. mustard powder
2 tsp. thyme
2 tsp. parsley
2 tsp. chives
Salt and pepper to taste
1 cup bread crumbs

Instructions

1. Pre-heat the Air Fryer at 390°F.
2. Drain any excess water out of the cauliflower on a kitchen towel.
3. Combine the cauliflower with all of ingredients bar the breadcrumbs, incorporating everything well.
4. Using your hands, shape 8 equal-sized amounts of the mixture into burger patties. Coat the patties in breadcrumbs before putting them in the basket of the fryer in a single layer.
5. Cook for 10-15 minutes, ensuring the patties crisp up.

Chili Potato Wedges

Prep + Cook Time: 50 minutes | Servings: 4

Ingredients

1 lb. fingerling potatoes, washed and cut into wedges
1 tsp. olive oil
1 tsp. salt
1 tsp. black pepper
1 tsp. cayenne pepper
1 tsp. nutritional yeast
½ tsp. garlic powder

Instructions

1. Pre-heat the Air Fryer at 400°F.
2. Coat the potatoes with the rest of the ingredients.
3. Transfer to the basket of your fryer and allow to cook for 16 minutes, shaking the basket at the halfway point.

Christmas Brussels Sprouts

Prep + Cook Time: 20 minutes | Servings: 2

Ingredients

2 cups Brussels sprouts, halved
1 tbsp. olive oil
1 tbsp. balsamic vinegar
1 tbsp. maple syrup
¼ tsp. sea salt

Instructions

1. Pre-heat the Air Fryer at 375°F.
2. Evenly coat the Brussels sprouts with the olive oil, balsamic vinegar, maple syrup, and salt.
3. Transfer to the basket of your fryer and cook for 5 minutes. Give the basket a good shake, turn the heat up to 400°F and continue to cook for another 8 minutes.

Summer Rolls

Prep + Cook Time: 25 minutes | Servings: 4

Ingredients

1 cup shiitake mushroom, sliced thinly
1 celery stalk, chopped
1 medium carrot, shredded
½ tsp. ginger, finely chopped
1 tsp. sugar
1 tbsp. soy sauce
1 tsp. nutritional yeast
8 spring roll sheets
1 tsp. corn starch
2 tbsp. water

Instructions

1. In a bowl, combine the ginger, soy sauce, nutritional yeast, carrots, celery, and sugar.
2. Mix together the cornstarch and water to create an adhesive for your spring rolls.
3. Scoop a tablespoonful of the vegetable mixture into the middle of the spring roll sheets. Brush the edges of the sheets with the cornstarch adhesive and enclose around the filling to make spring rolls.
4. Pre-heat your Air Fryer at 400°F. When warm, place the rolls inside and cook for 15 minutes or until crisp.

Rice Bowl

Prep + Cook Time: 55 minutes | Servings: 4

Ingredients

¼ cup cucumber, sliced
1 tsp. salt
1 tbsp. sugar
7 tbsp. Japanese rice vinegar
3 medium-sized eggplants, sliced
3 tbsp. sweet white miso paste
1 tbsp. mirin rice wine
4 cups sushi rice, cooked
4 spring onions
1 tbsp. sesame seeds, toasted

Instructions

1. Coat the cucumber slices with the rice wine vinegar, salt, and sugar.
2. Place a dish on top of the bowl to weight it down completely.
3. Pre-heat the Air Fryer at 400°F.
4. In a bowl, mix together the eggplants, mirin rice wine, and miso paste. Allow to marinate for half an hour.
5. Cook the eggplant in the fryer for 10 minutes.
6. Place the eggplant slices in the Air Fryer and cook for 10 minutes.
7. Fill the bottom of a serving bowl with rice and top with the eggplants and pickled cucumbers. Add the spring onions and sesame seeds for garnish.

Asian Tofu Bites

Prep + Cook Time: 20 minutes | Servings: 4

Ingredients

1 packaged firm tofu, cubed and pressed to remove excess water
1 tbsp. soy sauce
1 tbsp. ketchup
1 tbsp. maple syrup
½ tsp. vinegar
1 tsp. liquid smoke
1 tsp. hot sauce
2 tbsp. sesame seeds
1 tsp. garlic powder
Salt and pepper to taste

Instructions

1. Pre-heat the Air Fryer at 375°F.
2. Take a baking dish small enough to fit inside the fryer and spritz it with cooking spray.
3. Combine all the ingredients to coat the tofu completely and allow the marinade to absorb for half an hour.
4. Transfer the tofu to the baking dish, then cook for 15 minutes. Flip the tofu over and cook for another 15 minute on the other side.

Chickpeas

Prep + Cook Time: 20 minutes | Servings: 4

Ingredients

1 15-oz. can chickpeas, drained but not rinsed
2 tbsp. olive oil
1 tsp. salt
2 tbsp. lemon juice

Instructions

1. Pre-heat the Air Fryer at 400°F.
2. Add all the ingredients together in a bowl and mix. Transfer this mixture to the basket of the fryer.
3. Cook for 15 minutes, ensuring the chickpeas become nice and crispy.

Cauliflower Cheese Tater Tots

Prep + Cook Time: 25 minutes | Servings: 12

Ingredients

1 lb. cauliflower, steamed and chopped
½ cup nutritional yeast
1 tbsp. oats
1 flax egg [1 tbsp. desiccated coconuts + 3 tbsp. flaxseed meal
+ 3 tbsp. water]
1 onion, chopped
1 tsp. garlic, minced
1 tsp. parsley, chopped
1 tsp. oregano, chopped
1 tsp. chives, chopped
Salt and pepper to taste
½ cup bread crumbs

Instructions

1. Pre-heat the Air Fryer at 390°F.
2. Drain any excess water out of the cauliflower by wringing it with a paper towel.
3. In a bowl, combine the cauliflower with the remaining ingredients, save the bread crumbs. Using your hands, shape the mixture into several small balls.

4. Coat the balls in the bread crumbs and transfer to the basket of your fryer. Allow to cook for 6 minutes, after which you should raise the temperature to 400°F and then leave to cook for an additional 10 minutes.

Sweet Onions & Potatoes

Prep + Cook Time: 30 minutes | Servings: 6

Ingredients

2 large sweet potatoes, peeled and cut into chunks
2 medium sweet onions, cut into chunks
3 tbsp. olive oil
1 tsp. dried thyme
Salt and pepper to taste
¼ cup s, sliced and toasted

Instructions

1. Pre-heat the Air Fryer at 425°F.
2. In a bowl, combine all of the ingredients, except for the sliced s.
3. Transfer the vegetables and dressing to a ramekin and cook in the fryer for 20 minutes.
4. When ready to serve, add the s on top.

Mushroom Pizza Squares

Prep + Cook Time: 20 minutes | Servings: 10

Ingredients

1 vegan pizza dough
1 cup oyster mushrooms, chopped
1 shallot, chopped
¼ red bell pepper, chopped
2 tbsp. parsley
Salt and pepper

Instructions

1. Pre-heat the Air Fryer at 400°F.
2. Cut the vegan pizza dough into squares.
3. In a bowl, combine the oyster mushrooms, shallot, bell pepper and parsley. Sprinkle some salt and pepper as desired.
4. Spread this mixture on top of the pizza squares.
5. Cook in the Air Fryer for 10 minutes.

Tofu & Sweet Potatoes

Prep + Cook Time: 50 minutes | Servings: 8

Ingredients

8 sweet potatoes, scrubbed
2 tbsp. olive oil
1 large onion, chopped
2 green chilies, deseeded and chopped
½ lb. tofu, crumbled
2 tbsp. Cajun seasoning
cup tomatoes
1 can kidney beans, drained and rinsed
Salt and pepper to taste

Instructions

1. Pre-heat the Air Fryer at 400°F.
2. With a knife, pierce the skin of the sweet potatoes in numerous places and cook in the fryer for half an hour, making sure they become soft. Remove from the fryer, halve each potato, and set to one side.
3. Over a medium heat, fry the onions and chilis in a little oil for 2 minutes until fragrant.
4. Add in the tofu and Cajun seasoning and allow to cook for a further 3 minutes before incorporating the kidney beans and tomatoes. Sprinkle some salt and pepper as desire.
5. Top each sweet potato halve with a spoonful of the tofu mixture and serve.

Risotto

Prep + Cook Time: 40 minutes | Servings: 2

Ingredients

1 onion, diced
2 cups chicken stock, boiling
½ cup parmesan cheese or cheddar cheese, grated
1 clove garlic, minced
¾ cup arborio rice
1 tbsp. olive oil
1 tbsp. butter, unsalted

Instructions

1. Turn the Air Fryer to 390°F and set for 5 minutes to warm.
2. Grease a round baking tin with oil and stir in the butter, garlic, and onion.
3. Put the tin in the fryer and allow to cook for 4 minutes.
4. Pour in the rice and cook for a further 4 minutes, stirring three times throughout the cooking time.
5. Turn the temperature down to 320°F.
6. Add the chicken stock and give the dish a gentle stir. Cook for 22 minutes, leaving the fryer uncovered.
7. Pour in the cheese, stir once more and serve.

Chickpea & Avocado Mash

Prep + Cook Time: 30 minutes | Servings: 4

Ingredients

1 medium-sized head of cauliflower, cut into florets
1 can chickpeas, drained and rinsed
1 tbsp. extra-virgin olive oil
2 tbsp. lemon juice
Salt and pepper to taste
4 flatbreads, toasted
2 ripe avocados, mashed

Instructions

1. Pre-heat the Air Fryer at 425°F.
2. In a bowl, mix together the chickpeas, cauliflower, lemon juice and olive oil. Sprinkle salt and pepper as desired.
3. Put inside the Air Fryer basket and cook for 25 minutes.
4. Spread on top of the flatbread along with the mashed avocado. Sprinkle on more pepper and salt as desired and enjoy with hot sauce.

Fried Potatoes

Prep + Cook Time: 55 minutes | Servings: 1

Ingredients

1 medium russet potatoes, scrubbed and peeled
1 tsp. olive oil
¼ tsp. onion powder
1/8 tsp. salt
A dollop of vegan butter
A dollop of vegan cream cheese
1 tbsp. Kalamata olives
1 tbsp. chives, chopped

Instructions

1. Pre-heat the Air Fryer at 400°F.
2. In a bowl, coat the potatoes with the onion powder, salt, olive oil, and vegan butter.
3. Transfer to the fryer and allow to cook for 40 minutes, turning the potatoes over at the halfway point.
4. Take care when removing the potatoes from the fryer and enjoy with the vegan cream cheese, Kalamata olives and chives on top, plus any other vegan sides you desire.

French Green Beans

Prep + Cook Time: 20 minutes | Servings: 4

Ingredients

1 ½ lb. French green beans, stems removed and blanched
1 tbsp. salt
½ lb. shallots, peeled and cut into quarters
½ tsp. ground white pepper
2 tbsp. olive oil
¼ cup slivered s, toasted

Instructions

1. Pre-heat the Air Fryer at 400°F.
2. Coat the vegetables with the rest of the ingredients in a bowl.
3. Transfer to the basket of your fryer and cook for 10 minutes, making sure the green beans achieve a light brown color.

Black Bean Chili

Prep + Cook Time: 25 minutes | Servings: 6

Ingredients

1 tbsp. olive oil
1 medium onion, diced
3 cloves of garlic, minced
1 cup vegetable broth
3 cans black beans, drained and rinsed
2 cans diced tomatoes
2 chipotle peppers, chopped
2 tsp. cumin
2 tsp. chili powder
1 tsp. dried oregano
½ tsp. salt

Instructions

1. Over a medium heat, fry the garlic and onions in a little oil for 3 minutes.
2. Add in the remaining ingredients, stirring constantly and scraping the bottom to prevent sticking.
3. Pre-heat your Air Fryer at 400°F.
4. Take a heat-resistant dish small enough to fit inside the fryer and place the mixture inside. Put a sheet of aluminum foil on top.
5. Transfer to the air fryer and cook for 20 minutes.
6. When ready, plate up and serve with diced avocado, chopped cilantro, and chopped tomatoes.

Cauliflower

Prep + Cook Time: 20 minutes | Servings: 4

Ingredients

1 head cauliflower, cut into florets
1 tbsp. extra-virgin olive oil
2 scallions, chopped
5 cloves of garlic, sliced
1 ½ tbsp. tamari
1 tbsp. rice vinegar
½ tsp. sugar
1 tbsp. sriracha

Instructions

1.   Pre-heat the Air Fryer to 400°F.
2.   Put the cauliflower florets in the Air Fryer and drizzle some oil over them before cooking for 10 minutes.
3.   Turn the cauliflower over, throw in the onions and garlic, and stir. Cook for another 10 minutes.
4.   Mix together the rest of the ingredients in a bowl.
5.   Remove the cooked cauliflower from the fryer and coat it in the sauce.
6.   Return to the Air Fryer and allow to cook for another 5 minutes. Enjoy with a side of rice.

Tofu Bites

Prep + Cook Time: 65 minutes | Servings: 3

Ingredients

2 tbsp. sesame oil
¼ cup maple syrup
3 tbsp. peanut butter
¼ cup liquid aminos
3tbsp. chili garlic sauce
2 tbsp. rice wine vinegar
2 cloves of garlic, minced
1 inch fresh ginger, peeled and grated
1 tsp. red pepper flakes
1 block extra firm tofu, pressed to remove excess water and cubed
Toasted peanuts, chopped
1 tsp. sesame seeds
1 sprig cilantro, chopped

Instructions

1.   Whisk together the first 9 ingredients in a large bowl to well combine.
2.   Transfer to an airtight bag along with the cubed tofu. Allow to marinate for a minimum of a half hour.
3.   Pre-heat the Air Fryer to 425°F.
4.   Put the tofu cubes in the fryer, keep any excess marinade for the sauce. Cook for 15 minutes.
5.   In the meantime, heat the marinade over a medium heat to reduce by half.
6.   Plate up the cooked tofu with some cooked rice and serve with the sauce. Complete the dish with the sesame seeds, cilantro and peanuts.

Faux Rice

Prep + Cook Time: 60 minutes | Servings: 8

Ingredients

1 medium-to-large head of cauliflower

½ lemon, juiced
garlic cloves, minced
2 cans mushrooms, 8 oz. each
1 can water chestnuts, 8 oz.
¾ cup peas
½ cup egg substitute or 1 egg, beaten
4 tbsp. soy sauce
1 tbsp. peanut oil
1 tbsp. sesame oil
1 tbsp. ginger, fresh and minced
High quality cooking spray

Instructions

1.   Mix together the peanut oil, soy sauce, sesame oil, minced ginger, lemon juice, and minced garlic to combine well.
2.   Peel and wash the cauliflower head before cutting it into small florets.
3.   In a food processor, pulse the florets in small batches to break them down to resemble rice grains.
4.   Pour into your Air Fryer basket.
5.   Drain the can of water chestnuts and roughly chop them. Pour into the basket.
6.   Cook at 350°F for 20 minutes.
7.   In the meantime, drain the mushrooms. When the 20 minutes are up, add the mushrooms and the peas to the fryer and continue to cook for another 15 minutes.
8.   Lightly spritz a frying pan with cooking spray. Prepare an omelet with the egg substitute or the beaten egg, ensuring it is firm. Lay on a cutting board and slice it up.
9.   When the cauliflower is ready, throw in the omelet and cook for an additional 5 minutes. Serve hot.

Potato Croquettes

Prep + Cook Time: 25 minutes | Servings: 10

Ingredients

¼ cup nutritional yeast
2 cups boiled potatoes, mashed
1 flax egg [1 tbsp. flaxseed meal + 3 tbsp. water]
1 tbsp. flour
2 tbsp. chives, chopped
Salt and pepper to taste
2 tbsp. vegetable oil
¼ cup bread crumbs

Instructions

1.   Pre-heat the Air Fryer to 400°F.
2.   In a bowl, combine together the nutritional yeast, potatoes, flax eggs, flour, and chives. Sprinkle with salt and pepper as desired.
3.   In separate bowl mix together the vegetable oil and bread crumbs to achieve a crumbly consistency.
4.   Use your hands to shape the potato mixture into small balls and dip each one into the breadcrumb mixture.
5.   Place the croquettes inside the air fryer and cook for 15 minutes, ensuring the croquettes turn golden brown.

Sweet & Sour Tofu

Prep + Cook Time: 55 minutes | Servings: 2

Ingredients

2 tsp. apple cider vinegar
1 tbsp. sugar
1 tbsp. soy sauce
3 tsp. lime juice
1 tsp. ground ginger
1 tsp. garlic powder
½ block firm tofu, pressed to remove excess liquid and cut into cubes
1 tsp. cornstarch
2 green onions, chopped
Toasted sesame seeds for garnish

Instructions

1.   In a bowl, thoroughly combine the apple cider vinegar, sugar, soy sauce, lime juice, ground ginger, and garlic powder.
2.   Cover the tofu with this mixture and leave to marinate for at least 30 minutes.
3.   Transfer the tofu to the Air Fryer, keeping any excess marinade for the sauce. Cook at 400°F for 20 minutes or until crispy.
4.   In the meantime, thicken the sauce with the cornstarch over a medium-low heat.
5.   Serve the cooked tofu with the sauce, green onions, sesame seeds, and some rice.

Vegetable Salad

Prep + Cook Time: 20 minutes | Servings: 4

Ingredients

6 plum tomatoes, halved
2 large red onions, sliced
4 long red pepper, sliced
2 yellow pepper, sliced
6 cloves of garlic, crushed
1 tbsp. extra-virgin olive oil
1 tsp. paprika
½ lemon, juiced
Salt and pepper to taste
1 tbsp. baby capers

Instructions

1.   Pre-heat the Air Fryer at 420°F.
2.   Put the tomatoes, onions, peppers, and garlic in a large bowl and cover with the extra virgin olive oil, paprika, and lemon juice. Sprinkle with salt and pepper as desired.
3.   Line the inside of your fryer with aluminum foil. Place the vegetables inside and allow to cook for 10 minutes, ensuring the edges turn brown.
4.   Serve in a salad bowl with the baby capers. Make sure all the ingredients are well combined.

Mediterranean Vegetables

Prep + Cook Time: 30 minutes | Servings: 4

Ingredients

1 cup cherry tomatoes, halved
1 large zucchini, sliced
1 green pepper, sliced
1 parsnip, sliced
1 carrot, sliced
1 tsp. mixed herbs
1 tsp. mustard
1 tsp. garlic puree
6 tbsp. olive oil
Salt and pepper to taste

Instructions

1.   Pre-heat the Air Fryer at 400°F.
2.   Combine all the ingredients in a bowl, making sure to coat the vegetables well.
3.   Transfer to the fryer and cook for 6 minutes, ensuring the vegetables are tender and browned.

Sweet Potatoes

Prep + Cook Time: 55 minutes | Servings: 4

Ingredients

2 potatoes, peeled and cubed
4 carrots, cut into chunks
1 head broccoli, cut into florets
4 zucchinis, sliced thickly
Salt and pepper to taste
¼ cup olive oil
1 tbsp. dry onion powder

Instructions

1.   Pre-heat the Air Fryer to 400°F.
2.   In a baking dish small enough to fit inside the fryer, add all the ingredients and combine well.
3.   Cook for 45 minutes in the fryer, ensuring the vegetables are soft and the sides have browned before serving.

Sage Chicken Escallops

Prep + Cook Time: 45 minutes | Servings: 4

Ingredients

4 skinless chicken breasts
2 eggs, beaten
½ cup flour
6 sage leaves
¼ cup bread crumbs
¼ cup parmesan cheese
Cooking spray

Instructions

1.   Cut the chicken breasts into thin, flat slices.
2.   In a bowl, combine the parmesan with the sage.
3.   Add in the flour and eggs and sprinkle with salt and pepper as desired. Mix well.
4.   Dip chicken in the flour-egg mixture.
5.   Coat the chicken in the panko bread crumbs.
6.   Spritz the inside of the Air Fryer with cooking spray and set it to 390°F, allowing it to warm.
7.   Cook the chicken for 20 minutes.
8.   When golden, serve with fried rice.

Fried Pickles

Prep + Cook Time: 30 minutes | Servings: 4

Ingredients

14 dill pickles, sliced
¼ cup flour
1/8 tsp. baking powder
Pinch of salt
2 tbsp. cornstarch + 3 tbsp. water
6 tbsp. bread crumbs
½ tsp. paprika
Cooking spray

Instructions

1.   Pre-heat your Air Fryer at 400°F.
2.   Drain any excess moisture out of the dill pickles on a paper towel.
3.   In a bowl, combine the flour, baking powder and salt.
4.   Throw in the cornstarch and water mixture and combine well with a whisk.
5.   Put the panko bread crumbs in a shallow dish along with the paprika. Mix thoroughly.
6.   Dip the pickles in the flour batter, before coating in the bread crumbs. Spritz all the pickles with the cooking spray.
7.   Transfer to the fryer and cook for 15 minutes, until a golden brown color is achieved.

Cauliflower Bites

Prep + Cook Time: 30 minutes | Servings: 4

Ingredients
1 cup flour
⅓ cup desiccated coconut
Salt and pepper to taste
1 flax egg [1 tbsp. flaxseed meal + 3 tbsp. water]
1 small cauliflower, cut into florets
1 tsp. mixed spice
½ tsp. mustard powder
2 tbsp. maple syrup
1 clove of garlic, minced
2 tbsp. soy sauce

Instructions
1.   Pre-heat the Air Fryer to 400°F.
2.   In a bowl, mix together the oats, flour, and desiccated coconut, sprinkling with some salt and pepper as desired.
3.   In a separate bowl, season the flax egg with a pinch of salt.
4.   Coat the cauliflower with mixed spice and mustard powder.
5.   Dip the florets into the flax egg, then into the flour mixture. Cook for 15 minutes in the fryer.
6.   In the meantime, place a saucepan over medium heat and add in the maple syrup, garlic, and soy sauce. Boil first, before reducing the heat to allow the sauce to thicken.
7.   Remove the florets from the Air Fryer and transfer to the saucepan. Coat the florets in the sauce before returning to the fryer and allowing to cook for an additional 5 minutes.

Chicken & Veggies

Prep + Cook Time: 30 minutes | Servings: 4

Ingredients
8 chicken thighs
5 oz. mushrooms, sliced
1 red onion, diced
Fresh black pepper, to taste
10 medium asparagus
½ cup carrots, diced
¼ cup balsamic vinegar
2 red bell peppers, diced
½ tsp. sugar
2 tbsp. extra-virgin olive oil
1 ½ tbsp. fresh rosemary
2 cloves garlic, chopped
½ tbsp. dried oregano
1 tsp. kosher salt
2 fresh sage, chopped

Instructions
1.   Pre-heat the Air Fryer to 400°F.
2.   Grease the inside of a baking tray with the oil.
3.   Season the chicken with salt and pepper.
4.   Put all of the vegetables in a large bowl and throw in the oregano, garlic, sugar, mushrooms, vinegar, and sage. Combine everything well before transferring to the baking tray.
5.   Put the chicken thighs in the baking tray. Cook in the Air Fryer for about 20 minutes.
6.   Serve hot.

Falafel

Prep + Cook Time: 30 minutes | Servings: 8

Ingredients
1 tsp. cumin seeds
½ tsp. coriander seeds
2 cups chickpeas from can, drained and rinsed
½ tsp. red pepper flakes
3 cloves garlic
¼ cup parsley, chopped
¼ cup coriander, chopped
½ onion, diced
1 tbsp. juice from freshly squeezed lemon
3 tbsp. flour
½ tsp. salt cooking spray

Instructions
1.   Fry the cumin and coriander seeds over medium heat until fragrant.
2.   Grind using a mortar and pestle.
3.   Put all of ingredients, except for the cooking spray, in a food processor and blend until a fine consistency is achieved.
4.   Use your hands to mold the mixture into falafels and spritz with the cooking spray.
5.   Preheat your Air Fryer at 400°F.
6.   Transfer the falafels to the fryer in one single layer.
7.   Cook for 15 minutes, serving when they turn golden brown.

Easy Asparagus

Prep + Cook Time: 10 minutes | Servings: 4

Ingredients
1 lb. fresh asparagus spears, trimmed
1 tbsp. olive oil
Salt and pepper to taste

Instructions
1.   Pre-heat the Air Fryer at 375°F.
2.   Combine all of the ingredients and transfer to the Air Fryer.
3.   Cook for 5 minutes until soft.

Cauliflower Steak

Prep + Cook Time: 30 minutes | Servings: 2

Ingredients
1 cauliflower, sliced into two
1 tbsp. olive oil
2 tbsp. onion, chopped
¼ tsp. vegetable stock powder
¼ cup milk
Salt and pepper to taste

Instructions
1.   Place the cauliflower in a bowl of salted water and allow to absorb for at least 2 hours.
2.   Pre-heat the Air Fryer to 400°F.
3.   Rinse off the cauliflower, put inside the fryer and cook for 15 minutes.
4.   In the meantime, fry the onions over medium heat, stirring constantly, until they turn translucent. Pour in the vegetable stock powder and milk. Bring to a boil and then lower the heat.
5.   Let the sauce reduce and add in salt and pepper.
6.   Plate up the cauliflower steak and top with the sauce.

Rocket Salad

Prep + Cook Time: 35 minutes | Servings: 4

Ingredients

8 fresh figs, halved
1 ½ cups chickpeas, cooked
1 tsp. cumin seeds, roasted then crushed
4 tbsp. balsamic vinegar
2 tbsp. extra-virgin olive oil
Salt and pepper to taste
3 cups arugula rocket, washed and dried

Instructions

1.   Pre-heat the Air Fryer to 375°F.
2.   Cover the Air Fryer basket with aluminum foil and grease lightly with oil. Put the figs in the fryer and allow to cook for 10 minutes.
3.   In a bowl, combine the chickpeas and cumin seeds.
4.   Remove the cooked figs from the fryer and replace with chickpeas. Cook for 10 minutes. Leave to cool.
5.   In the meantime, prepare the dressing. Mix together the balsamic vinegar, olive oil, salt and pepper.
6.   In a salad bowl combine the arugula rocket with the cooled figs and chickpeas.
7.   Toss with the sauce and serve right away.

Vegan Ravioli

Prep + Cook Time: 15 minutes | Servings: 4

Ingredients

½ cup bread crumbs
2 tsp. nutritional yeast
1 tsp. dried basil
1 tsp. dried oregano
1 tsp. garlic powder
Salt and pepper to taste
¼ cup aquafaba
8 oz. vegan ravioli
Cooking spray

Instructions

1.   Cover the Air Fryer basket with aluminum foil and coat with a light brushing of oil.
2.   Pre-heat the Air Fryer to 400°F. Combine together the panko breadcrumbs, nutritional yeast, basil, oregano, and garlic powder. Sprinkle on salt and pepper to taste.
3.   Put the aquafaba in a separate bowl. Dip the ravioli in the aquafaba before coating it in the panko mixture. Spritz with cooking spray and transfer to the Air Fryer.
4.   Cook for 6 minutes ensuring to shake the Air Fryer basket halfway.

Thanksgiving Sprouts

Prep + Cook Time: 20 minutes | Servings: 6

Ingredients

1 ½ lb. Brussels sprouts, cleaned and trimmed
3 tbsp. olive oil
1 tsp. salt
1 tsp. black pepper

Instructions

1.   Pre-heat the Air Fryer to 375°F. Cover the basket with aluminum foil and coat with a light brushing of oil.
2.   In a mixing bowl, combine all ingredients, coating the sprouts well.
3.   Put in the fryer basket and cook for 10 minutes. Shake the Air Fryer basket throughout the duration to ensure even cooking.

Roasted Garlic, Broccoli & Lemon

Prep + Cook Time: 25 minutes | Servings: 6

Ingredients

2 heads broccoli, cut into florets
2 tsp. extra virgin olive oil
1 tsp. salt
½ tsp. black pepper
1 clove garlic, minced
½ tsp. lemon juice

Instructions

1.   Cover the Air Fryer basket with aluminum foil and coat with a light brushing of oil.
2.   Pre-heat the fryer to 375°F.
3.   In a bowl, combine all ingredients save for the lemon juice and transfer to the fryer basket. Allow to cook for 15 minutes.
4.   Serve with the lemon juice.

Pepperoni Pizza

Prep + Cook Time: 15 minutes | Servings: 3

Ingredients

3 portobello mushroom caps, cleaned and scooped
3 tbsp. olive oil
3 tbsp. tomato sauce
3 tbsp. mozzarella, shredded
12 slices pepperoni
1 pinch salt
1 pinch dried Italian seasonings

Instructions

1.   Pre-heat the Air Fryer to 330°F.
2.   Season both sides of the portobello mushrooms with a drizzle of olive oil, then sprinkle salt and the Italian seasonings on the insides.
3.   With a knife, spread the tomato sauce evenly over the mushroom, before adding the mozzarella on top.
4.   Put the portobello in the cooking basket and place in the Air Fryer.
5.   Cook for 1 minute, before taking the cooking basket out of the fryer and putting the pepperoni slices on top.
6.   Cook for another 3 to 5 minutes. Garnish with freshly grated parmesan cheese and crushed red pepper flakes and serve.

Baby Corn Pakodas

Prep + Cook Time: 20 minutes | Servings: 5

Ingredients
1 cup flour
¼ tsp. baking soda
¼ tsp. salt
½ tsp. curry powder
½ tsp. red chili powder
¼ tsp. turmeric powder
¼ cup water
10 pc. baby corn, blanched

Instructions
1.   Pre-heat the Air Fryer to 425°F.
2.   Cover the Air Fryer basket with aluminum foil and coat with a light brushing of oil.
3.   In a bowl, combine all ingredients save for the corn. Stir with a whisk until well combined.
4.   Coat the corn in the batter and put inside the Air Fryer.
5.   Cook for 8 minutes until a golden brown color is achieved.

Chicken-Mushroom Casserole

Prep + Cook Time: 30 minutes | Servings: 4

Ingredients
4 chicken breasts
½ cup shredded cheese
Salt to taste
1 cup coconut milk
1 cup mushrooms
1 broccoli, cut into florets
1 tbsp. curry powder

Instructions
1.   Pre-heat your Air Fryer to 350°F. Spritz a casserole dish with some cooking spray.
2.   Cube the chicken breasts and combine with curry powder and coconut milk in a bowl. Season with salt.
3.   Add in the broccoli and mushroom and mix well.
4.   Pour the mixture into the casserole dish. Top with the cheese.
5.   Transfer to your Air Fryer and cook for about 20 minutes.
6.   Serve warm.

Pita Bread Pizza

Prep + Cook Time: 15 minutes | Servings: 1

Ingredients
1 friendly pita bread
1 tbsp. pizza sauce
6 pepperoni slices
¼ cup grated mozzarella cheese
1 tsp. olive oil
¼ tsp. garlic powder
¼ tsp. dried oregano

Instructions
1.   Pre-heat your Air Fryer to 350°F.
2.   Spread the pizza sauce on top of the pita bread. Place the pepperoni slices over the sauce, followed by the mozzarella cheese.
3.   Season with garlic powder and oregano.
4.   Put the pita pizza inside the Air Fryer and place a trivet on top.
5.   Cook for 6 minutes and enjoy.

Paprika Tofu

Prep + Cook Time: 25 minutes | Servings: 4

Ingredients
2 block extra firm tofu, pressed to remove excess water and cubed
¼ cup cornstarch
1 tbsp. smoked paprika
Salt and pepper to taste

Instructions
1.   Cover the Air Fryer basket with aluminum foil and coat with a light brushing of oil.
2.   Pre-heat the Air Fryer to 370°F.
3.   Combine all ingredients in a bowl, coating the tofu well.
4.   Put in the Air Fryer basket and allow to cook for 12 minutes.

Mac & Cheese

Prep + Cook Time: 15 minutes | Servings: 2

Ingredients
1 cup cooked macaroni
½ cup warm milk
1 tbsp. parmesan cheese
1 cup grated cheddar cheese
Salt and pepper, to taste

Instructions
1.   Pre-heat the Air Fryer to 350°F.
2.   In a baking dish, mix together all of the ingredients, except for Parmesan.
3.   Put the dish inside the Air Fryer and allow to cook for 10 minutes.
4.   Add the Parmesan cheese on top and serve.

Pasta Salad

Prep + Cook Time: 2 hours 25 minutes | Servings: 8

Ingredients
4 tomatoes, medium and cut in eighths
3 eggplants, small
3 zucchinis, medium sized
2 bell peppers, any color
4 cups large pasta, uncooked in any shape
1 cup cherry tomatoes, sliced
½ cup Italian dressing, fat-free
8 tbsp. parmesan, grated
2 tbsp. extra virgin olive oil
2 tsp. pink Himalayan salt
1 tsp. basil, dried
High quality cooking spray

Instructions
1.   Wash and dry the eggplant. Cut off the stem and throw it away. Do not peel the eggplant. Cut it into half-inch-thick round slices.
2.   Coat the eggplant slices with 1 tbsp. of extra virgin olive oil, and transfer to the Air Fryer basket.
3.   Cook the eggplant for 40 minutes at 350°F. Once it is tender and cooked through, remove from the fryer and set to one side.
4.   Wash and dry the zucchini. Cut off the stem and throw it away. Do not peel the zucchini. Cut the zucchini into half-inch-thick round slices.
5.   Combine with the olive oil to coat, and put it in the Air Fryer basket.
6.   Cook the zucchini for about 25 minutes at 350°F. Once it is tender and cooked through, remove from the fryer and set to one side.
7.   Wash the tomatoes and cut them into eight equal slices. Transfer them to the fryer basket and spritz lightly with high quality cooking spray. Cook the tomatoes for 30 minutes at 350°F. Once they have shrunk and are beginning to turn brown, set them to one side.
8.   Cook the pasta and drain it. Rinse with cold water and set it aside to cool.
9.   Wash, dry and halve the bell peppers. Remove the stems and seeds.
10.   Wash and halve the cherry tomatoes.
11.   In a large bowl, mix together the bell peppers and cherry tomatoes. Stir in the roasted vegetables, cooked pasta, pink Himalayan salt, dressing, chopped basil leaves, and grated parmesan, ensuring to incorporate everything well.
12.   Let the salad cool and marinate in the refrigerator.
13.   Serve the salad cold or at room temperature.

Prosciutto & Potato Salad

Prep + Cook Time: 15 minutes | Servings: 8

Ingredients

4 lb. potatoes, boiled and cubed
15 slices prosciutto, diced
15 oz. sour cream
2 cups shredded cheddar cheese
2 tbsp. mayonnaise
1 tsp. salt
1 tsp. black pepper
1 tsp. dried basil

Instructions

1.   Pre-heat the Air Fryer to 350°F.
2.   Place the potatoes, prosciutto, and cheddar in a baking dish. Put it in the Air Fryer and allow to cook for 7 minutes.
3.   In a separate bowl, mix together the sour cream, mayonnaise, salt, pepper, and basil using a whisk.
4.   Coat the salad with the dressing and serve.

Chicken Quesadillas

Prep + Cook Time: 20 minutes | Servings: 4

Ingredients

2 soft taco shells
1 lb. boneless chicken breasts
1 large green pepper, sliced
1 medium-sized onion, sliced
½ cup Cheddar cheese, shredded
½ cup salsa sauce
2 tbsp. olive oil
Salt and pepper, to taste

Instructions

1.   Pre-heat the Air Fryer to 370°F and drizzle the basket with 1 tablespoon of olive oil.
2.   Lay one taco shell into the bottom of the fryer and spread some salsa inside the taco. Slice the chicken breast into strips and put the strips into taco shell.
3.   Top the chicken with the onions and peppers.
4.   Season with salt and pepper. Add the shredded cheese and top with the second taco shell.
5.   Drizzle with another tablespoon of olive oil. Put the rack over the taco to keep it in place.
6.   Cook for 4 – 6 minutes, until it turns lightly brown and is cooked through. Serve either hot or cold.

Mozzarella Bruschetta

Prep + Cook Time: 10 minutes | Servings: 1

Ingredients

6 small loaf slices
½ cup tomatoes, finely chopped
3 oz. mozzarella cheese, grated
1 tbsp. fresh basil, chopped
1 tbsp. olive oil

Instructions

1.   Pre-heat the Air Fryer to 350°F. Place the bread inside and cook for about 3 minutes.
2.   Add the tomato, mozzarella, prosciutto, and a drizzle of olive oil on top.

3.   Cook the bruschetta for an additional minute before serving.

Sausage-Chicken Casserole

Prep + Cook Time: 30 minutes | Servings: 8

Ingredients

2 cloves minced garlic
10 eggs
1 cup broccoli, chopped
½ tbsp. salt
1 cup cheddar, shredded and divided
¼ tbsp. pepper
¾ cup whipping cream
1 x 12-oz. package cooked chicken sausage

Instructions

1.   Pre-heat the Air Fryer to 400°F.
2.   In a large bowl, beat the eggs with a whisk. Pour in the whipping cream and cheese. Combine well.
3.   In a separate bowl, mix together the garlic, broccoli, salt, pepper and cooked sausage.
4.   Place the chicken sausage mix in a casserole dish. Top with the cheese mixture.
5.   Transfer to the Air Fryer and cook for about 20 minutes.

Cashew & Chicken Manchurian

Prep + Cook Time: 30 minutes | Servings: 6

Ingredients

1 cup chicken boneless
1 spring onions, chopped
1 onion, chopped
3 green chili
6 cashew nuts
1 tsp. ginger, chopped
½ tsp. garlic, chopped
1 Egg
2 tbsp. flour
1 tbsp. cornstarch
1 tsp. soy sauce
2 tsp. chili paste
1 tsp. pepper
Pinch MSG
sugar as needed
1 tbsp. oil

Instructions

1.   Pre-heat your Air Fryer at 360°F
2.   Toss together the chicken, egg, salt and pepper to coat well.
3.   Combine the cornstarch and flour and use this to cover the chicken.
4.   Cook in the fryer for 10 minutes.
5.   In the meantime, toast the nuts in a frying pan. Add in the onions and cook until they turn translucent. Combine with the remaining ingredients to create the sauce.
6.   Finally, add in the chicken. When piping hot, garnish with the spring onions and serve.

Cheese & Bacon Rolls

Prep + Cook Time: 25 minutes | Servings: 4

Ingredients

8 oz. refrigerated crescent roll dough [usually 1 can]
6 oz. very sharp cheddar cheese, grated
1 lb. bacon, cooked and chopped

Instructions

1.   Roll out the crescent dough flat and slice it into 1" x 1 ½" pieces.
2.   In a bowl, mix together the cheese and bacon. Take about ¼ cup of this mixture and spread it across one slice of dough. Repeat with the rest of the mixture and dough.
3.   Set your Air Fryer to 330°F and allow to warm.
4.   Place the rolls on the Air Fry tray and transfer to the fryer. Alternatively, you can put them in the food basket.
5.   Bake for roughly 6 – 8 minutes until a golden brown color is achieved. Watch them carefully to prevent burning, as they may cook very quickly.

Kidney Beans Oatmeal

Prep + Cook Time: 25 minutes | Servings: 2 – 4

Ingredients

2 large bell peppers, halved lengthwise, deseeded
2 tbsp. cooked kidney beans
2 tbsp. cooked chick peas
2 cups oatmeal, cooked
1 tsp. ground cumin
½ tsp. paprika
½ tsp. salt or to taste
¼ tsp. black pepper powder
¼ cup yogurt

Instructions

1.   Pre-heat the Air Fryer at 355°F.
2.   Put the bell peppers, cut-side-down, in the fryer. Allow to cook for 2 – 3 minutes.
3.   Take the peppers out of the Air Fryer and let cool.
4.   In a bowl, combine together the rest of the ingredients.
5.   Divide the mixture evenly and use each portion to stuff a pepper.
6.   Return to the Air Fryer and continue to air fry for 4 minutes. Serve hot.

Chicken Fillets & Brie

Prep + Cook Time: 40 minutes | Servings: 4

Ingredients

4 slices turkey, cured
2 large chicken fillets
4 slices brie cheese
1 tbsp. chives, chopped
Salt and pepper to taste

Instructions

1.   Pre-heat Air Fryer to 360°F. Slice each chicken fillet in half and sprinkle on salt and pepper. Coat with the brie and chives.
2.   Wrap the turkey around the chicken and secure with toothpick.
3.   Cook for 15 minutes until a brown color is achieved.

Cheese & Macaroni Balls

Prep + Cook Time: 25 minutes | Servings: 2

Ingredients

2 cups leftover macaroni
1 cup cheddar cheese, shredded
3 large eggs
1 cup milk
½ cup flour
1 cup bread crumbs
½ tsp. salt
¼ tsp. black pepper

Instructions

1.   In a bowl, combine the leftover macaroni and shredded cheese.
2.   Pour the flour in a separate bowl. Put the bread crumbs in a third bowl. Finally, in a fourth bowl, mix together the eggs and milk with a whisk.
3.   With an ice-cream scoop, create balls from the macaroni mixture. Coat them the flour, then in the egg mixture, and lastly in the bread crumbs.
4.   Pre-heat the Air Fryer to 365°F and cook the balls for about 10 minutes, giving them an occasional stir. Ensure they crisp up nicely.
5.   Serve with the sauce of your choice.

Cheese Pizza

Prep + Cook Time: 15 minutes | Servings: 4

Ingredients

1 pc. bread
½ lb. mozzarella cheese
1 tbsp. olive oil
2 tbsp. ketchup
⅓ cup sausage
1 tsp. garlic powder

Instructions

1.   Using a tablespoon, spread the ketchup over the pita bread.
2.   Top with the sausage and cheese. Season with the garlic powder and 1 tablespoon of olive oil.
3.   Pre-heat the Air Fryer to 340°F.
4.   Put the pizza in the fryer basket and cook for 6 minutes. Enjoy!

Portabella Pizza

Prep + Cook Time: 15 minutes | Servings: 3

Ingredients

3 tbsp. olive oil
3 portobello mushroom caps, cleaned and scooped
3 tbsp. mozzarella, shredded
3 tbsp. tomato sauce
Pinch of salt
12 slices pepperoni
Pinch of dried Italian seasonings

Instructions

1.   Pre-heat the Air Fryer to 330°F.
2.   Coat both sides of the mushroom cap with a drizzle of oil, before seasoning the inside with the Italian seasonings and salt. Evenly spread the tomato sauce over the mushroom and add the cheese on top.
3.   Put the mushroom into the cooking basket of the Air Fryer. Place the slices of pepperoni on top of the portobello pizza after a minute of cooking and continue to cook for another 3-5 minutes.

American Hot Dogs

Prep + Cook Time: 20 minutes | Servings: 4

Ingredients

3 brazilian sausages, cut into 3 equal pieces
9 bacon fillets, raw
Black pepper to taste
Salt to taste

Instructions

1.　Pre-heat the Air Fryer for 5 minutes at 355°F.
2.　Take a slice of bacon and wrap it around each piece of sausage. Sprinkle with some salt and pepper as desired, as well as a half-teaspoon of Italian herbs if you like.
3.　Fry the sausages for 15 minutes and serve warm.

Garlic Bacon

Prep + Cook Time: 40 minutes | Servings: 4

Ingredients

4 potatoes, peeled and cut into bite-size chunks
6 cloves garlic, unpeeled
strips bacon, chopped
1 tbsp. fresh rosemary, finely chopped

Instructions

1.　In a large bowl, thoroughly combine the potatoes, garlic, bacon, and rosemary. Place the ingredients in a baking dish.
2.　Set your Air Fryer to 350°F and briefly allow to warm.
3.　Cook the potatoes for 25-30 minutes until a golden brown color is achieved.

Mexican Pizza

Prep + Cook Time: 15 minutes | Servings: 4

Ingredients

¾ cup refried beans
1 cup salsa
12 frozen beef meatballs, pre-cooked
2 jalapeno peppers, sliced
6 bread
1 cup pepper Jack cheese, shredded
1 cup Colby cheese, shredded

Instructions

1.　Pre-heat the Air Fryer for 4 minutes at 370°F.
2.　In a bowl, mix together the salsa, meatball, jalapeno pepper and beans.
3.　Place a spoonful of this mixture on top of each pita bread, along with a topping of pepper Jack and Colby cheese.
4.　Bake in the fryer for 10 minutes. Serve hot.

Pesto Gnocchi

Prep + Cook Time: 30 minutes | Servings: 4

Ingredients

1 package [16-oz.] shelf-stable gnocchi
1 medium-sized onion, chopped
3 cloves garlic, minced
1 jar [8 oz.] pesto
⅓ cup parmesan cheese, grated
1 tbsp. extra virgin olive oil

Salt and black pepper to taste

Instructions

1.　Pre-heat the Air Fryer to 340°F.
2.　In a large bowl combine the onion, garlic, and gnocchi, and drizzle with the olive oil. Mix thoroughly.
3.　Transfer the mixture to the fryer and cook for 15 – 20 minutes, stirring occasionally, making sure the gnocchi become lightly brown and crispy.
4.　Add in the pesto and Parmesan cheese, and give everything a good stir before serving straightaway.

Cheeseburger Sliders

Prep + Cook Time: 20 minutes | Servings: 3

Ingredients

1 lb. ground beef
6 slices cheddar cheese
6 dinner rolls
Salt and pepper

Instructions

1.　Pre-heat the Air Fryer to 390°F.
2.　With your hands, shape the ground beef into 6 x 2.5-oz. patties. Sprinkle on some salt and pepper to taste.
3.　Place the burgers in the cooking basket and cook for 10 minutes. Take care when removing them from the Air Fryer.
4.　Top the patties with the cheese. Put them back in the Air Fryer and allow to cook for another minute before serving.

SIDE DISHES

Low-Carb Pizza Crust

Prep + Cook Time: 20 minutes | Servings: 4

Ingredients

1 tbsp. full-fat cream cheese
½ cup whole-milk mozzarella cheese, shredded
2 tbsp. flour
1 egg white

Instructions

1.	In a microwave-safe bowl, combine the cream cheese, mozzarella, and flour and heat in the microwave for half a minute. Mix well to create a smooth consistency. Add in the egg white and stir to form a soft ball of dough.
2.	With slightly wet hands, press the dough into a pizza crust about six inches in diameter.
3.	Place a sheet of parchment paper in the bottom of your fryer and lay the crust on top. Cook for ten minutes at 350°F, turning the crust over halfway through the cooking time.
4.	Top the pizza base with the toppings of your choice and enjoy!

Bacon-Wrapped Onion Rings

Prep + Cook Time: 15 minutes | Servings: 8

Ingredients

1 large onion, peeled
8 slices sugar-free bacon
1 tbsp. sriracha

Instructions

1.	Chop up the onion into slices a quarter-inch thick. Gently pull apart the rings. Take a slice of bacon and wrap it around an onion ring. Repeat with the rest of the ingredients. Place each onion ring in your fryer.
2.	Cut the onion rings at 350°F for ten minutes, turning them halfway through to ensure the bacon crisps up.
3.	Serve hot with the sriracha.

Smoked BBQ Toasted s

Prep + Cook Time: 10 minutes | Servings: 1

Ingredients

2 tsp. coconut oil, melted
¼ tsp. smoked paprika
1 tsp. chili powder
¼ tsp. cumin
1 cup raw s

Instructions

1.	Mix the melted coconut oil with the paprika, chili powder, and cumin. Place the s in a large bowl and pour the coconut oil over them, tossing them to cover them evenly.
2.	Place the s in the basket of your fryer and spread them out across the base.
3.	Cook for six minutes at 320°F, giving the basket an occasional shake to make sure everything is cooked evenly.
4.	Leave to cool and serve.

Roasted Eggplant

Prep + Cook Time: 20 minutes | Servings: 1

Ingredients

1 large eggplant
2 tbsp. olive oil
¼ tsp. salt
½ tsp. garlic powder

Instructions

1.	Prepare the eggplant by slicing off the top and bottom and cutting it into slices around a quarter-inch thick.
2.	Apply olive oil to the slices with a brush, coating both sides. Season each side with sprinklings of salt and garlic powder.
3.	Place the slices in the fryer and cook for fifteen minutes at 390°F.
4.	Serve right away.

Low-Carb Pita Chips

Prep + Cook Time: 15 minutes | Servings: 1

Ingredients

1 cup mozzarella cheese, shredded
1 egg
¼ cup blanched finely ground flour
½ oz. pork rinds, finely ground

Instructions

1.	Melt the mozzarella in the microwave. Add the egg, flour, and pork rinds and combine together to form a smooth paste. Microwave the cheese again if it begins to set.
2.	Put the dough between two sheets of parchment paper and use a rolling pin to flatten it out into a rectangle. The thickness is up to you. With a sharp knife, cut into the dough to form triangles. It may be necessary to complete this step-in multiple batches.
3.	Place the chips in the fryer and cook for five minutes at 350°F. Turn them over and cook on the other side for another five minutes, or until the chips are golden and firm.
4.	Allow the chips to cool and harden further. They can be stored in an airtight container.

Flatbread

Prep + Cook Time: 20 minutes | Servings: 1

Ingredients

1 cup mozzarella cheese, shredded
¼ cup blanched finely ground flour
1 oz. full-fat cream cheese, softened

Instructions

1.	Microwave the mozzarella for half a minute until melted. Combine with the flour to achieve a smooth consistency, before adding the cream cheese. Keep mixing to create a dough, microwaving the mixture again if the cheese begins to harden.
2.	Divide the dough into two equal pieces. Between two sheets of parchment paper, roll out the dough until it is about a quarter-inch thick. Cover the bottom of your fryer with another sheet of parchment.
3.	Transfer the dough into the fryer and cook at 320°F for seven minutes. You may need to complete this step in two batches. Make sure to turn the flatbread halfway through cooking. Take care when removing it from the fryer and serve warm.

Buffalo Cauliflower

Prep + Cook Time: 10 minutes | Servings: 1

Ingredients
½ packet dry ranch seasoning
2 tbsp. salted butter, melted
Cauliflower florets
¼ cup buffalo sauce

Instructions
1.   In a bowl, combine the dry ranch seasoning and butter. Toss with the cauliflower florets to coat and transfer them to the fryer.
2.   Cook at 400°F for five minutes, shaking the basket occasionally to ensure the florets cook evenly.
3.   Remove the cauliflower from the fryer, pour the buffalo sauce over it, and enjoy.

Brussels Sprout Chips

Prep + Cook Time: 15 minutes | Servings: 1

Ingredients
1 lb. Brussels sprouts
1 tbsp. coconut oil, melted
1 tbsp. unsalted butter, melted

Instructions
1.   Prepare the Brussels sprouts by halving them, discarding any loose leaves.
2.   Combine with the melted coconut oil and transfer to your air fryer.
3.   Cook at 400°F for ten minutes, giving the basket a good shake throughout the cooking time to brown them up if desired.
4.   The sprouts are ready when they are partially caramelized. Remove them from the fryer and serve with a topping of melted butter before serving.

Cauliflower Tots

Prep + Cook Time: 20 minutes | Servings: 8

Ingredients
1 large head cauliflower
½ cup parmesan cheese, grated
1 cup mozzarella cheese, shredded
1 tsp. seasoned salt
1 egg

Instructions
1.   Place a steamer basket over a pot of boiling water, ensuring the water is not high enough to enter the basket.
2.   Cut up the cauliflower into florets and transfer to the steamer basket. Cover the pot with a lid and leave to steam for seven minutes, making sure the cauliflower softens.
3.   Place the florets on a cheesecloth and leave to cool. Remove as much moisture as possible. This is crucial as it ensures the cauliflower will harden.
4.   In a bowl, break up the cauliflower with a fork.
5.   Stir in the parmesan, mozzarella, seasoned salt, and egg, incorporating the cauliflower well with all of the other ingredients. Make sure the mixture is firm enough to be moldable.
6.   Using your hand, mold about two tablespoons of the mixture into tots and repeat until you have used up all of the mixture. Put each tot into your air fryer basket. They may need to be cooked in multiple batches.
7.   Cook at 320°F for twelve minutes, turning them halfway through. Ensure they are brown in color before serving.

Herbed Garlic Radishes

Prep + Cook Time: 15 minutes | Servings: 2

Ingredients
1 lb. radishes
2 tbsp. unsalted butter, melted
¼ tsp. dried oregano
½ tsp. dried parsley
½ tsp. garlic powder

Instructions
1.   Prepare the radishes by cutting off their tops and bottoms and quartering them.
2.   In a bowl, combine the butter, dried oregano, dried parsley, and garlic powder. Toss with the radishes to coat.
3.   Transfer the radishes to your air fryer and cook at 350°F for ten minutes, shaking the basket at the halfway point to ensure the radishes cook evenly through. The radishes are ready when they begin to turn brown.

Jicama Fries

Prep + Cook Time: 25 minutes | Servings: 1

Ingredients
1 small jicama, peeled
¼ tsp. onion powder
¾ tsp. chili powder
¼ tsp. garlic powder
¼ tsp. ground black pepper

Instructions
1.   To make the fries, cut the jicama into matchsticks of your desired thickness.
2.   In a bowl, toss them with the onion powder, chili powder, garlic powder, and black pepper to coat. Transfer the fries into the basket of your air fryer.
3.   Cook at 350°F for twenty minutes, giving the basket an occasional shake throughout the cooking process. The fries are ready when they are hot and golden in color. Enjoy!

Zesty Salmon Jerky

Prep + Cook Time: 6 hours | Servings: 2

Ingredients
1 lb. boneless skinless salmon
½ tsp. liquid smoke
½ tsp. ground ginger
¼ cup soy sauce
¼ tsp. red pepper flakes

Instructions
1.   Cut the salmon into strips about four inches long and a quarter-inch thick.
2.   Put the salmon in an airtight container or bag along with the liquid smoke, ginger, soy sauce, and red pepper flakes, combining everything to coat the salmon completely. Leave the salmon in the refrigerator for at least two hours.
3.   Transfer the salmon slices in the fryer, taking care not to overlap any pieces. This step may need to be completed in multiple batches.
4.   Cook at 140°F for four hours.
5.   Take care when removing the salmon from the fryer and leave it to cool. This jerky makes a good snack and can be stored in an airtight container.

Zucchini Bites

Prep + Cook Time: 15 minutes | Servings: 4

Ingredients

4 zucchinis
1 egg
½ cup parmesan cheese, grated
1 tbsp. Italian herbs
1 cup coconut, grated

Instructions

1 Thinly grate the zucchini and dry with a cheesecloth, ensuring to remove all of the moisture.
2 In a bowl, combine the zucchini with the egg, parmesan, Italian herbs, and grated coconut, mixing well to incorporate everything. Using your hands, mold the mixture into balls.
3 Pre-heat the fryer at 400°F and place a rack inside. Lay the zucchini balls on the rack and cook for ten minutes. Serve hot.

Pop Corn Broccoli

Prep + Cook Time: 10 minutes | Servings: 1

Ingredients

4 egg yolks
¼ cup butter, melted
2 cups coconut flower
Salt and pepper
2 cups broccoli florets

Instructions

1. In a bowl, whisk the egg yolks and melted butter together. Throw in the coconut flour, salt and pepper, then stir again to combine well.
2. Pre-heat the fryer at 400°F.
3. Dip each broccoli floret into the mixture and place in the fryer. Cook for six minutes, in multiple batches if necessary. Take care when removing them from the fryer and enjoy!

Rosemary Green Beans

Prep + Cook Time: 10 minutes | Servings: 1

Ingredients

1 tbsp. butter, melted
2 tbsp. rosemary
½ tsp. salt
3 cloves garlic, minced
¾ cup green beans, chopped

Instructions

1. Pre-heat your fryer at 390°F.
2. Combine the melted butter with the rosemary, salt, and minced garlic. Toss in the green beans, making sure to coat them well.
3. Cook in the fryer for five minutes.

Carrot Croquettes

Prep + Cook Time: 10 minutes | Servings: 4

Ingredients

2 medium-sized carrots, trimmed and grated
2 medium-sized celery stalks, trimmed and grated
½ cup of leek, finely chopped
1 tbsp. garlic paste
¼ tsp. freshly cracked black pepper
1 tsp. fine sea salt
1 tbsp. fresh dill, finely chopped
1 egg, lightly whisked
¼ cup flour
¼ tsp. baking powder
½ cup bread crumbs [seasoned or regular]

Chive mayo to serve

Instructions

1. Drain any excess liquid from the carrots and celery by placing them on a paper towel.
2. Stir together the vegetables with all of the other ingredients, save for the bread crumbs and chive mayo.
3. Use your hands to mold 1 tablespoon of the vegetable mixture into a ball and repeat until all of the mixture has been used up. Press down on each ball with your hand or a palette knife. Cover completely with bread crumbs. Spritz the croquettes with a non-stick cooking spray.
4. Arrange the croquettes in a single layer in your Air Fryer and fry for 6 minutes at 360°F.
5. Serve warm with the chive mayo on the side.

Peppered Puff Pastry

Prep + Cook Time: 25 minutes | Servings: 4

Ingredients

1 ½ tbsp. sesame oil
1 cup white mushrooms, sliced
2 cloves garlic, minced
1 bell pepper, seeded and chopped
¼ tsp. sea salt
¼ tsp. dried rosemary
½ tsp. ground black pepper, or more to taste
11 oz. puff pastry sheets
½ cup crème fraiche
1 egg, well whisked
½ cup parmesan cheese, preferably freshly grated

Instructions

1. Pre-heat your Air Fryer to 400°F.
2. In a skillet, heat the sesame oil over a moderate heat and fry the mushrooms, garlic, and pepper until soft and fragrant.
3. Sprinkle on the salt, rosemary, and pepper.
4. In the meantime, unroll the puff pastry and slice it into 4-inch squares.
5. Spread the crème fraiche across each square.
6. Spoon equal amounts of the vegetables into the puff pastry squares. Enclose each square around the filling in a triangle shape, pressing the edges with your fingertips.
7. Brush each triangle with some whisked egg and cover with grated Parmesan.
8. Cook for 22-25 minutes.

Sautéed Green Beans

Prep + Cook Time: 12 minutes | Servings: 4

Ingredients

¾ lb. green beans, cleaned
1 tbsp. balsamic vinegar
¼ tsp. kosher salt
½ tsp. mixed peppercorns, freshly cracked
1 tbsp. butter
Sesame seeds to serve

Instructions

1. Pre-heat your Air Fryer at 390°F.
2. Combine the green beans with the rest of the ingredients, except for the sesame seeds. Transfer to the fryer and cook for 10 minutes.
3. In the meantime, heat the sesame seeds in a small skillet to toast all over, stirring constantly to prevent burning.
4. Serve the green beans accompanied by the toasted sesame seeds.

Horseradish Mayo & Gorgonzola Mushrooms

Prep + Cook Time: 15 minutes | Servings: 5

Ingredients

½ cup of bread crumbs
2 cloves garlic, pressed
2 tbsp. fresh coriander, chopped
⅓ tsp. kosher salt
½ tsp. crushed red pepper flakes
1 ½ tbsp. olive oil
20 medium-sized mushrooms, stems removed
½ cup Gorgonzola cheese, grated
¼ cup low-fat mayonnaise
1 tsp. prepared horseradish, well-drained
tbsp. fresh parsley, finely chopped

Instructions

1. Combine the bread crumbs together with the garlic, coriander, salt, red pepper, and the olive oil.
2. Take equal-sized amounts of the bread crumb mixture and use them to stuff the mushroom caps. Add the grated Gorgonzola on top of each.
3. Put the mushrooms in the Air Fryer grill pan and transfer to the fryer.
4. Grill them at 380°F for 8-12 minutes, ensuring the stuffing is warm throughout.
5. In the meantime, prepare the horseradish mayo. Mix together the mayonnaise, horseradish and parsley.
6. When the mushrooms are ready, serve with the mayo.

Scallion & Ricotta Potatoes

Prep + Cook Time: 15 minutes | Servings: 4

Ingredients

4 baking potatoes
2 tbsp. olive oil
½ cup Ricotta cheese, room temperature
2 tbsp. scallions, chopped
1 heaped tbsp. fresh parsley, roughly chopped
1 heaped tbsp. coriander, minced
2 oz. Cheddar cheese, preferably freshly grated
1 tsp. celery seeds
½ tsp. salt
½ tsp. garlic pepper

Instructions

1. Pierce the skin of the potatoes with a knife.
2. Cook in the Air Fryer basket for roughly 13 minutes at 350°F. If they are not cooked through by this time, leave for 2 – 3 minutes longer.
3. In the meantime, make the stuffing by combining all the other ingredients.
4. Cut halfway into the cooked potatoes to open them.
5. Spoon equal amounts of the stuffing into each potato and serve hot.

Crumbed Beans

Prep + Cook Time: 10 minutes | Servings: 4

Ingredients

½ cup flour
1 tsp. smoky chipotle powder
½ tsp. ground black pepper
1 tsp. sea salt flakes
2 eggs, beaten
½ cup crushed saltines
10 oz. wax beans

Instructions

1. Combine the flour, chipotle powder, black pepper, and salt in a bowl. Put the eggs in a second bowl. Place the crushed saltines in a third bowl.
2. Wash the beans with cold water and discard any tough strings.
3. Coat the beans with the flour mixture, before dipping them into the beaten egg. Lastly cover them with the crushed saltines.
4. Spritz the beans with a cooking spray.
5. Air-fry at 360°F for 4 minutes. Give the cooking basket a good shake and continue to cook for 3 minutes. Serve hot.

Colby Potato Patties

Prep + Cook Time: 15 minutes | Servings: 8

Ingredients

2 lb. white potatoes, peeled and grated
½ cup scallions, finely chopped
½ tsp. freshly ground black pepper, or more to taste
1tbsp. fine sea salt
½ tsp. hot paprika
2 cups Colby cheese, shredded
¼ cup canola oil
1 cup crushed crackers

Instructions

1. Boil the potatoes until soft. Dry them off and peel them before mashing thoroughly, leaving no lumps.
2. Combine the mashed potatoes with scallions, pepper, salt, paprika, and cheese.
3. Mold the mixture into balls with your hands and press with your palm to flatten them into patties.
4. In a shallow dish, combine the canola oil and crushed crackers. Coat the patties in the crumb mixture.
5. Cook the patties at 360°F for about 10 minutes, in multiple batches if necessary.
6. Serve with tabasco mayo or the sauce of your choice.

Turkey Garlic Potatoes

Prep + Cook Time: 45 minutes | Servings: 2

Ingredients

3 unsmoked turkey strips
6 small potatoes
1 tsp. garlic, minced
2 tsp. olive oil
Salt to taste
Pepper to taste

Instructions

1. Peel the potatoes and cube them finely.
2. Coat in 1 teaspoon of oil and cook in the Air Fryer for 10 minutes at 350°F.
3. In a separate bowl, slice the turkey finely and combine with the garlic, oil, salt and pepper. Pour the potatoes into the bowl and mix well.
4. Lay the mixture on some silver aluminum foil, transfer to the fryer and cook for about 10 minutes.
5. Serve with raita.

Croutons

Prep + Cook Time: 25 minutes | Servings: 4

Ingredients

2 slices friendly bread
1 tbsp. olive oil

Instructions

1. Cut the slices of bread into medium-size chunks.
2. Coat the inside of the Air Fryer with the oil. Set it to 390°F and allow it to heat up.
3. Place the chunks inside and shallow fry for at least 8 minutes.
4. Serve with hot soup.

Garlic Stuffed Mushrooms

Prep + Cook Time: 25 minutes | Servings: 4

Ingredients

6 small mushrooms
1 oz. onion, peeled and diced
1 tbsp. friendly bread crumbs
1 tbsp. olive oil
1 tsp. garlic, pureed
1 tsp. parsley
Salt and pepper to taste

Instructions

1. Combine the bread crumbs, oil, onion, parsley, salt, pepper and garlic in a bowl. Cut out the mushrooms' stalks and stuff each cap with the crumb mixture.
2. Cook in the Air Fryer for 10 minutes at 350°F.
3. Serve with a side of mayo dip.

Zucchini Sweet Potatoes

Prep + Cook Time: 20 minutes | Servings: 4

Ingredients

2 large-sized sweet potatoes, peeled and quartered
1 medium-sized zucchini, sliced
1 Serrano pepper, deveined and thinly sliced
1 bell pepper, deveined and thinly sliced
1 – 2 carrots, cut into matchsticks
¼ cup olive oil
1 ½ tbsp. maple syrup
½ tsp. porcini powder
¼ tsp. mustard powder
½ tsp. fennel seeds
1 tbsp. garlic powder
½ tsp. fine sea salt
¼ tsp. ground black pepper
Tomato ketchup to serve

Instructions

1. Put the sweet potatoes, zucchini, peppers, and the carrot into the basket of your Air Fryer. Coat with a drizzling of olive oil.
2. Pre-heat the fryer at 350°F.
3. Cook the vegetables for 15 minutes.
4. In the meantime, prepare the sauce by vigorously combining the other ingredients, save for the tomato ketchup, with a whisk.
5. Lightly grease a baking dish small enough to fit inside your fryer.
6. Move the cooked vegetables to the baking dish, pour over the sauce and make sure to coat the vegetables well.
7. Raise the temperature to 390°F and cook the vegetables for an additional 5 minutes.
8. Serve warm with a side of ketchup.

Cheese Lings

Prep + Cook Time: 25 minutes | Servings: 6

Ingredients

1 cup flour
small cubes cheese, grated
¼ tsp. chili powder
1 tsp. butter
Salt to taste
1 tsp. baking powder

Instructions

1. Combine all the ingredients to form a dough, along with a small amount water as necessary.
2. Divide the dough into equal portions and roll each one into a ball.
3. Pre-heat Air Fryer at 360°F.
4. Transfer the balls to the fryer and air fry for 5 minutes, stirring periodically.

Potato Side Dish

Prep + Cook Time: 30 minutes | Servings: 2

Ingredients

2 medium potatoes
1 tsp. butter
3 tbsp. sour cream
1 tsp. chives
1 ½ tbsp. cheese, grated
Salt and pepper to taste

Instructions

1. Pierce the potatoes with a fork and boil them in water until they are cooked.
2. Transfer to the Air Fryer and cook for 15 minutes at 350°F.
3. In the meantime, combine the sour cream, cheese and chives in a bowl. Cut the potatoes halfway to open them up and fill with the butter and toppings.
4. Serve with salad.

Roasted Potatoes & Cheese

Prep + Cook Time: 55 minutes | Servings: 4

Ingredients

4 medium potatoes
1 asparagus bunch
⅓ cup cottage cheese
⅓ cup low-fat crème fraiche
1 tbsp. wholegrain mustard

Instructions

1. Pour some oil into your Air Fryer and pre-heat to 390°F.
2. Cook potatoes for 20 minutes.
3. Boil the asparagus in salted water for 3 minutes.
4. Remove the potatoes and mash them with rest of ingredients. Sprinkle on salt and pepper.
5. Serve with rice.

Vegetable & Cheese Omelet

Prep + Cook Time: 15 minutes | Servings: 2

Ingredients

3 tbsp. plain milk
4 eggs, whisked
1 tsp. melted butter
Kosher salt and freshly ground black pepper, to taste
1 red bell pepper, deveined and chopped
1 green bell pepper, deveined and chopped
1 white onion, finely chopped
½ cup baby spinach leaves, roughly chopped
½ cup Halloumi cheese, shaved

Instructions

1.   Grease the Air Fryer baking pan with some canola oil.
2.   Place all of the ingredients in the baking pan and stir well.
3.   Transfer to the fryer and cook at 350°F for 13 minutes.
4.   Serve warm.

Scrambled Eggs

Prep + Cook Time: 15 minutes | Servings: 2

Ingredients

2 tbsp. olive oil, melted
4 eggs, whisked
5 oz. fresh spinach, chopped
1 medium-sized tomato, chopped
1 tsp. fresh lemon juice
½ tsp. coarse salt
½ tsp. ground black pepper
½ cup of fresh basil, roughly chopped

Instructions

1.   Grease the Air Fryer baking pan with the oil, tilting it to spread the oil around. Pre-heat the fryer at 280°F.
2.   Mix the remaining ingredients, apart from the basil leaves, whisking well until everything is completely combined.
3.   Cook in the fryer for 8 - 12 minutes.
4.   Top with fresh basil leaves before serving with a little sour cream if desired.

Sweet Corn Fritters

Prep + Cook Time: 20 minutes | Servings: 4

Ingredients

1 medium-sized carrot, grated
1 yellow onion, finely chopped
4 oz. canned sweet corn kernels, drained
1 tsp. sea salt flakes
1 heaping tbsp. fresh cilantro, chopped
1 medium-sized egg, whisked
2 tbsp. plain milk
1 cup of Parmesan cheese, grated
¼ cup flour
⅓ tsp. baking powder
⅓ tsp. sugar

Instructions

1.   Place the grated carrot in a colander and press down to squeeze out any excess moisture. Dry it with a paper towel.
2.   Combine the carrots with the remaining ingredients.

3.   Mold 1 tablespoon of the mixture into a ball and press it down with your hand or a spoon to flatten it. Repeat until the rest of the mixture is used up.
4.   Spritz the balls with cooking spray.
5.   Arrange in the basket of your Air Fryer, taking care not to overlap any balls. Cook at 350°F for 8 to 11 minutes or until they're firm.
6.   Serve warm.

Rosemary Cornbread

Prep + Cook Time: 1 hr. | Servings: 6

Ingredients

1 cup cornmeal
1 ½ cups flour
½ tsp. baking soda
½ tsp. baking powder
¼ tsp. kosher salt
1 tsp. dried rosemary
¼ tsp. garlic powder
2 tbsp. sugar
2 eggs
¼ cup melted butter
1 cup buttermilk
½ cup corn kernels

Instructions

1.   In a bowl, combine all the dry ingredients. In a separate bowl, mix together all the wet ingredients. Combine the two.
2.   Fold in the corn kernels and stir vigorously.
3.   Pour the batter into a lightly greased round loaf pan that is lightly greased.
4.   Cook for 1 hour at 380°F.

Veggie Rolls

Prep + Cook Time: 30 minutes | Servings: 6

Ingredients

2 potatoes, mashed
¼ cup peas
¼ cup carrots, mashed
1 small cabbage, sliced
¼ beans
2 tbsp. sweetcorn
1 small onion, chopped
1 tsp. capsicum
1 tsp. coriander
2 tbsp. butter
Ginger
Garlic to taste
½ tsp. masala powder
½ tsp. chili powder
½ cup bread crumbs
1 packet spring roll sheets
½ cup cornstarch slurry

Instructions

1.   Boil all the vegetables in water over a low heat. Rinse and allow to dry.
2.   Unroll the spring roll sheets and spoon equal amounts of vegetable onto the center of each one. Fold into spring rolls and coat each one with the slurry and bread crumbs.
3.   Pre-heat the Air Fryer to 390°F. Cook the rolls for 10 minutes.
4.   Serve with a side of boiled rice.

Grilled Cheese

Prep + Cook Time: 25 minutes | Servings: 2

Ingredients

4 slices bread
½ cup sharp cheddar cheese
¼ cup butter, melted

Instructions

1. Pre-heat the Air Fryer at 360°F.
2. Put cheese and butter in separate bowls.
3. Apply the butter to each side of the bread slices with a brush.
4. Spread the cheese across two of the slices of bread and make two sandwiches. Transfer both to the fryer.
5. Cook for 5 – 7 minutes or until a golden brown color is achieved and the cheese is melted.

Potato Gratin

Prep + Cook Time: 55 minutes | Servings: 6

Ingredients

½ cup milk
7 medium russet potatoes, peeled
1 tsp. black pepper
½ cup cream
½ cup semi-mature cheese, grated
½ tsp. nutmeg

Instructions

1. Pre-heat the Air Fryer to 390°F.
2. Cut the potatoes into wafer-thin slices.
3. In a bowl, combine the milk and cream and sprinkle with salt, pepper, and nutmeg as desired.
4. Use the milk mixture to coat the slices of potatoes. Place in an 8" heat-resistant baking dish. Top the potatoes with the rest of the cream mixture.
5. Put the baking dish into the basket of the fryer and cook for 25 minutes.
6. Pour the cheese over the potatoes.
7. Cook for an additional 10 minutes, ensuring the top is nicely browned before serving.

Roasted Vegetables

Prep + Cook Time: 30 minutes | Servings: 6

Ingredients

1 ⅓ cup small parsnips
1 ⅓ cup celery [3 – 4 stalks]
2 red onions
1 ⅓ cup small butternut squash
1 tbsp. fresh thyme needles
1 tbsp. olive oil
Salt and pepper to taste

Instructions

1. Pre-heat the Air Fryer to 390°F.
2. Peel the parsnips and onions and cut them into 2-cm cubes. Slice the onions into wedges.
3. Do not peel the butternut squash. Cut it in half, de-seed it, and cube.
4. Combine the cut vegetables with the thyme, olive oil, salt and pepper.
5. Put the vegetables in the basket and transfer the basket to the Air Fryer.

6. Cook for 20 minutes, stirring once throughout the cooking time, until the vegetables are nicely browned and cooked through.

Sweet Potato Curry Fries

Prep + Cook Time: 55 minutes | Servings: 4

Ingredients

2.2 lb. sweet potatoes
1 tsp. curry powder
2 tbsp. olive oil
Salt to taste

Instructions

1. Pre-heat Air Fryer to 390°F.
2. Wash the sweet potatoes before slicing them into matchsticks.
3. Drizzle the oil in the pan, place the fries inside and bake for 25 minutes.
4. Sprinkle with curry and salt before serving with ketchup if desired.

FISH & SEAFOOD

Crab Legs

Prep + Cook Time: 20 minutes | Servings: 3

Ingredients

3 lb. crab legs
¼ cup salted butter, melted and divided
½ lemon, juiced
¼ tsp. garlic powder

Instructions

1.   In a bowl, toss the crab legs and two tablespoons of the melted butter together. Place the crab legs in the basket of the fryer.
2.   Cook at 400°F for fifteen minutes, giving the basket a good shake halfway through.
3.   Combine the remaining butter with the lemon juice and garlic powder.
4.   Crack open the cooked crab legs and remove the meat. Serve with the butter dip on the side and enjoy!

Crusty Pesto Salmon

Prep + Cook Time: 15 minutes | Servings: 2

Ingredients

¼ cup s, roughly chopped
¼ cup pesto
2 x 4-oz. salmon fillets
2 tbsp. unsalted butter, melted

Instructions

1.   Mix the s and pesto together.
2.   Place the salmon fillets in a round baking dish, roughly six inches in diameter.
3.   Brush the fillets with butter, followed by the pesto mixture, ensuring to coat both the top and bottom. Put the baking dish inside the fryer.
4.   Cook for twelve minutes at 390°F.
5.   The salmon is ready when it flakes easily when prodded with a fork. Serve warm.

Buttery Cod

Prep + Cook Time: 12 minutes | Servings: 2

Ingredients

2 x 4-oz. cod fillets
2 tbsp. salted butter, melted
1 tsp. Old Bay seasoning
½ medium lemon, sliced

Instructions

1.   Place the cod fillets in a baking dish.
2.   Brush with melted butter, season with Old Bay, and top with some lemon slices.
3.   Wrap the fish in aluminum foil and put into your fryer.
4.   Cook for eight minutes at 350°F.
5.   The cod is ready when it flakes easily. Serve hot.

Sesame Tuna Steak

Prep + Cook Time: 12 minutes | Servings: 2

Ingredients

1 tbsp. coconut oil, melted
2 x 6-oz. tuna steaks
½ tsp. garlic powder
2 tsp. black sesame seeds
2 tsp. white sesame seeds

Instructions

1.   Apply the coconut oil to the tuna steaks with a brunch, then season with garlic powder.
2.   Combine the black and white sesame seeds. Embed them in the tuna steaks, covering the fish all over. Place the tuna into your air fryer.
3.   Cook for eight minutes at 400°F, turning the fish halfway through.
4.   The tuna steaks are ready when they have reached a temperature of 145°F. Serve straightaway.

Lemon Garlic Shrimp

Prep + Cook Time: 15 minutes | Servings: 2

Ingredients

1 medium lemon
½ lb. medium shrimp, shelled and deveined
½ tsp. Old Bay seasoning
2 tbsp. unsalted butter, melted
½ tsp. minced garlic

Instructions

1.   Grate the rind of the lemon into a bowl. Cut the lemon in half and juice it over the same bowl. Toss in the shrimp, Old Bay, and butter, mixing everything to make sure the shrimp is completely covered.
2.   Transfer to a round baking dish roughly six inches wide, then place this dish in your fryer.
3.   Cook at 400°F for six minutes. The shrimp is cooked when it turns a bright pink color.
4.   Serve hot, drizzling any leftover sauce over the shrimp.

Foil Packet Salmon

Prep + Cook Time: 15 minutes | Servings: 2

Ingredients

2 x 4-oz. skinless salmon fillets
2 tbsp. unsalted butter, melted
½ tsp. garlic powder
1 medium lemon
½ tsp. dried dill

Instructions

1.   Take a sheet of aluminum foil and cut into two squares measuring roughly 5" x 5". Lay each of the salmon fillets at the center of each piece. Brush both fillets with a tablespoon of bullet and season with a quarter-teaspoon of garlic powder.
2.   Halve the lemon and grate the skin of one half over the fish. Cut four half-slices of lemon, using two to top each fillet. Season each fillet with a quarter-teaspoon of dill.
3.   Fold the tops and sides of the aluminum foil over the fish to create a kind of packet. Place each one in the fryer.
4.   Cook for twelve minutes at 400°F.
5.   The salmon is ready when it flakes easily. Serve hot.

Foil Packet Lobster Tail

Prep + Cook Time: 15 minutes | Servings: 2

Ingredients

2 x 6-oz. lobster tail halves
2 tbsp. salted butter, melted
½ medium lemon, juiced
½ tsp. Old Bay seasoning
1 tsp. dried parsley

Instructions

1.   Lay each lobster on a sheet of aluminum foil. Pour a light drizzle of melted butter and lemon juice over each one, and season with Old Bay.
2.   Fold down the sides and ends of the foil to seal the lobster. Place each one in the fryer.
3.   Cook at 375°F for twelve minutes.
4.   Just before serving, top the lobster with dried parsley.

Avocado Shrimp

Prep + Cook Time: 20 minutes | Servings: 2

Ingredients

½ cup onion, chopped
2 lb. shrimp
1 tbsp. seasoned salt
1 avocado
½ cup pecans, chopped

Instructions

1.   Pre-heat the fryer at 400°F.
2.   Put the chopped onion in the basket of the fryer and spritz with some cooking spray. Leave to cook for five minutes.
3.   Add the shrimp and set the timer for a further five minutes. Sprinkle with some seasoned salt, then allow to cook for an additional five minutes.
4.   During these last five minutes, halve your avocado and remove the pit. Cube each half, then scoop out the flesh.
5.   Take care when removing the shrimp from the fryer. Place it on a dish and top with the avocado and the chopped pecans.

Lemon Butter Scallops

Prep + Cook Time: 30 minutes | Servings: 1

Ingredients

1 lemon
1 lb. scallops
½ cup butter
¼ cup parsley, chopped

Instructions

1.   Juice the lemon into a Ziploc bag.
2.   Wash your scallops, dry them, and season to taste. Put them in the bag with the lemon juice. Refrigerate for an hour.
3.   Remove the bag from the refrigerator and leave for about twenty minutes until it returns to room temperature. Transfer the scallops into a foil pan that is small enough to be placed inside the fryer.
4.   Pre-heat the fryer at 400°F and put the rack inside.
5.   Place the foil pan on the rack and cook for five minutes.
6.   In the meantime, melt the butter in a saucepan over a medium heat. Zest the lemon over the saucepan, then add in the chopped parsley. Mix well.

7.   Take care when removing the pan from the fryer. Transfer the contents to a plate and drizzle with the lemon-butter mixture. Serve hot.

Cheesy Lemon Halibut

Prep + Cook Time: 20 minutes | Servings: 2

Ingredients

1 lb. halibut fillet
½ cup butter
2 ½ tbsp. mayonnaise
2 ½ tbsp. lemon juice
¾ cup parmesan cheese, grated

Instructions

1.   Pre-heat your fryer at 375°F.
2.   Spritz the halibut fillets with cooking spray and season as desired.
3.   Put the halibut in the fryer and cook for twelve minutes.
4.   In the meantime, combine the butter, mayonnaise, and lemon juice in a bowl with a hand mixer. Ensure a creamy texture is achieved.
5.   Stir in the grated parmesan.
6.   When the halibut is ready, open the drawer and spread the butter over the fish with a butter knife. Allow to cook for a further two minutes, then serve hot.

Spicy Mackerel

Prep + Cook Time: 20 minutes | Servings: 2

Ingredients

2 mackerel fillets
2 tbsp. red chili flakes
2 tsp. garlic, minced
1 tsp. lemon juice

Instructions

1.   Season the mackerel fillets with the red pepper flakes, minced garlic, and a drizzle of lemon juice. Allow to sit for five minutes.
2.   Preheat your fryer at 350°F.
3.   Cook the mackerel for five minutes, before opening the drawer, flipping the fillets, and allowing to cook on the other side for another five minutes.
4.   Plate the fillets, making sure to spoon any remaining juice over them before serving.

Thyme Scallops

Prep + Cook Time: 12 minutes | Servings: 1

Ingredients

1 lb. scallops
Salt and pepper
½ tbsp. butter
½ cup thyme, chopped

Instructions

1.   Wash the scallops and dry them completely. Season with pepper and salt, then set aside while you prepare the pan.
2.   Grease a foil pan in several spots with the butter and cover the bottom with the thyme. Place the scallops on top.
3.   Pre-heat the fryer at 400°F and set the rack inside.
4.   Place the foil pan on the rack and allow to cook for seven minutes.
5.   Take care when removing the pan from the fryer and transfer the scallops to a serving dish. Spoon any remaining butter in the pan over the fish and enjoy.

Crispy Calamari

Prep + Cook Time: 15 minutes | Servings: 4

Ingredients

1 lb. fresh squid
Salt and pepper
2 cups flour
1 cup water
2 cloves garlic, minced
½ cup mayonnaise

Instructions

1.   Remove the skin from the squid and discard any ink. Slice the squid into rings and season with some salt and pepper.
2.   Put the flour and water in separate bowls. Dip the squid firstly in the flour, then into the water, then into the flour again, ensuring that it is entirely covered with flour.
3.   Pre-heat the fryer at 400°F. Put the squid inside and cook for six minutes.
4.   In the meantime, prepare the aioli by combining the garlic with the mayonnaise in a bowl.
5.   Once the squid is ready, plate up and serve with the aioli.

Filipino Bistek

Prep + Cook Time: 10 minutes + marinating time | Servings: 4

Ingredients

2 milkfish bellies, deboned and sliced into 4 portions
¾ tsp. salt
¼ tsp. ground black pepper
¼ tsp. cumin powder
2 tbsp. calamansi juice
2 lemongrass, trimmed and cut crosswise into small pieces
½ cup tamari sauce
2 tbsp. fish sauce [Patis]
2 tbsp. sugar
1 tsp. garlic powder
½ cup chicken broth
2 tbsp. olive oil

Instructions

1.   Dry the fish using some paper towels.
2.   Put the fish in a large bowl and coat with the rest of the ingredients. Allow to marinate for 3 hours in the refrigerator.
3.   Cook the fish steaks on an Air Fryer grill basket at 340°F for 5 minutes.
4.   Turn the steaks over and allow to grill for an additional 4 minutes. Cook until medium brown.
5.   Serve with steamed white rice.

Saltine Fish Fillets

Prep + Cook Time: 15 minutes | Servings: 4

Ingredients

1 cup crushed saltines
¼ cup extra-virgin olive oil
1 tsp. garlic powder
½ tsp. shallot powder
1 egg, well whisked
4 white fish fillets
Salt and ground black pepper to taste

Fresh Italian parsley to serve

Instructions

1.   In a shallow bowl, combine the crushed saltines and olive oil.
2.   In a separate bowl, mix together the garlic powder, shallot powder, and the beaten egg.
3.   Sprinkle a good amount of salt and pepper over the fish, before dipping each fillet into the egg mixture.
4.   Coat the fillets with the crumb mixture.
5.   Air fry the fish at 370°F for 10 - 12 minutes.
6.   Serve with fresh parsley.

Cod Nuggets

Prep + Cook Time: 25 minutes | Servings: 4

Ingredients

1 lb. cod fillet, cut into chunks
1 tbsp. olive oil
1 cup cracker crumbs
1 tbsp. egg and water
½ cup flour
Salt and pepper

Instructions

1.   Place the cracker crumbs and oil in food processor and pulse together. Sprinkle the cod pieces with salt and pepper.
2.   Roll the cod pieces in the flour before dredging them in egg and coating them in the cracker crumbs.
3.   Pre-heat the Air Fryer to 350°F.
4.   Put the fish in the basket and air fry to 350°F for 15 minutes or until a light golden-brown color is achieved.
5.   Serve hot.

Sweet Potatoes & Salmon

Prep + Cook Time: 45 minutes | Servings: 4

Ingredients

For the Salmon Fillets:
4 x 6-oz. skin-on salmon fillets
1 tbsp. extra-virgin olive oil
1 tsp. celery salt
¼ tsp. ground black pepper, or more to taste
2 tbsp. capers
Pinch of dry mustard
Pinch of ground mace
1 tsp. smoked cayenne pepper

For the Potatoes:
4 sweet potatoes, peeled and cut into wedges
1 tbsp. sesame oil
Kosher salt and pepper, to taste

Instructions

1.   Coat all sides of the salmon filets with a brushing of oil. Cover with all the seasonings for the fillets.
2.   Air-fry at 360°F for 5 minutes, flip them over, and proceed to cook for 5 more minutes.
3.   In the meantime, coat the sweet potatoes with the sesame oil, salt, and pepper.
4.   Cook the potatoes at 380°F for 15 minutes.
5.   Turn the potatoes over and cook for another 15 - 20 minutes.
6.   Serve the potatoes and salmon together.

Grilled Shrimp

Prep + Cook Time: 35 minutes | Servings: 4

Ingredients
18 shrimps, shelled and deveined
2 tbsp. freshly squeezed lemon juice
½ tsp. hot paprika
½ tsp. salt
1 tsp. lemon-pepper seasoning
2 tbsp. extra-virgin olive oil
2 garlic cloves, peeled and minced
1 tsp. onion powder
¼ tsp. cumin powder
½ cup fresh parsley, coarsely chopped

Instructions
1. Put all the ingredients in a bowl, making sure to coat the shrimp well. Refrigerate for 30 minutes.
2. Pre-heat the Air Fryer at 400°F
3. Air-fry the shrimp for 5 minutes, ensuring that the shrimps turn pink.
4. Serve with pasta or rice.

Homemade Cod Fillets

Prep + Cook Time: 15 minutes | Servings: 4

Ingredients
4 cod fillets
¼ tsp. fine sea salt
¼ tsp. ground black pepper, or more to taste
1 tsp. cayenne pepper
½ cup non-dairy milk
½ cup fresh Italian parsley, coarsely chopped
1 tsp. dried basil
½ tsp. dried oregano
1 Italian pepper, chopped
4 garlic cloves, minced

Instructions
1. Lightly grease a baking dish with some vegetable oil.
2. Coat the cod fillets with salt, pepper, and cayenne pepper.
3. Blend the rest of the ingredients in a food processor. Cover the fish fillets in this mixture.
4. Transfer the fillets to the Air Fryer and cook at 380°F for 10 to 12 minutes, ensure the cod is flaky before serving.

Christmas Flounder

Prep + Cook Time: 15 minutes + marinating time | Servings: 4

Ingredients
4 flounder fillets
Sea salt and freshly cracked mixed peppercorns, to taste
1 ½ tbsp. dark sesame oil
2 tbsp. sake
¼ cup soy sauce
1 tbsp. grated lemon rind
2 garlic cloves, minced
1 tsp. sugar
Fresh chopped chives, to serve

Instructions
1. Put all of the ingredients, except for the chives, in a large bowl. Coat the fillets well with the seasoning.
2. Refrigerate for 2 hours to let it marinate.
3. Place the fish fillets in the Air Fryer cooking basket and cook at 360°F for 10 to 12 minutes, turning once during the cooking time.

4. Simmer the rest of the marinade over a medium-to-low heat, stirring constantly, allowing it to thicken.
5. Plate up the flounder and add the glaze on top. Serve with fresh chives.

Coconut Prawns

Prep + Cook Time: 10 minutes | Servings: 4

Ingredients
12 prawns, cleaned and deveined
Salt and ground black pepper, to taste
½ tsp. cumin powder
1 tsp. fresh lemon juice
1 medium egg, whisked
⅓ cup of beer
½ cup flour
1 tsp. baking powder
1 tbsp. curry powder
½ tsp. grated fresh ginger
1 cup flaked coconut

Instructions
1. Coat the prawns in the salt, pepper, cumin powder, and lemon juice.
2. In a bowl, combine together the whisked egg, beer, a quarter-cup of the flour, baking powder, curry, and ginger.
3. In a second bowl, put the remaining quarter-cup of flour, and in a third bowl, the flaked coconut.
4. Dredge the prawns in the flour, before coating them in the beer mixture. Finally, coat your prawns in the flaked coconut.
5. Air-fry at 360°F for 5 minutes. Flip them and allow to cook on the other side for another 2 to 3 minutes before serving.

Cajun Shrimp

Prep + Cook Time: 25 minutes | Servings: 4

Ingredients
¼ tsp. cayenne pepper
¼ tsp. smoked paprika
½ tsp. old bay seasoning
1 tbsp. olive oil
Pinch of salt
1 ¼ lb. tiger shrimp

Instructions
1. Pre-heat your Air Fryer to 390°F.
2. In a large bowl, combine together all the ingredients, ensuring to coat the shrimps well.
3. Transfer to the fryer and cook for 5 minutes.
4. Serve over boiled rice.

Catfish

Prep + Cook Time: 30 minutes | Servings: 4

Ingredients
2 catfish fillets [catfish]
1 medium egg, beaten
1 cup friendly bread crumbs
1 cup tortilla chips
1 lemon, juiced and peeled
1 tsp. parsley
Salt and pepper to taste

Instructions
1. Slice up the catfish fillets neatly and drizzle lightly with the lemon juice.
2. In a separate bowl, combine the bread crumbs with the lemon rind, parsley, tortillas, salt and pepper. Pour into your food processor and pulse.
3. Put the fillets in a tray and spread it evenly across the base. Pour the mixture over the fish to cover well.
4. Transfer to your Air Fryer and cook at 350°F for 15 minutes. Serve with chips and a refreshing drink.

Fish Fillets

Prep + Cook Time: 25 minutes | Servings: 4

Ingredients

4 fish fillets
1 egg, beaten
1 cup bread crumbs
4 tbsp. olive oil
Pepper and salt to taste

Instructions

1.   Pre-heat the Air Fryer at 350°F.
2.   In a shallow dish, combine together the bread crumbs, oil, pepper, and salt.
3.   Pour the beaten egg into a second dish.
4.   Dredge each fish fillet in the egg before rolling them in the bread crumbs. Place in the Air Fryer basket.
5.   Allow to cook in the Air Fryer for 12 minutes.

Bean Burritos

Prep + Cook Time: 15 minutes | Servings: 4

Ingredients

4 tortillas
1 can beans
1 cup cheddar cheese, grated
¼ tsp. paprika
¼ tsp. chili powder
¼ tsp. garlic powder
Salt and pepper to taste

Instructions

1.   Pre-heat the Air Fryer to 350°F.
2.   In a bowl, mix together the paprika, chili powder, garlic powder, salt and pepper.
3.   Fill each tortilla with an equal portion of beans before adding the spice mixture and the cheddar cheese. Roll the tortilla wraps into burritos.
4.   Cover the base of a baking dish with parchment paper.
5.   Transfer the burritos to the baking dish.
6.   Put in the Air Fryer and cook for roughly 5 minutes. Serve hot.

Fishman Cakes

Prep + Cook Time: 35 minutes | Servings: 4

Ingredients

2 cups white fish
1 cup potatoes, mashed
1 tsp. mix herbs
1 tsp. mix spice
1 tsp. coriander
1 tsp. Worcestershire sauce
2 tsp. chili powder
1 tsp. milk
1 tsp. butter
1 small onion, diced
¼ cup bread crumbs
Pepper and salt to taste

Instructions

1.   Place all of the ingredients in a bowl and combine.
2.   Using your hands, mold equal portions of the mixture into small patties and refrigerate for 2 hours.
3.   Put the fish cakes in the Air Fryer basket and cook at 400°F for 15 minutes. Serve hot.

Sunday's Salmon

Prep + Cook Time: 20 minutes | Servings: 3

Ingredients

½ lb. salmon fillet, chopped
2 egg whites
2 tbsp. chives, chopped
2 tbsp. garlic, minced
½ cup onion, chopped
2/3 cup carrots, grated
2/3 cup potato, grated
½ cup friendly bread crumbs
¼ cup flour
Pepper and salt

Instructions

1.   In a shallow dish, combine the bread crumbs with the pepper and salt.
2.   Pour the flour into another dish.
3.   In a third dish, add the egg whites.
4.   Put all of the other ingredients in a large mixing bowl and stir together to combine.
5.   Using your hands, shape equal amounts of the mixture into small balls. Roll each ball in the flour before dredging it in the egg and lastly covering it with bread crumbs. Transfer all the coated croquettes to the Air Fryer basket and air fry at 320°F for 6 minutes.
6.   Reduce the heat to 350°F and allow to cook for another 4 minutes.
7.   Serve hot.

Whitefish Cakes

Prep + Cook Time: 1 hr. 20 minutes | Servings: 4

Ingredients

1 ½ cups whitefish fillets, minced
1 ½ cups green beans, finely chopped
½ cup scallions, chopped
1 chili pepper, deveined and minced
1 tbsp. red curry paste
1 tsp. sugar
1 tbsp. fish sauce
2 tbsp. apple cider vinegar
1 tsp. water
Sea salt flakes, to taste
½ tsp. cracked black peppercorns
1 ½ teaspoons butter, at room temperature
1 lemon

Instructions

1.   Place all of the ingredients a bowl, following the order in which they are listed.
2.   Combine well with a spatula or your hands.
3.   Mold the mixture into several small cakes and refrigerate for 1 hour.
4.   Put a piece of aluminum foil in the cooking basket and lay the cakes on top.
5.   Cook at 390°F for 10 minutes. Turn each fish cake over before air-frying for another 5 minutes.
6.   Serve the fish cakes with a side of cucumber relish.

Marinated Sardines

Prep + Cook Time: 1 hr. 15 minutes | Servings: 4

Ingredients

¾ lb. sardines, cleaned and rinsed
Salt and ground black pepper, to taste
1 tsp. smoked cayenne pepper
1 tbsp. lemon juice
1 tbsp. soy sauce
2 tbsp. olive oil

For the Potatoes:

8 medium Russet potatoes, peeled and quartered
½ stick melted butter
Salt and pepper, to taste
1 tsp. granulated garlic

Instructions

1. Dry the sardines with a paper towel.
2. Cover the sardines in the salt, black pepper, cayenne pepper, lemon juice, soy sauce, and olive oil, and leave to marinate for half an hour.
3. Air-fry the sardines at 350°F for roughly 5 minutes.
4. Raise the heat to 385°F and cook for an additional 7 - 8 minutes. Remove the sardines and plate up.
5. Wipe the cooking basket clean and pour in the potatoes, butter, salt, pepper, and garlic.
6. Roast at 390°F for 30 minutes. Serve the vegetables and the sardines together.

Halibut Steaks

Prep + Cook Time: 15 minutes | Servings: 4

Ingredients

1 lb. halibut steaks
Salt and pepper to taste
1 tsp. dried basil
2 tbsp. honey
¼ cup vegetable oil
2 ½ tbsp. Worcester sauce
1 tbsp. freshly squeezed lemon juice
2 tbsp. vermouth
1 tbsp. fresh parsley leaves, coarsely chopped

Instructions

1. Put all of the ingredients in a large bowl. Combine and cover the fish completely with the seasoning.
2. Transfer to your Air Fryer and cook at 390°F for 5 minutes.
3. Turn the fish over and allow to cook for a further 5 minutes.
4. Ensure the fish is cooked through, leaving it in the fryer for a few more minutes if necessary.
5. Serve with a side of potato salad.

Fisherman's Fish Fingers

Prep + Cook Time: 40 minutes | Servings: 4

Ingredients

¾ lb. fish, cut into fingers
1 cup friendly bread crumbs
2 tsp. mixed herbs
¼ tsp. baking soda
2 eggs, beaten
3 tsp. flour
2 tbsp. Maida
1 tsp. garlic ginger puree
½ tsp. black pepper
2 tsp. garlic powder
½ tsp. red chili flakes
½ tsp. turmeric powder
2 tbsp. lemon juice
½ tsp. salt

Instructions

1. Put the fish, garlic ginger puree, garlic powder, red chili flakes, turmeric powder, lemon juice, 1 teaspoon of the mixed herbs, and salt in a bowl and combine well.
2. In a separate bowl, combine the flour, Maida, and baking soda.
3. In a third bowl pour in the beaten eggs.
4. In a fourth bowl, stir together the bread crumbs, black pepper, and another teaspoon of mixed herbs.
5. Pre-heat the Air Fryer to 350°F.
6. Coat the fish fingers in the flour. Dredge in the egg, then roll in the breadcrumb mixture.
7. Put the fish fingers in the fryer's basket and allow to cook for 10 minutes, ensuring they crisp up nicely.

Fish Taco

Prep + Cook Time: 30 minutes | Servings: 4

Ingredients

12 oz. cod filet
1 cup friendly bread crumbs
4 – 6 friendly flour tortillas
1 cup tempura butter
½ cup salsa
½ cup guacamole
2 tbsp. freshly chopped cilantro
½ tsp. salt
¼ tsp. black pepper
Lemon wedges for garnish

Instructions

1. Slice the cod filets lengthwise and sprinkle salt and pepper on all sides.
2. Put the tempura butter in a bowl and coat each cod piece in it. Dip the fillets into the bread crumbs.
3. Pre-heat the Air Fryer to 340°F.
4. Fry the cod sticks for about 10 – 13 minutes in the fryer. Flip each one once while cooking.
5. In the meantime, coat one side of each tortilla with an even spreading of guacamole.
6. Put a cod stick in each tortilla and add the chopped cilantro and salsa on top. Lightly drizzle over the lemon juice. Fold into tacos.

Crispy Fish Fillet

Prep + Cook Time: 15 minutes | Servings: 4

Ingredients

2 fish fillets, each sliced into 4 pieces
1 tbsp. lemon juice
1 tsp. chili powder
4 tbsp. mayonnaise
3 tbsp. cornmeal
¼ tsp. black pepper
4 tbsp. flour
¼ tsp. salt

Instructions

1. Pre-heat the Air Fryer at 400°F.
2. Combine together the flour, pepper, cornmeal, salt, and chili powder.
3. In a shallow bowl, stir together the lemon juice and mayonnaise.
4. Coat the fillets in the mayonnaise mixture, before covering with the flour mixture.
5. Put the coated fish into the fryer's basket and cook for 5 minutes, ensuring they crisp up nicely. Serve hot.

Crispy Shrimp

Prep + Cook Time: 20 minutes | Servings: 8

Ingredients

2 lb. shrimp, peeled and deveined
4 egg whites
2 tbsp. olive oil
1 cup flour
½ tsp. cayenne pepper
1 cup friendly bread crumbs
Salt and pepper to taste

Instructions

1.   Combine together the flour, pepper, and salt in a shallow bowl.
2.   In a separate bowl mix the egg whites using a whisk.
3.   In a third bowl, combine the bread crumbs, cayenne pepper, and salt.
4.   Pre-heat your Air Fryer to 400°F.
5.   Cover the shrimp with the flour mixture before dipping it in the egg white and lastly rolling in the bread crumbs.
6.   Put the coated shrimp in the fryer's basket and top with a light drizzle of olive oil. Air fry the shrimp at 400°F for 8 minutes, in multiple batches if necessary.

Fish Sticks

Prep + Cook Time: 20 minutes | Servings: 4

Ingredients

1 lb. tilapia fillets, cut into strips
1 large egg, beaten
2 tsp. Old Bay seasoning
1 tbsp. olive oil
1 cup friendly bread crumbs

Instructions

1.   Pre-heat the Air Fryer at 400°F.
2.   In a shallow dish, combine together the bread crumbs, Old Bay, and oil. Put the egg in a small bowl.
3.   Dredge the fish sticks in the egg. Cover them with bread crumbs and put them in the fryer's basket.
4.   Cook the fish for 10 minutes or until they turn golden brown.
5.   Serve hot.

Crab Herb Croquettes

Prep + Cook Time: 30 minutes | Servings: 6

Ingredients

1 lb. crab meat
1 cup friendly bread crumbs
2 egg whites
½ tsp. parsley
¼ tsp. chives
¼ tsp. tarragon
2 tbsp. celery, chopped
¼ cup red pepper, chopped
1 tsp. olive oil
½ tsp. lime juice
4 tbsp. sour cream
4 tbsp. mayonnaise
¼ cup onion, chopped
¼ tsp. salt

Instructions

1.   Put the bread crumbs and salt in a bowl.
2.   Pour the egg whites in a separate bowl.
3.   Place the rest of the ingredients in a third bowl and combine thoroughly.
4.   Using your hands, shape equal amounts of the mixture into small balls and dredge each ball in the egg white before coating with the bread crumbs.
5.   Put the croquettes in the Air Fryer basket and cook at 400°F for 18 minutes. Serve hot.

Broiled Tilapia

Prep + Cook Time: 10 minutes | Servings: 4

Ingredients

1 lb. tilapia fillets
½ tsp. lemon pepper
Salt to taste

Instructions

1.   Spritz the Air Fryer basket with some cooking spray.
2.   Put the tilapia fillets in basket and sprinkle on the lemon pepper and salt.
3.   Cook at 400°F for 7 minutes.
4.   Serve with a side of vegetables.

Salmon Patties

Prep + Cook Time: 20 minutes | Servings: 4

Ingredients

1 egg
14 oz. canned salmon, drained
4 tbsp. flour
4 tbsp. cup cornmeal
4 tbsp. onion, minced
½ tsp. garlic powder
2 tbsp. mayonnaise
Salt and pepper to taste

Instructions

1.   Flake apart the salmon with a fork.
2.   Put the flakes in a bowl and combine with the garlic powder, mayonnaise, flour, cornmeal, egg, onion, pepper, and salt.
3.   Use your hands to shape equal portions of the mixture into small patties and put each one in the Air Fryer basket.
4.   Air fry the salmon patties at 350°F for 15 minutes. Serve hot.

Lemon Fish

Prep + Cook Time: 25 minutes | Servings: 2

Ingredients

2 tsp. green chili sauce
2 tsp. oil
2 egg white
Salt to taste
1 tsp. red chili sauce
2 – 3 lettuce leaves
4 tsp. flour
2 lemons
¼ cup sugar
4 fish fillets

Instructions

1. Slice up one of the lemons and set aside.
2. Boil a half-cup water in a saucepan. Stir in the sugar, ensuring it dissolves completely.
3. Put 1 cup of the flour, salt, green chili sauce, 2 teaspoons of oil and the egg white in a bowl and combine well.
4. Add 3 tbsp. of water and mix with a whisk until a smooth, thick consistency is achieved. Evenly spread the refined flour across a plate.
5. Dredge the fish fillets in the batter and cover with the refined flour.
6. Coat the Air Fryer's basket with a brushing of oil. Put the fish fillets in the basket and cook at 180°F for 10 – 15 minutes.
7. Add salt to the saucepan and combine well. Pour in the corn flour slurry and mix once more.
8. Add in the red chili sauce and stir.
9. Add the lemon slices. Squeeze the juice of the other lemon into the saucepan. Continue to cook, ensuring the sauce thickens well, stirring all the time.
10. Take the fish out of the fryer, coat with a light brushing of oil and return to the fryer basket.
11. Allow to cook for 5 additional minutes.
12. Shred up the lettuce leaves with your hands and arrange them on a serving platter.
13. Serve the fish over the lettuce and with the lemon sauce drizzled on top.

Jumbo Shrimp

Prep + Cook Time: 10 minutes | Servings: 4

Ingredients

12 jumbo shrimps
½ tsp. garlic salt
¼ tsp. freshly cracked mixed peppercorns
For the Sauce:
1 tsp. Dijon mustard
4 tbsp. mayonnaise
1 tsp. lemon zest
1 tsp. chipotle powder
½ tsp. cumin powder

Instructions

1. Sprinkle the garlic salt over the shrimp and coat with the cracked peppercorns.
2. Fry the shrimp in the cooking basket at 395°F for 5 minutes.
3. Turn the shrimp over and allow to cook for a further 2 minutes.
4. In the meantime, mix together all ingredients for the sauce with a whisk.

5. Serve over the shrimp.

Cod

Prep + Cook Time: 20 minutes | Servings: 5

Ingredients

1 lb. cod
3 tbsp. milk
1 cup meal
2 cups friendly bread crumbs
2 large eggs, beaten
½ tsp. pepper
¼ tsp. salt

Instructions

1. Combine together the milk and eggs in a bowl.
2. In a shallow dish, stir together bread crumbs, pepper, and salt.
3. Pour the meal into a second shallow dish.
4. Coat the cod sticks with the meal before dipping each one in the egg and rolling in bread crumbs.
5. Put the fish sticks in the Air Fryer basket. Cook at 350°F for 12 minutes, shaking the basket halfway through cooking.

Cheese Tilapia

Prep + Cook Time: 20 minutes | Servings: 4

Ingredients

1 lb. tilapia fillets
¾ cup parmesan cheese, grated
1 tbsp. parsley, chopped
2 tsp. paprika
1 tbsp. olive oil
Pepper and salt to taste

Instructions

1. Pre-heat the Air Fryer to 400°F.
2. In a shallow dish, combine together the paprika, grated cheese, pepper, salt and parsley.
3. Pour a light drizzle of olive oil over the tilapia fillets. Cover the fillets with the paprika and cheese mixture.
4. Lay the fillets on a sheet of aluminum foil and transfer to the Air Fryer basket. Fry for 10 minutes. Serve hot.

Cheese Crust Salmon

Prep + Cook Time: 20 minutes | Servings: 5

Ingredients

2 lb. salmon fillet
2 garlic cloves, minced
¼ cup fresh parsley, chopped
½ cup parmesan cheese, grated
Salt and pepper to taste

Instructions

1. Pre-heat the Air Fryer to 350°F.
2. Lay the salmon, skin-side-down, on a sheet of aluminum foil. Place another sheet of foil on top.
3. Transfer the salmon to the fryer and cook for 10 minutes.
4. Remove the salmon from the fryer. Take off the top layer of foil and add the minced garlic, parmesan cheese, pepper, salt and parsley on top of the fish.
5. Return the salmon to the Air Fryer and resume cooking for another minute.

Parmesan Crusted Tilapia

Prep + Cook Time: 15 minutes | Servings: 4

Ingredients

¾ cup grated parmesan cheese
4 tilapia fillets
1 tbsp. olive oil
1 tbsp. chopped parsley
2 tsp. paprika
Pinch garlic powder

Instructions

1 Pre-heat your Air Fryer at 350°F.
2 Coat each of the tilapia fillets with a light brushing of olive oil.
3 Combine all of the other ingredients together in a bowl.
4 Cover the fillets with the parmesan mixture.
5 Line the base of a baking dish with a sheet of parchment paper and place the fillets in the dish.
6 Transfer to the Air Fryer and cook for 5 minutes. Serve hot.

Salmon Croquettes

Prep + Cook Time: 15 minutes | Servings: 4

Ingredients

1 lb. can red salmon, drained and mashed
⅓ cup olive oil
2 eggs, beaten
1 cup friendly bread crumbs
½ bunch parsley, chopped

Instructions

1 Pre-heat the Air Fryer to 400°F.
2 In a mixing bowl, combine together the drained salmon, eggs, and parsley.
3 In a shallow dish, stir together the bread crumbs and oil to combine well.
4 Mold equal-sized amounts of the mixture into small balls and coat each one with bread crumbs.
5 Put the croquettes in the fryer's basket and air fry for 7 minutes.

Creamy Salmon

Prep + Cook Time: 20 minutes | Servings: 2

Ingredients

¾ lb. salmon, cut into 6 pieces
¼ cup yogurt
1 tbsp. olive oil
1 tbsp. dill, chopped
3 tbsp. sour cream
Salt to taste

Instructions

1 Sprinkle some salt on the salmon.
2 Put the salmon slices in the Air Fryer basket and add in a drizzle of olive oil.
3 Air fry the salmon at 285°F for 10 minutes.
4 In the meantime, combine together the cream, dill, yogurt, and salt.
5 Plate up the salmon and pour the creamy sauce over it. Serve hot.

Fried Cajun Shrimp

Prep + Cook Time: 10 minutes | Servings: 4

Ingredients

1 ¼ lb. shrimp, peeled and deveined
½ tsp. old bay seasoning

¼ tsp. cayenne pepper
1 tbsp. olive oil
½ tsp. paprika
¼ tsp. salt

Instructions

1 Pre-heat the Air Fryer to 400°F.
2 Place all of the ingredients in a bowl and mix well to coat the shrimp evenly.
3 Put the seasoned shrimp in the fryer's basket and air fry for 5 minutes. Serve hot.

Grilled Salmon Fillets

Prep + Cook Time: 20 minutes | Servings: 2

Ingredients

2 salmon fillets
⅓ cup of water
⅓ cup of light soy sauce
⅓ cup sugar
2 tbsp. olive oil
Black pepper and salt to taste
Garlic powder [optional]

Instructions

1 Sprinkle some salt and pepper on top of the salmon fillets. Season with some garlic powder if desired.
2 In a medium bowl, mix together the remaining ingredients with a whisk and use this mixture to coat the salmon fillets. Leave to marinate for 2 hours.
3 Pre-heat the Air Fryer at 355°F.
4 Remove any excess liquid from the salmon fillets and transfer to the fryer. Cook for 8 minutes before serving warm.

Prawns

Prep + Cook Time: 30 minutes | Servings: 4

Ingredients

1 lb. prawns, peeled
1 lb. bacon slices

Instructions

Pre-heat the Air Fryer to 400°F.
Wrap the bacon slices around the prawns and put them in fryer's basket.
Air fry for 5 minutes and serve hot.

Chunky Fish

Prep + Cook Time: 10 minutes + chilling time | Servings: 4

Ingredients

2 cans canned fish
2 celery stalks, trimmed and finely chopped
1 egg, whisked
1 cup friendly bread crumbs
1 tsp. whole-grain mustard
½ tsp. sea salt
¼ tsp. freshly cracked black peppercorns
1 tsp. paprika

Instructions

1 Combine all of the ingredients in the order in which they appear. Mold the mixture into four equal-sized cakes. Leave to chill in the refrigerator for 50 minutes.
2 Put on an Air Fryer grill pan. Spritz all sides of each cake with cooking spray.
3 Grill at 360°F for 5 minutes. Turn the cakes over and resume cooking for an additional 3 minutes.
4 Serve with mashed potatoes if desired.

Glazed Halibut Steak

Prep + Cook Time: 70 minutes | Servings: 3

Ingredients

1 lb. halibut steak
2/3 cup low-sodium soy sauce
½ cup mirin
2 tbsp. lime juice
¼ cup sugar
¼ tsp. crushed red pepper flakes
¼ cup orange juice
1 garlic clove, smashed
¼ tsp. ginger, ground

Instructions

1 Make the teriyaki glaze by mixing together all of the ingredients except for the halibut in a saucepan.
2 Bring it to a boil and lower the heat, stirring constantly until the mixture reduces by half. Remove from the heat and leave to cool.
3 Pour half of the cooled glaze into a Ziploc bag. Add in the halibut, making sure to coat it well in the sauce. Place in the refrigerator for 30 minutes.
4 Pre-heat the Air Fryer to 390°F.
5 Put the marinated halibut in the fryer and allow to cook for 10 – 12 minutes.
6 Use any the remaining glaze to lightly brush the halibut steak with.
7 Serve with white rice or shredded vegetables.

Breadcrumbed Fish

Prep + Cook Time: 25 minutes | Servings: 2 – 4

Ingredients

4 tbsp. vegetable oil
5 oz. friendly bread crumbs
1 egg
4 medium fish fillets

Instructions

1 Pre-heat your Air Fryer to 350°F.
2 In a bowl, combine the bread crumbs and oil.
3 In a separate bowl, stir the egg with a whisk. Dredge each fish fillet in the egg before coating it in the crumbs mixture. Put them in Air Fryer basket.
4 Cook for 12 minutes and serve hot.

Cajun Lemon Salmon

Prep + Cook Time: 15 minutes | Servings: 1

Ingredients

1 salmon fillet
1 tsp. Cajun seasoning
½ lemon, juiced
¼ tsp. sugar
2 lemon wedges, for serving

Instructions

1 Pre-heat the Air Fryer to 350°F.
2 Combine the lemon juice and sugar.
3 Cover the salmon with the sugar mixture.
4 Coat the salmon with the Cajun seasoning.
5 Line the base of your fryer with a sheet of parchment paper.
6 Transfer the salmon to the fryer and allow to cook for 7 minutes.

Breaded Salmon

Prep + Cook Time: 25 minutes | Servings: 4

Ingredients

2 cups friendly bread crumbs
4 fillets of salmon
1 cup Swiss cheese, shredded
2 eggs, beaten

Instructions

1 Pre-heat your Air Fryer to 390°F.
2 Dredge the salmon fillets into the eggs. Add the Swiss cheese on top of each fillet.
3 Coat all sides of the fish with bread crumbs. Put in an oven safe dish, transfer to the fryer, and cook for 20 minutes.

Asian Style Fish

Prep + Cook Time: 35 minutes | Servings: 2

Ingredients

1 medium sea bass, halibut or fish cutlet [11 – 12 oz.]
1 tomato, cut into quarters
1 lime, cut thinly
1 stalk green onion, chopped
3 slices of ginger, julienned
2 garlic cloves, minced
1 chili, sliced
2 tbsp. cooking wine
1 tbsp. olive oil
Steamed rice [optional]

Instructions

1 Fry the ginger and garlic in the oil until they turn golden brown.
2 Pre-heat the Air Fryer to 360°F.
3 Wash and dry the fish. Halve it, ensuring each half is small enough to fit inside the fryer.
4 Put the fish in the basket of the fryer. Pour in a drizzle of the cooking wine.
5 Place the tomato and lime slices on top of the fish slices.
6 Add the garlic ginger oil mixture on top, followed by the green onion and chili slices.
7 Top with a sheet of aluminum foil. Cook for 15 minutes, or longer if necessary.
8 Serve hot with a side of steamed rice if desired.

Seafood Fritters

Prep + Cook Time: 50 minutes | Servings: 2 – 4

Ingredients

2 cups clam meat
1 cup shredded carrot
½ cup shredded zucchini
1 cup flour, combined with 3/4 cup water to make a batter
2 tbsp. olive oil
¼ tsp. pepper

Instructions

1 Pre-heat your Air Fryer to 390°F.
2 Combine the clam meat with the olive oil, shredded carrot, pepper and zucchini.
3 Using your hands, shape equal portions of the mixture into balls and roll each ball in the chickpea mixture.
4 Put the balls in the fryer and cook for 30 minutes, ensuring they turn nice and crispy before serving.

Calamari

Prep + Cook Time: 25 minutes | Servings: 2

Ingredients

1 cup club soda
½ lb. calamari tubes [or tentacles], about ¼ inch wide, rinsed and dried
½ cup honey
1 – 2 tbsp. sriracha
1 cup flour
Sea salt to taste
Red pepper and black pepper to taste
Red pepper flakes to taste

Instructions

1 In a bowl, cover the calamari rings with club soda and mix well. Leave to sit for 10 minutes.
2 In another bowl, combine the flour, salt, red and black pepper.
3 In a third bowl mix together the honey, pepper flakes, and Sriracha to create the sauce.
4 Remove any excess liquid from the calamari and coat each one with the flour mixture.
5 Spritz the fryer basket with the cooking spray.
6 Arrange the calamari in the basket, well-spaced out and in a single layer.
7 Cook at 380°F for 11 minutes, shaking the basket at least two times during the cooking time.
8 Take the calamari out of the fryer, coat it with half of the sauce and return to the fryer. Cook for an additional 2 minutes.
9 Plate up the calamari and pour the rest of the sauce over it.

Salmon & Dill Sauce

Prep + Cook Time: 45 minutes | Servings: 4

Ingredients

For the Salmon:
1 ½ lb. salmon
1 tsp. olive oil
1 pinch salt
For the Dill Sauce:
½ cup non-fat Greek yogurt
½ cup sour cream
Pinch of salt
2 tbsp. dill, finely chopped

Instructions

1 Pre-heat the Air Fryer to 270°F.
2 Slice the salmon into four 6-oz. pieces and pour a light drizzling of olive oil over each slice. Sprinkle on the salt.
3 Put the salmon in the cooking basket and allow to cook for 20 - 23 minutes.
4 Prepare the dill sauce by mixing together the yogurt, sour cream, chopped dill and salt.
5 Pour the sauce over the salmon and top with another sprinkling of chopped dill before serving.

Black Cod

Prep + Cook Time: 30 minutes | Servings: 2

Ingredients

2 [6- to 8-oz.] fillets of black cod or sablefish
Salt
Freshly ground black pepper

Olive oil
1 cup grapes, halved
1 small bulb fennel, sliced ¼-inch thick
½ cup pecans
3 cups shredded kale
2 tsp. white balsamic vinegar or white wine vinegar
2 tbsp. extra-virgin olive oil

Instructions

1 Pre-heat the Air Fryer to 400°F.
2 Sprinkle the cod fillets with salt and pepper and drizzle some olive oil over the fish.
3 Put the fish skin-side-down in the Air Fryer basket. Air fry for 10 minutes. Transfer the fillets to a side plate and loosely cover with aluminum foil.
4 Coat the grapes, fennel and pecans with a drizzle of olive oil and sprinkle on some salt and pepper.
5 Place the grapes, fennel and pecans in the fryer's basket and cook for 5 minutes at 400°F. Shake the basket occasionally throughout the cooking time.
6 Put the grapes, fennel and pecans in a bowl and add the kale.
7 Pour over the balsamic vinegar and olive oil and sprinkle with salt and pepper as desired. Serve with the fish and enjoy.

Tilapia Fillets

Prep + Cook Time: 25 minutes | Servings: 3

Ingredients

1 lb. tilapia fillets, sliced
4 wheat buns
2 egg yolks
1 tbsp. fish sauce
2 tbsp. mayonnaise
3 sweet pickle relish
1 tbsp. hot sauce
1 tbsp. nectar

Instructions

1 In a bowl, mix together the egg yolks and fish sauce.
2 Throw in the mayonnaise, sweet pickle relish, hot sauce and nectar.
3 Transfer the mixture to a round baking tray.
4 Put it in the Air Fryer and line the sides with the tilapia fillets. Cook for 15 minutes at 300°F.
5 Remove and serve on hamburger buns if desired.

Salmon Mixed Eggs

Prep + Cook Time: 25 minutes | Servings: 2

Ingredients

1 lb. salmon, cooked
2 eggs
1 onion, chopped
1 cup celery, chopped
1 tbsp. oil
Salt and pepper to taste

Instructions

1 In a bowl, mix the eggs with a whisk. Stir in the celery, onion, salt and pepper.
2 Grease a round baking tray with the oil. Transfer the egg mixture to the tray. Cook in the Air Fryer on 300°F for 10 minutes.
3 Serve with cooked salmon.

Cajun Salmon

Prep + Cook Time: 20 minutes | Servings: 1

Ingredients
1 salmon fillet
Cajun seasoning
Light sprinkle of sugar
¼ lemon, juiced, to serve

Instructions
1 Pre-heat Air Fryer to 355°F.
2 Lightly cover all sides of the salmon with Cajun seasoning. Sprinkle conservatively with sugar.
3 For a salmon fillet about three-quarters of an inch thick, cook in the fryer for 7 minutes, skin-side-up on the grill pan.
4 Serve with the lemon juice.

Fish Fingers

Prep + Cook Time: 40 minutes | Servings: 2

Ingredients
2 eggs
10 oz. fish, such as mackerel, cut into fingers
½ tsp. Turmeric Powder
½ Lemon, juiced
1 + 1 tsp. mixed dried herbs
1 + 1 tsp. Garlic Powder, separately
½ tsp. Red Chili Flakes
1 cup friendly bread crumbs
2 tbsp. Maida
3 tsp. flour
¼ tsp. baking soda
1 tsp. ginger garlic paste
½ tsp. black pepper
½ tsp. sea salt
1 – 2 tbsp. olive oil
Ketchup or tartar sauce [optional]

Instructions
1 Put the fish fingers in a bowl. Cover with 1 teaspoon of mixed herbs, 1 teaspoon of garlic powder, salt, red chili flakes, turmeric powder, black pepper, ginger garlic paste, and lemon juice. Leave to absorb for at least 10 minutes.
2 In a separate bowl, mix together the flour and baking soda. Crack the eggs in the mixture and stir again.
3 Throw in the marinated fish and set aside again for at least 10 minutes.
4 Combine the bread crumbs and the remaining teaspoon of mixed herbs and teaspoon of garlic powder.
5 Roll the fish sticks with the bread crumb and herb mixture.
6 Pre-heat the Air Fyer at 360°F.
7 Line the basket of the fryer with a sheet of aluminum foil. Place the fish fingers inside the fryer and pour over a drizzle of the olive oil.
8 Cook for 10 minutes, ensuring the fish is brown and crispy before serving. Enjoy with ketchup or tartar sauce if desired.

Mediterranean Salad

Prep + Cook Time: 15 minutes | Servings: 2

Ingredients
1 cup cooked quinoa
1 red bell pepper, chopped
2 prosciutto slices, chopped
¼ cup chopped kalamata olives
½ cup crumbled feta cheese
1 tsp. olive oil
1 tsp. dried oregano
6 cherry tomatoes, halved
Salt and pepper, to taste

Instructions
1 Pre-heat your Air Fryer to 350°F.
2 Drizzle the inside of the fryer with the olive oil. Place the red bell pepper inside and allow to cook for roughly 2 minutes. Put the prosciutto slices in the fryer and cook for an additional 3 minutes.
3 Put the ham and pepper in an oven-proof bowl and remove any excess grease. Combine with the remaining ingredients, save for the tomatoes.
4 Finally, stir in the cherry tomato halves.

APPETIZERS

Curly's Cauliflower

Prep + Cook Time: 30 minutes | Servings: 4

Ingredients

4 cups bite-sized cauliflower florets
1 cup friendly bread crumbs, mixed with 1 tsp. salt
¼ cup melted butter [vegan/other]
¼ cup buffalo sauce [vegan/other]
Mayo [vegan/other] or creamy dressing for dipping

Instructions

1 In a bowl, combine the butter and buffalo sauce to create a creamy paste.
2 Completely cover each floret with the sauce.
3 Coat the florets with the bread crumb mixture. Cook the florets in the Air Fryer for approximately 15 minutes at 350°F, shaking the basket occasionally.
4 Serve with a raw vegetable salad, mayo or creamy dressing.

Fried Mushrooms

Prep + Cook Time: 40 minutes | Servings: 4

Ingredients

2 lb. button mushrooms
3 tbsp. white or French vermouth [optional]
1 tbsp. coconut oil
2 tsp. herbs of your choice
½ tsp. garlic powder

Instructions

1 Wash and dry the mushrooms. Slice them into quarters.
2 Pre-heat your Air Fryer at 320°F and add the coconut oil, garlic powder, and herbs to the basket.
3 Briefly cook the ingredients for 2 minutes and give them a stir. Put the mushrooms in the air fryer and cook for 25 minutes, stirring occasionally throughout.
4 Pour in the white vermouth and mix. Cook for an additional 5 minutes.
5 Serve hot.

Cheesy Garlic Bread

Prep + Cook Time: 20 minutes | Servings: 2

Ingredients

1 friendly baguette
4 tsp. butter, melted
3 chopped garlic cloves
5 tsp. sundried tomato pesto
1 cup mozzarella cheese, grated

Instructions

1 Cut your baguette into 5 thick round slices.
2 Add the garlic cloves to the melted butter and brush onto each slice of bread.
3 Spread a teaspoon of sun dried tomato pesto onto each slice.
4 Top each slice with the grated mozzarella.
5 Transfer the bread slices to the Air Fryer and cook them at 180°F for 6 – 8 minutes.
6 Top with some freshly chopped basil leaves, chili flakes and oregano if desired.

Stuffed Mushrooms

Prep + Cook Time: 25 minutes | Servings: 4

Ingredients

6 small mushrooms
1 tbsp. onion, peeled and diced
1 tbsp. friendly bread crumbs
1 tbsp. olive oil
1 tsp. garlic, pureed
1 tsp. parsley
Salt and pepper to taste

Instructions

1 Combine the bread crumbs, oil, onion, parsley, salt, pepper and garlic in a bowl.
2 Scoop the stalks out of the mushrooms and spoon equal portions of the crumb mixture in the caps. Transfer to the Air Fryer and cook for 10 minutes at 350°F.
3 Serve with mayo dip if desired.

Grilled Tomatoes

Prep + Cook Time: 25 minutes | Servings: 2

Ingredients

2 tomatoes, medium to large
Herbs of your choice, to taste
Pepper to taste
High quality cooking spray

Instructions

1 Wash and dry the tomatoes, before chopping them in half.
2 Lightly spritz them all over with cooking spray.
3 Season each half with herbs (oregano, basil, parsley, rosemary, thyme, sage, etc.) as desired and black pepper.
4 Put the halves in the tray of your Air Fryer. Cook for 20 minutes at 320°F, or longer if necessary. Larger tomatoes will take longer to cook.

Carrots & Rhubarb

Prep + Cook Time: 35 minutes | Servings: 4

Ingredients

1 lb. heritage carrots
1 lb. rhubarb
1 medium orange
½ cup walnuts, halved
2 tsp. walnut oil
½ tsp. sugar or a few drops of sugar extract

Instructions

1 Rinse the carrots to wash. Dry and chop them into 1-inch pieces.
2 Transfer them to the Air Fryer basket and drizzle over the walnut oil.
3 Cook at 320°F for about 20 minutes.
4 In the meantime, wash the rhubarb and chop it into ½-inch pieces.
5 Coarsely dice the walnuts.
6 Wash the orange and grate its skin into a small bowl. Peel the rest of the orange and cut it up into wedges.
7 Place the rhubarb, walnuts and sugar in the fryer and allow to cook for an additional 5 minutes.
8 Add in 2 tbsp. of the orange zest, along with the orange wedges. Serve immediately.

Broccoli

Prep + Cook Time: 30 minutes | Servings: 4

Ingredients
1 large head broccoli
½ lemon, juiced
3 cloves garlic, minced
1 tbsp. coconut oil
1 tbsp. white sesame seeds
2 tsp. Maggi sauce or other seasonings to taste

Instructions
1 Wash and dry the broccoli. Chop it up into small florets.
2 Place the minced garlic in your Air Fryer basket, along with the coconut oil, lemon juice and Maggi sauce.
3 Heat for 2 minutes at 320°F and give it a stir. Put the garlic and broccoli in the basket and cook for another 13 minutes.
4 Top the broccoli with the white sesame seeds and resume cooking for 5 more minutes, ensuring the seeds become nice and toasty.

Maple Glazed Beets

Prep + Cook Time: 60 minutes | Servings: 8

Ingredients
3 ½ lb. beetroots
4 tbsp. maple syrup
1 tbsp. coconut oil

Instructions
1 Wash and peel the beets. Cut them up into 1-inch pieces.
2 Put the coconut oil in the Air Fryer and melt for 1 minute at 320°F.
3 Place the beet cubes to the Air Fryer Basket and allow to cook for 40 minutes. Coat the beetroots in two tbsp. of the maple syrup and cook for another 10 minutes, ensuring the beets become soft.
4 Toss the cooked beets with the remaining two tbsp. of maple syrup and serve right away.

Endive Marinated in Curried Yogurt

Prep + Cook Time: 20 minutes | Servings: 6

Ingredients
6 heads endive
½ cup plain and fat-free yogurt
3 tbsp. lemon juice
1 tsp. garlic powder [or 2 minced cloves of garlic]
½ tsp. curry powder
Salt and ground black pepper to taste

Instructions
1 Wash the endives, and slice them in half lengthwise.
2 In a bowl, mix together the yogurt, lemon juice, garlic powder [or minced garlic], curry powder, salt and pepper. If you would like you marinade to be thinner, add some more lemon juice.
3 Brush the endive halves with the marinade, coating them completely. Allow to sit for a minimum of a half-hour and a maximum of one day.
4 Pre-heat Air Fryer to 320°F. Allow the endives to cook for 10 minutes and serve hot.

Tasty Tofu

Prep + Cook Time: 35 minutes | Servings: 4

Ingredients
1x 12 oz. package low-fat and extra firm tofu
2 tbsp. low-sodium soy sauce
2 tbsp. fish sauce
1 tbsp. coriander paste
1 tsp. sesame oil
1 tsp. duck fat or coconut oil
1 tsp. Maggi sauce

Instructions
1 Remove the liquid from the package of tofu and chop the tofu into 1-inch cubes. Line a plate with paper towels and spread the tofu out on top in one layer. Place another paper towel on top, followed by another plate, weighting it down with a heavier object if necessary. This is to dry the tofu out completely. Leave for a minimum of 30 minutes or a maximum of 24 hours, replacing the paper towels once or twice throughout the duration.
2 In a medium bowl, mix together the sesame oil, Maggi sauce, coriander paste, fish sauce, and soy sauce. Stir to combine fully.
3 Coat the tofu cubes with this mixture and allow to marinate for at least a half-hour, tossing the cubes a few times throughout to ensure even coating. Add another few drops of fish sauce or soy sauce to thin out the marinade if necessary.
4 Melt the duck fat/coconut oil in your Air Fryer at 350°F for about 2 minutes. Place the tofu cubes in the basket and cook for about 20 minutes or longer to achieve a crispier texture. Flip the tofu over or shake the basket every 10 minutes.
5 Serve hot with the dipping sauce of your choosing.

Roasted Peppers

Prep + Cook Time: 40 minutes | Servings: 4

Ingredients
12 medium bell peppers
1 sweet onion, small
1 tbsp. Maggi sauce
1 tbsp. extra virgin olive oil

Instructions
1 Warm up the olive oil and Maggi sauce in Air Fryer at 320°F.
2 Peel the onion, slice it into 1-inch pieces, and add it to the Air Fryer.
3 Wash and de-stem the peppers. Slice them into 1-inch pieces and remove all the seeds, with water if necessary [ensuring to dry the peppers afterwards].
4 Place the peppers in the Air Fryer.
5 Cook for about 25 minutes, or longer if desired. Serve hot.

Roasted Parsnip

Prep + Cook Time: 55 minutes | Servings: 5

Ingredients
2 lb. parsnips [about 6 large parsnips]
2 tbsp. maple syrup
1 tbsp. coconut oil
1 tbsp. parsley, dried flakes

Instructions
1 Melt the duck fat or coconut oil in your Air Fryer for 2 minutes at 320°F.
2 Rinse the parsnips to clean them and dry them. Chop into 1-inch cubes. Transfer to the fryer.
3 Cook the parsnip cubes in the fat/oil for 35 minutes, tossing them regularly.
4 Season the parsnips with parsley and maple syrup and allow to cook for another 5 minutes or longer to achieve a soft texture throughout. Serve straightaway.

Cheese Boats

Prep + Cook Time: 30 minutes | Servings: 2

Ingredients

1 cup ground chicken
1 zucchini
1 ½ cups crushed tomatoes
½ tsp. salt
¼ tsp. pepper
½ tsp. garlic powder
2 tbsp. butter or olive oil
½ cup cheese, grated
¼ tsp. dried oregano

Instructions

1 Peel and halve the zucchini. Use a spoon to scoop out the flesh.
2 In a bowl, combine the ground chicken, tomato, garlic powder, butter, cheese, oregano, salt, and pepper. Fill in the hollowed-out zucchini with this mixture.
3 Transfer to the Air Fryer and bake for about 10 minutes at 400°F. Serve warm.

Eggplant

Prep + Cook Time: 45 minutes | Servings: 6

Ingredients

3 eggplants, medium
½ lemon, juiced
1 tbsp. duck fat, or coconut oil
1 tbsp. Maggi sauce
3 tsp. za'atar
1 tsp. sumac
1 tsp. garlic powder
1 tsp. onion powder
1 tsp. extra virgin olive oil
2 bay leaves

Instructions

1 Wash, dry and destem the eggplants. Chop them into 1-inch cubes.
2 In the Air Fryer basket, combine duck fat [or coconut oil], maggi sauce, za'atar, onion powder, garlic powder, sumac and bay leaves.
3 Melt the ingredients for 2 minutes at 320°F, stirring well.
4 Place the eggplant in the Air Fryer basket and allow to cook for 25 minutes.
5 In a large bowl, mix together the lemon juice and extra virgin olive oil. Add the cooked eggplant and stir to coat evenly.
6 Serve immediately with grated parmesan or fresh chopped basil if desired.

Sweet Potato Fries

Prep + Cook Time: 35 minutes | Servings: 5

Ingredients

2 large sweet potatoes
1 tbsp. extra virgin olive oil

Instructions

1 Wash the sweet potatoes. Dry and peel them before chopping them into shoestring fries. In a bowl, toss the fries with the olive oil to coat well.
2 Set your Air Fryer to 320°F and briefly allow to warm. Put the sweet potatoes in the Air Fryer basket and fry for 15 minutes, stirring them at the halfway point.
3 Once done, toss again to make sure no fries are sticking to each other.
4 Turn the heat to 350°F and cook for a further 10 minutes, again giving them a good stir halfway through the cooking time.
5 Serve your fries straightaway.

Chicken, Mushroom & Spinach Pizza

Prep + Cook Time: 25 minutes | Servings: 4

Ingredients

10 ½ oz. minced chicken
1 tsp. garlic powder
1 tsp. black pepper
2 tbsp. tomato basil sauce
5 button mushrooms, sliced thinly
Handful of spinach

Instructions

1 Pre-heat your Air Fryer at 450°F.
2 Add parchment paper onto your baking tray.
3 In a large bowl add the chicken with the black pepper and garlic powder.
4 Add one spoonful of the chicken mix onto your baking tray.
5 Flatten them into 7-inch rounds.
6 Bake in the Air Fryer for about 10 minutes.
7 Take out off the Air Fryer and add the tomato basil sauce onto each round.
8 Add the mushroom on top. Bake again for 5 minutes.
9 Serve immediately.

Turkey Sausage Patties

Prep + Cook Time: 20 minutes | Servings: 6

Ingredients

1 lb. lean ground turkey
1 tsp. olive oil
1 tbsp. chopped chives
1 small onion, diced
1 large garlic clove, chopped
¾ tsp. paprika
Kosher salt and pepper to taste
Pinch of raw sugar
1 tbsp. vinegar
1 tsp. fennel seed
Pinch of nutmeg

Instructions

1 Pre-heat the Air Fryer to 375°F.
2 Add a half-teaspoon of the oil to the fryer, along with the onion and garlic. Air fry for 30 seconds before adding in the fennel. Place everything on a plate.
3 In a bowl, combine the ground turkey with the sugar, paprika, nutmeg, vinegar, chives and the onion mixture. Divide into equal portions and shape each one into a patty.
4 Add another teaspoon of oil to the fryer. Put the patties in the fryer and cook for roughly 3 minutes.
5 Serve with salad or on hamburger buns.

Bacon Fries

Prep + Cook Time: 60 minutes | Servings: 2 – 4

Ingredients

2 large russet potatoes, peeled and cut into ½ inch sticks
5 slices of bacon, diced
2 tbsp. vegetable oil
2 ½ cups cheddar cheese, shredded
3 oz. cream cheese, melted
Salt and freshly ground black pepper
¼ cup chopped scallions
Ranch dressing

Instructions

1 Boil a large pot of salted water.
2 Briefly cook the potato sticks in the boiling water for 4 minutes.
3 Drain the potatoes and run some cold water over them in order to wash off the starch. Pat them dry with a kitchen towel.
4 Pre-heat the Air Fryer to 400°F.
5 Put the chopped bacon in the Air Fryer and air-fry for 4 minutes. Shake the basket at the halfway point.
6 Place the bacon on paper towels to drain any excess fat and remove the grease from the Air Fryer drawer.
7 Coat the dried potatoes with oil and put them in the Air Fryer basket. Air-fry at 360°F for 25 minutes, giving the basket the occasional shake throughout the cooking time and sprinkling the fries with salt and freshly ground black pepper at the halfway point.
8 Take a casserole dish or baking pan that is small enough to fit inside your Air Fryer and place the fries inside.
9 Mix together the 2 cups of the Cheddar cheese and the melted cream cheese.
10 Pour the cheese mixture over the fries and top them with the rest of the Cheddar cheese and the cooked bacon crumbles.
11 Take absolute care when placing the baking pan inside the cooker. Use a foil sling [a sheet of aluminum foil folded into a strip about 2 inches wide by 24 inches long].
12 Cook the fries at 340°F for 5 minutes, ensuring the cheese melts.
13 Garnish the fries with the chopped scallions and serve straight from in the baking dish with some ranch dressing.

Toasted Pumpkin Seeds

Prep + Cook Time: 25 minutes | Servings: 4

Ingredients

1 ½ cups pumpkin seeds [cut a whole pumpkin & scrape out the insides
using a large spoon, separating the seeds from the flesh]
1 tsp. smoked paprika
1 ½ tsp. salt
Olive oil

Instructions

1 Run the pumpkin seeds under some cold water.
2 Over a medium heat, boil two quarts of salted water in a pot.
3 Add in the pumpkin seeds and cook in the water for 8 to 10 minutes.
4 Dump the contents of the pot into a sieve to drain the seeds. Place them on paper towels and allow them to dry for at least 20 minutes.
5 Pre-heat your Air Fryer to 350°F.
6 In a medium bowl coat the pumpkin seeds with olive oil, smoked paprika and salt.
7 Put them in the fryer's basket and air fry for at least 30 minutes until slightly browned and crispy. Shake the basket a few times during the cooking time.
8 Allow the seeds to cool. Serve with a salad or keep in an airtight container for snacking.

Banana Peppers

Prep + Cook Time: 20 minutes | Servings: 8

Ingredients:

1 cup full-fat cream cheese
Cooking spray
16 avocado slices
16 slices salami
Salt and pepper to taste
16 banana peppers

Instructions

1 Pre-heat the Air Fryer to 400°F.
2 Spritz a baking tray with cooking spray.
3 Remove the stems from the banana peppers with a knife.
4 Cut a slit into one side of each banana pepper.
5 Season the cream cheese with the salt and pepper and combine well.
6 Fill each pepper with one spoonful of the cream cheese, followed by one slice of avocado.
7 Wrap the banana peppers in the slices of salami and secure with a toothpick.
8 Place the banana peppers in the baking tray and transfer it to the Air Fryer. Bake for roughly 8 - 10 minutes.

Barbecue Sauce

Prep + Cook Time: 20 minutes | Servings: 6

Ingredients

For the Sauce:
1 tbsp. yellow mustard
1 tbsp. apple cider vinegar
1 tbsp. olive oil
¼ cup unsulfured blackstrap molasses
¼ cup ketchup
2 tbsp. sugar
1 garlic clove, minced
Salt and ground black pepper, to taste
1/8 tsp. ground allspice
¼ cup water

For the Wings

2 lb. chicken wings
¼ tsp. celery salt
¼ cup habanero hot sauce
Chopped fresh parsley, or garnish

Instructions:

1 Put all the ingredients for the sauce in a pan over a medium-to-high heat and bring the mixture to a boil.
2 Lower the heat and allow to simmer and thicken.
3 In the meantime, pre-heat your Air Fryer to 400°F.
4 Place the chicken wings in the fryer and cook for 6 minutes.
5 Turn the wings and cook for another 6 minutes on the other side. Sprinkle some celery salt over them.
6 Serve the chicken wings with the prepared sauce, along with habanero sauce or any other accompaniment of your choice.

Coconut Shrimp

Prep + Cook Time: 20 minutes | Servings: 16

Ingredients

½ tsp. salt
1 lb. large shrimp [about 16 to 20 peeled/de-veined]
½ cup flour
2 egg whites
½ cup friendly (panko) bread crumbs
½ cup unsweetened coconut, shredded
Zest of 1 lime
¼ tsp. cayenne pepper
Spray can of vegetable or canola oil
Sweet chili sauce or duck sauce, to serve

Instructions

1 In a shallow dish, beat the eggs with a whisk.
2 Combine the bread crumbs, coconut, lime zest, salt and cayenne pepper in a separate dish.
3 Pre-heat the Air Fryer to 400°F.
4 Coat the shrimp in the flour. Dip the shrimp into the egg mixture, and then into the breadcrumb coconut mixture, ensuring to coat the shrimp all over.
5 Place the shrimp on a plate and spritz with oil. Move the shrimp to the basket of your fryer, taking care not to overlap the fish.
6 Air fry the shrimp for 5 - 6 minutes, ensuring that each shrimp is cooked through and firm before serving.

Tortilla Chips

Prep + Cook Time: 5 minutes | Servings: 2

Ingredients

8 corn tortillas
Salt to taste
1 tbsp. olive oil

Instructions

1 Pre-heat your Air Fryer to 390°F.
2 Slice the corn tortillas into triangles. Coat with a light brushing of olive oil.
3 Put the tortilla pieces in the wire basket and air fry for 3 minutes. You may need to do this in multiple batches.
4 Season with salt before serving.

Naan Bread Dippers

Prep + Cook Time: 50 minutes | Servings: 10

Ingredients

4 naan bread, cut into 2-inch strips
3 tbsp. butter, melted
12 oz. light cream cheese, softened
1 cup plain yogurt
2 tsp. curry powder
2 cups cooked chicken, shredded
4 scallions, minced
⅓ cup golden raisins
6 oz. Monterey Jack cheese, grated [about 2 cups]
¼ cup fresh cilantro, chopped
Salt and freshly ground black pepper
½ cup sliced s
½ cup Major Grey's Chutney

Instructions

1 Pre-heat Air Fryer to 400°F.
2 Slice up the naan in thirds lengthwise before cutting crosswise into 2-inch strips. In a bowl, toss the strips with the melted butter.
3 Move the naan strips to Air Fryer basket. Toast for 5 minutes, shaking the basket halfway through. You will have to do this in two batches.

4 Mix together the softened cream cheese and yogurt with a hand mixer or in a food processor. Add in the curry powder and combine evenly.
5 Fold in the shredded chicken, scallions, golden raisins, Monterey Jack cheese and chopped cilantro.
6 Sprinkle with salt and freshly ground black pepper as desired.
7 Pour the mixture into a 1-quart baking dish and spread out evenly. Arrange the sliced s on top. Air-fry at 300°F for 25 minutes.
8 Put a dollop of Major Grey's chutney in the center of the dip and scatter the scallions on top.
9 Serve the naan dippers with the hot dip.

Snack Mix

Prep + Cook Time: 30 minutes | Servings: 10

Ingredients

½ cup honey
3 tbsp. butter, melted
1 tsp. salt
2 cups sesame sticks
2 cup pepitas [pumpkin seeds]
2 cups granola
1 cup cashews
2 cups crispy corn puff cereal [Kix or Corn Pops]
2 cup mini pretzel crisps

Instructions

1 In a bowl, combine the honey, butter, and salt.
2 In another bowl, mix together the sesame sticks, pepitas, granola, cashews, corn puff cereal, and pretzel crisps.
3 Combine the contents of the two bowls.
4 Pre-heat your Air Fryer to 370°F.
5 Put the mixture in the fryer basket and air-fry for 10 - 12 minutes to toast the snack mixture, shaking the basket frequently. You will have to do this in two batches.
6 Place the snack mix on a cookie sheet and allow it to cool fully.
7 Store in an airtight container for up to one week. Makes a great holiday gift!

Feta Triangles

Prep + Cook Time: 55 minutes | Servings: 5

Ingredients

1 egg yolk, beaten
4 oz. feta cheese
2 tbsp. flat-leafed parsley, finely chopped
1 scallion, finely chopped
2 sheets of frozen filo pastry, defrosted
2 tbsp. olive oil ground black pepper to taste

Instructions

1 In a bowl, combine the beaten egg yolk with the feta, parsley and scallion. Sprinkle on some pepper to taste.
2 Slice each sheet of filo dough into three strips.
3 Place a teaspoonful of the feta mixture on each strip of pastry.
4 Pinch the tip of the pastry and fold it up to enclose the filling and create a triangle. Continue folding the strip in zig-zags until the filling is wrapped in a triangle. Repeat with all of the strips of pastry.
5 Pre-heat the Air Fryer to 390°F.
6 Coat the pastry with a light coating of oil and arrange in the cooking basket.
7 Place the basket in the Air Fryer and cook for 3 minutes.
8 Lower the heat to 360°F and cook for a further 2 minutes or until a golden brown color is achieved

Sage & Onion Stuffing

Prep + Cook Time: 35 minutes | Servings: 6

Ingredients
2 lb. sausage meat
½ onion
½ tsp. garlic puree
1 tsp. sage
3 tbsp. friendly bread crumbs
Pinch of salt
Black pepper

Instructions
1 Combine all of the ingredients in a large bowl.
2 Take equal portions of the mixture, mold them into medium sized balls and put them in the Air Fryer.
3 Cook at 355°F for 15 minutes.

Puppy Poppers

Prep + Cook Time: 25 minutes | Servings: 50 treats

Ingredients
½ cup unsweetened applesauce
1 cup peanut butter
2 cup oats
1 cup flour
1 tsp. baking powder

Instructions
1 Combine the applesauce and peanut butter in a bowl to create a smooth consistency.
2 Pour in the oats, flour and baking powder. Continue mixing to form a soft dough.
3 Shape a half-teaspoon of dough into a ball and continue with the rest of the dough.
4 Pre-heat the Air Fryer to 350°F.
5 Grease the bottom of the basket with oil.
6 Place the poppers in the fryer and cook for 8 minutes, flipping the balls at the halfway point. You may need to cook the poppers in batches.
7 Let the poppers cool and serve immediately or keep in an airtight container for up to 2 weeks.

Masala Cashew

Prep + Cook Time: 20 minutes | Servings: 3

Ingredients
½ lb. cashew nuts
½ tsp. garam masala powder
1 tsp. coriander powder
1 tsp. ghee
1 tsp. red chili powder
½ tsp. black pepper
2 tsp. dry mango powder
1 tsp. sea salt

Instructions
1 Put all the ingredients in a large bowl and toss together well.
2 Arrange the cashew nuts in the basket of your Air Fryer.
3 Cook at 250°F for 15 minutes until the nuts are brown and crispy.
4 Let the nuts cool before serving or transferring to an airtight container to be stored for up to 2 weeks.

Bacon Wrapped Shrimp

Prep + Cook Time: 50 minutes | Servings: 4

Ingredients
1 ¼ lb. tiger shrimp, peeled and deveined [16 pieces]
1 lb. bacon, thinly sliced, room temperature [16 slices]

Instructions
1 Wrap each bacon slice around a piece of shrimp, from the head to the tail. Refrigerate for 20 minutes.
2 Pre-heat the Air Fryer to 390°F.
3 Place the shrimp in the fryer's basket and cook for 5 – 7 minutes.
4 Allow to dry on a paper towel before serving.

Tomato & Avocado Egg Rolls

Prep + Cook Time: 20 minutes | Servings: 5

Ingredients
10 egg roll wrappers
3 avocados, peeled and pitted
1 tomato, diced
Salt and pepper, to taste

Instructions
1 Pre-heat your Air Fryer to 350°F.
2 Put the tomato and avocados in a bowl. Sprinkle on some salt and pepper and mash together with a fork until a smooth consistency is achieved.
3 Spoon equal amounts of the mixture onto the wrappers. Roll the wrappers around the filling, enclosing them entirely.
4 Transfer the rolls to a lined baking dish and cook for 5 minutes.

Meatballs in Tomato Sauce

Prep + Cook Time: 35 minutes | Servings: 4

Ingredients
1 small onion, finely chopped
¾ lb. [12 oz] ground beef
1 tbsp. chopped fresh parsley
½ tbsp. chopped fresh thyme leaves
1 egg
3 tbsp. friendly bread crumbs
Pepper and salt to taste
10 oz. your favorite tomato sauce if desired

Instructions
1 Put all the ingredients in a bowl and combine well. Use your hands to mold the mixture into 10 - 12 balls.
2 Pre-heat the Air Fryer to 390°F.
3 Put the meatballs in the Air Fryer basket and place the basket in the Air Fryer. Cook the meatballs for 8 minutes.
4 Put the meatballs in an oven dish, pour in the tomato sauce and set the dish in the basket of the Air Fryer.
5 Reduce the temperature to 330°F and warm the meatballs for 5 minutes.

Amazing Blooming Onion

Prep + Cook Time: 40 minutes | Servings: 4

Ingredients
4 medium/small onions
1 tbsp. olive oil
4 dollops of butter

Instructions
1 Peel the onion. Cut off the top and bottom.
2 To make it bloom, cut as deeply as possible without slicing through it completely. 4 cuts [i.e. 8 segments] should do it.
3 Place the onions in a bowl of salted water and allow to absorb for 4 hours to help eliminate the sharp taste and induce the blooming process.
4 Pre-heat your Air Fryer to 355°F.
5 Transfer the onions to the Air Fryer. Pour over a light drizzle of olive oil and place a dollop of butter on top of each onion.
6 Cook or roast for 30 minutes. Remove the outer layer before serving if it is too brown.

Crab Croquettes

Prep + Cook Time: 5 minutes | Servings: 6

Ingredients
For the Filling:
1 lb. lump crab meat
2 egg whites, beaten
1 tbsp. olive oil
¼ cup red onion, finely chopped
¼ red bell pepper, finely chopped
2 tbsp. celery, finely chopped
¼ tsp. tarragon, finely chopped
¼ tsp. chives, finely chopped
½ tsp. parsley, finely chopped
½ tsp. cayenne pepper
¼ cup mayonnaise
¼ cup sour cream

For the Breading
3 eggs, beaten
1 cup flour
1 cup friendly bread crumbs
1 tsp. olive oil
½ tsp. salt

Instructions
1 Sauté the olive oil, onions, peppers, and celery over a medium heat, allowing to sweat until the vegetables turn translucent. This should take about 4 – 5 minutes.
2 Take off the heat and allow to cool.
3 In a food processor, pulse the bread crumbs, olive oil and salt to form a fine crumb.
4 Place the eggs, panko mixture and flour in three separate bowls.
5 Combine the crabmeat, egg whites, mayonnaise, sour cream, spices and vegetables in a large bowl.
6 Pre-heat the Air Fryer to 390°F.
7 Take equal amounts of the crab mixture and shape into golf balls. Coat the balls in the flour, before dipping them in the eggs and finally in the panko, making sure the bread crumbs stick well.
8 Put croquettes in the fryer basket in a single layer and well-spaced.
9 Cook the croquettes for 8 – 10 minutes or until a golden brown color is achieved.

Pumpkin Seeds

Prep + Cook Time: 55 minutes | Servings: 1 ½ cups

Ingredients
1 ½ cups pumpkin seeds from a large whole pumpkin
Olive oil
1 ½ tsp. salt
1 tsp. smoked paprika

Instructions
1 Boil two quarts of well-salted water in a pot. Cook the pumpkin seeds in the boiling water for 10 minutes.
2 Dump the content of the pot into a sieve and dry the seeds on paper towels for at least 20 minutes.
3 Pre-heat the Air Fryer to 350°F.
4 Cover the seeds with olive oil, salt and smoked paprika, before placing them in the Air Fryer basket.
5 Air fry for 35 minutes. Give the basket a good shake several times throughout the cooking process to ensure the pumpkin seeds are crispy and lightly browned.

6 Let the seeds cool before serving. Alternatively, you can keep them in an air-tight container or bag for snacking or for use as a yogurt topping.

Cocktail Flanks

Prep + Cook Time: 45 minutes | Servings: 4

Ingredients
1x 12-oz. package cocktail franks
1x 8-oz. can crescent rolls

Instructions
1 Drain the cocktail franks and dry with paper towels.
2 Unroll the crescent rolls and slice the dough into rectangular strips, roughly 1" by 1.5".
3 Wrap the franks in the strips with the ends poking out. Leave in the freezer for 5 minutes.
4 Pre-heat the Air Fryer to 330°F.
5 Take the franks out of the freezer and put them in the cooking basket. Cook for 6 – 8 minutes.
6 Reduce the heat to 390°F and cook for another 3 minutes or until a golden-brown color is achieved.

Garlic Mushrooms

Prep + Cook Time: 30 minutes | Servings: 4

Ingredients
16 small button mushrooms

For the Stuffing:
1 ½ slices bread
1 garlic clove, crushed
1 tbsp. flat-leafed parsley, finely chopped
Ground black pepper to taste
1 ½ tbsp. olive oil

Instructions
1 Pre-heat the Air Fryer to 390°F.
2 Blend together the bread slices, garlic, parsley and pepper until a fine crumb is formed.
3 Mix in the olive oil.
4 Remove the mushroom stalks and spoon even amounts of the filling into the caps. Press the crumbs in well to make sure none fall out
5 Put the mushroom caps in the cooking basket and place it in the Air Fryer.
6 Cook the mushrooms for 7 – 8 minutes or until they turn golden and crispy.

Eggplant Chips

Prep + Cook Time: 45 minutes | Servings: 4

Ingredients
2 eggplants, peeled and thinly sliced
Salt
½ cup tapioca starch
¼ cup canola oil
½ cup water
1 tsp. garlic powder
½ tsp. dried dill weed
½ tsp. ground black pepper, to taste

Instructions
1 Season the eggplant slices with salt and leave for half an hour.
2 Run them under cold water to rinse off any excess salt.
3 In a bowl, coat the eggplant slices with all of the other ingredients.
4 Cook at 390°F for 13 minutes. You may need to do this in batches.
5 Serve with the dipping sauce of your choice.

Sage Potatoes

Prep + Cook Time: 45 minutes | Servings: 8

Ingredients

1 ½ lb. fingerling potatoes, halved lengthwise
2 tbsp. melted butter
¼ cup fresh sage leaves, finely chopped
2 sprigs thyme, chopped
1 tsp. lemon zest, finely grated
¼ tsp. ground pepper
1 tbsp. sea salt flakes
½ tsp. grated ginger

Instructions

1 Place the potatoes in a bowl of cold water and allow to absorb for about half an hour.
2 Dry them with a clean kitchen towel.
3 Transfer to the Air Fryer and roast at 400°F for 15 minutes.
4 Serve with tomato ketchup and mayonnaise if desired.

Dijon & Quinoa Cocktail Meatballs

Prep + Cook Time: 20 minutes | Servings: 6

Ingredients

½ lb. ground pork
½ lb. ground beef
1 cup quinoa, cooked
1 egg, beaten
2 scallions, finely chopped
½ tsp. onion powder
1 ½ tbsp. Dijon mustard
¾ cup ketchup
1 tsp. ancho chili powder
1 tbsp. sesame oil
2 tbsp. tamari sauce
¼ cup balsamic vinegar
2 tbsp. sugar

Instructions

1 In a bowl, stir together all the ingredients and combine well.
2 Use your hands to shape equal amounts of the mixture into small meatballs.
3 Place the meatballs in the Air Fryer and cook at 370°F for 10 minutes. Give the basket a good shake and allow to cook for another 5 minutes.

Ricotta Balls

Prep + Cook Time: 25 minutes | Servings: 2 – 4

Ingredients

2 cups ricotta, grated
2 eggs, separated
2 tbsp. chives, finely chopped
2 tbsp. fresh basil, finely chopped
4 tbsp. flour
¼ tsp. salt to taste
¼ tsp. pepper powder to taste
1 tsp. orange zest, grated

For coating

¼ cup friendly bread crumbs
1 tbsp. vegetable oil

Instructions

1. Pre-heat your Air Fryer at 390°F.
2. In a bowl, combine the yolks, flour, salt, pepper, chives and orange zest. Throw in the ricotta and incorporate with your hands.
3. Mold equal amounts of the mixture into balls.
4. Mix the oil with the bread crumbs until a crumbly consistency is achieved.
5. Coat the balls in the bread crumbs and transfer each one to the fryer's basket.
6. Put the basket in the fryer. Air fry for 8 minutes or until a golden brown color is achieved.
7. Serve with a sauce of your choosing, such as ketchup.

Spiced Nuts

Prep + Cook Time: 40 minutes | Servings: 3 cups

Ingredients

1 egg white, lightly beaten
¼ cup sugar
1 tsp. salt
½ tsp. ground cinnamon
¼ tsp. ground cloves
¼ tsp. ground allspice
Pinch ground cayenne pepper
1 cup pecan halves
1 cup cashews
1 cup s

Instructions

1. In a bowl, combine the egg white with the sugar and spices.
2. Pre-heat the Air Fryer to 300°F.
3. Coat the inside of the fryer's basket with vegetable oil.
4. Cover the nuts with the spiced egg white. Place half of them in the fryer.
5. Air fry for 25 minutes, giving the nuts a few good stirs throughout the cooking time, until they are crunchy and toasted.
6. Repeat with the other half of the nuts.
7. Serve immediately or store in an airtight container for up to two weeks.

Shrimp Bites

Prep + Cook Time: 45 minutes | Servings: 10

Ingredients

1 ¼ lb. shrimp, peeled and deveined
1 tsp. paprika
½ tsp. ground black pepper
½ tsp. red pepper flakes, crushed
1 tbsp. salt
1 tsp. chili powder
1 tbsp. shallot powder
¼ tsp. cumin powder
1 ¼ lb. thin bacon slices

Instructions

1. Coat the shrimps with all of the seasonings.
2. Wrap a slice of bacon around each shrimp, and hold it in place with a toothpick. Refrigerate for half an hour.
3. Transfer to the Air Fryer and fry at 360°F for 7 - 8 minutes.

Cajun Spiced Snack

Prep + Cook Time: 30 minutes | Servings: 5

Ingredients

2 tbsp. Cajun or Creole seasoning
½ cup butter, melted
2 cups peanut
2 cups mini wheat thin crackers
2 cups mini pretzels
2 tsp. salt
1 tsp. cayenne pepper
4 cups plain popcorn
1 tsp. paprika
1 tsp. garlic
½ tsp. thyme
½ tsp. oregano
1 tsp. black pepper
½ tsp. onion powder

Instructions

1.   Pre-heat the Air Fryer to 370°F.
2.   In a bowl, combine the Cajun spice with the melted butter.
3.   In a separate bowl, stir together the peanuts, crackers, popcorn and pretzels. Coat the snacks with the butter mixture.
4.   Place in the fryer and fry for 8 - 10 minutes, shaking the basket frequently during the cooking time. You will have to complete this step in two batches.
5.   Put the snack mix on a cookie sheet and leave to cool.
6.   The snacks can be kept in an airtight container for up to one week.

Cheesy Broccoli Balls

Prep + Cook Time: 20 minutes | Servings: 6

Ingredients

2 eggs, well whisked
2 cups Colby cheese, shredded
1 cup flour
Seasoned salt, to taste
¼ tsp. ground black pepper, or more if preferred
1 head broccoli, chopped into florets
1 cup crushed saltines

Instructions

1.   Mix together the eggs, cheese, flour, salt, pepper, and broccoli until a dough-like paste is formed.
2.   Refrigerate for 1 hour. Divide the mixture evenly and mold each portion into small balls. Coat the balls in the crushed saltines and spritz them all over with cooking spray.
3.   Cook at 360°F for 10 minutes. At this point, you should check how far along in the cooking process they are and allow to cook for a further 8 - 10 minutes as needed.
4.   Serve with the dipping sauce of your choice.

POULTRY

Goulash

Prep + Cook Time: 20 minutes | Servings: 2

Ingredients

2 chopped bell peppers
2 diced tomatoes
1 lb. ground chicken
½ cup chicken broth
Salt and pepper

Instructions

1. Pre-heat your fryer at 365°F and spray with cooking spray.
2. Cook the bell pepper for five minutes.
3. Add in the diced tomatoes and ground chicken. Combine well, then allow to cook for a further six minutes.
4. Pour in chicken broth, and season to taste with salt and pepper. Cook for another six minutes before serving.

Garlicky Meatballs

Prep + Cook Time: 20 minutes | Servings: 2

Ingredients

½ lb. boneless chicken thighs
1 tsp. minced garlic
1 ¼ cup roasted pecans
½ cup mushrooms
1 tsp. extra virgin olive oil

Instructions

1. Preheat your fryer to 375°F.
2. Cube the chicken thighs.
3. Place them in the food processor along with the garlic, pecans, and other seasonings as desired. Pulse until a smooth consistency is achieved.
4. Chop the mushrooms finely. Add to the chicken mixture and combine.
5. Using your hands, shape the mixture into balls and brush them with olive oil.
6. Put the balls into the fryer and cook for eighteen minutes. Serve hot.

Cilantro Drumsticks

Prep + Cook Time: 30 minutes | Servings: 4

Ingredients:

8 chicken drumsticks
½ cup chimichurri sauce
¼ cup lemon juice

Instructions

1. Coat the chicken drumsticks with chimichurri sauce and refrigerate in an airtight container for no less than an hour, ideally overnight.
2. When it's time to cook, pre-heat your fryer to 400°F.
3. Remove the chicken from refrigerator and allow return to room temperature for roughly twenty minutes.
4. Cook for eighteen minutes in the fryer. Drizzle with lemon juice to taste and enjoy.

Poppin' Pop Corn Chicken

Prep + Cook Time: 20 minutes | Servings: 1

Ingredients

1 lb. skinless, boneless chicken breast
1 tsp. chili flakes
1 tsp. garlic powder
½ cup flour
1 tbsp. olive oil cooking spray

Instructions

1. Pre-heat your fryer at 365°F. Spray with olive oil.
2. Cut the chicken breasts into cubes and place in a bowl. Toss with the chili flakes, garlic powder, and additional seasonings to taste and make sure to coat entirely.
3. Add the coconut flour and toss once more.
4. Cook the chicken in the fryer for ten minutes. Turnover and cook for a further five minutes before serving.

Crispy Chicken

Prep + Cook Time: 10 minutes | Servings: 2

Ingredients

1 lb. chicken skin
1 tsp. butter
½ tsp. chili flakes
1 tsp. dill

Instructions

1. Pre-heat the fryer at 360°F.
2. Cut the chicken skin into slices.
3. Heat the butter until melted and pour it over the chicken skin. Toss with chili flakes, dill, and any additional seasonings to taste, making sure to coat well.
4. Cook the skins in the fryer for three minutes. Turn them over and cook on the other side for another three minutes.
5. Serve immediately or save them for later – they can be eaten hot or at room temperature.

Southern Fried Chicken

Prep + Cook Time: 30 minutes | Servings: 2

Ingredients

2 x 6-oz. boneless skinless chicken breasts
2 tbsp. hot sauce
½ tsp. onion powder
1 tbsp. chili powder
2 oz. pork rinds, finely ground

Instructions

1. Cut the chicken breasts in half lengthwise and rub in the hot sauce. Combine the onion powder with the chili powder, then rub into the chicken. Leave to marinate for at least a half hour.
2. Use the ground pork rinds to coat the chicken breasts in the ground pork rinds, covering them thoroughly. Place the chicken in your fryer.
3. Set the fryer at 350°F and cook the chicken for 13 minutes. Flip the chicken and cook the other side for another 13 minutes or until golden.
4. Test the chicken with a meat thermometer. When fully cooked, it should reach 165°F. Serve hot, with the sides of your choice.

Jalapeno Chicken Breasts

Prep + Cook Time: 25 minutes | Servings: 2

Ingredients

2 oz. full-fat cream cheese, softened
4 slices sugar-free bacon, cooked and crumbled
¼ cup pickled jalapenos, sliced
½ cup sharp cheddar cheese, shredded and divided
2 x 6-oz. boneless skinless chicken breasts

Instructions

1. In a bowl, mix the cream cheese, bacon, jalapeno slices, and half of the cheddar cheese until well-combined.
2. Cut parallel slits in the chicken breasts of about ¾ the length – make sure not to cut all the way down. You should be able to make between six and eight slices, depending on the size of the chicken breast.
3. Insert evenly sized dollops of the cheese mixture into the slits of the chicken breasts. Top the chicken with sprinkles of the rest of the cheddar cheese. Place the chicken in the basket of your air fryer.
4. Set the fryer to 350°F and cook the chicken breasts for twenty minutes.
5. Test with a meat thermometer. The chicken should be at 165°F when fully cooked. Serve hot and enjoy!

Fajita Style Chicken Breast

Prep + Cook Time: 35 minutes | Servings: 2

Ingredients

2 x 6-oz. boneless skinless chicken breasts
1 green bell pepper, sliced
¼ medium white onion, sliced
1 tbsp. coconut oil, melted
3 tsp. taco seasoning mix

Instructions

1. Cut each chicken breast in half and place each one between two sheets of cooking parchment. Using a mallet, pound the chicken to flatten to a quarter-inch thick.
2. Place the chicken on a flat surface, with the short end facing you. Place four slices of pepper and three slices of onion at the end of each piece of chicken. Roll up the chicken tightly, making sure not to let any veggies fall out. Secure with some toothpicks or with butcher's string.
3. Coat the chicken with coconut oil and then with taco seasoning. Place into your air fryer.
4. Turn the fryer to 350°F and cook the chicken for twenty-five minutes.
5. Serve the rolls immediately with your favorite dips and sides.

Lemon Pepper Chicken Legs

Prep + Cook Time: 30 minutes | Servings: 4

Ingredients

½ tsp. garlic powder
2 tsp. baking powder
8 chicken legs
4 tbsp. salted butter, melted
1 tbsp. lemon pepper seasoning

Instructions

1. In a small bowl combine the garlic powder and baking powder, then use this mixture to coat the chicken legs. Lay the chicken in the basket of your fryer.
2. Cook the chicken legs at 375°F for twenty-five minutes. Halfway through, turn them over and allow to cook on the other side.
3. When the chicken has turned golden brown, test with a thermometer to ensure it has reached an ideal temperature of 165°F. Remove from the fryer.
4. Mix together the melted butter and lemon pepper seasoning and toss with the chicken legs until the chicken is coated all over. Serve hot.

Greek Chicken Meatballs

Prep + Cook Time: 15 minutes | Servings: 1

Ingredients

½ oz. finely ground pork rinds
1 lb. ground chicken
1 tsp. Greek seasoning
1/3 cup feta, crumbled
1/3 cup frozen spinach, drained and thawed

Instructions

1. Place all the ingredients in a large bowl and combine using your hands. Take equal-sized portions of this mixture and roll each into a 2-inch ball. Place the balls in your fryer.
2. Cook the meatballs at 350°F for twelve minutes, in several batches if necessary.
3. Once they are golden, ensure they have reached an ideal temperature of 165°F and remove from the fryer. Keep each batch warm while you move on to the next one. Serve with Tzatziki if desired.

-Crusted Chicken

Ingredients: Prep + Cook Time: 30 minutes | Servings: 2

Ingredients

¼ cup slivered s
2x 6-oz. boneless skinless chicken breasts
2 tbsp. full-fat mayonnaise
1 tbsp. Dijon mustard

Instructions

1. Pulse the s in a food processor until they are finely chopped. Spread the s on a plate and set aside.
2. Cut each chicken breast in half lengthwise.
3. Mix the mayonnaise and mustard together and then spread evenly on top of the chicken slices.
4. Place the chicken into the plate of chopped s to coat completely, laying each coated slice into the basket of your fryer.
5. Cook for 25 minutes at 350°F until golden. Test the temperature, making sure the chicken has reached 165°F. Serve hot.

Buffalo Chicken Tenders

Ingredients: Prep + Cook Time: 20 minutes | Servings: 4

Ingredients
1 egg
1 cup mozzarella cheese, shredded
¼ cup buffalo sauce
1 cup cooked chicken, shredded
¼ cup feta cheese

Instructions
1.   Combine all ingredients (except for the feta). Line the basket of your fryer with a suitably sized piece of parchment paper. Lay the mixture into the fryer and press it into a circle about half an inch thick. Crumble the feta cheese over it.
2.   Cook for eight minutes at 400°F. Turn the fryer off and allow the chicken to rest inside before removing with care.
3.   Cut the mixture into slices and serve hot.

Buffalo Chicken Strips

Ingredients: Prep + Cook Time: 30 minutes | Servings: 1

Ingredients
¼ cup hot sauce
1 lb. boneless skinless chicken tenders
1 tsp. garlic powder
1 ½ oz. pork rinds, finely ground
1 tsp chili powder

Instructions
1.   Toss the hot sauce and chicken tenders together in a bowl, ensuring the chicken is completely coated.
2.   In another bowl, combine the garlic powder, ground pork rinds, and chili powder. Use this mixture to coat the tenders, covering them well. Place the chicken into your fryer, taking care not to layer pieces on top of one another.
3.   Cook the chicken at 375°F for twenty minutes until cooked all the way through and golden. Serve warm with your favorite dips and sides.

Chicken & Pepperoni Pizza

Ingredients: Prep + Cook Time: 20 minutes | Servings: 6

Ingredients:
2 cups cooked chicken, cubed
20 slices pepperoni
1 cup sugar-free pizza sauce
1 cup mozzarella cheese, shredded
¼ cup parmesan cheese, grated

Instructions
1.   Place the chicken into the base of a four-cup baking dish and add the pepperoni and pizza sauce on top. Mix well so as to completely coat the meat with the sauce.
2.   Add the parmesan and mozzarella on top of the chicken, then place the baking dish into your fryer.
3.   Cook for 15 minutes at 375°F.
4.   When everything is bubbling and melted, remove from the fryer. Serve hot.

Italian Chicken Thighs

Ingredients: Prep + Cook Time: 30 minutes | Servings: 4

Ingredients
4 skin-on bone-in chicken thighs
2 tbsp. unsalted butter, melted

3 tsp. Italian herbs
½ tsp. garlic powder
¼ tsp. onion powder

Instructions
1.   Using a brush, coat the chicken thighs with the melted butter. Combine the herbs with the garlic powder and onion powder, then massage into the chicken thighs. Place the thighs in the fryer.
2.   Cook at 380°F for 20 minutes, turning the chicken halfway through to cook on the other side.
3.   When the thighs have achieved a golden color, test the temperature with a meat thermometer. Once they have reached 165°F, remove from the fryer and serve.

Teriyaki Chicken Wings

Ingredients: Prep + Cook Time: 45 minutes | Servings: 4

Ingredients:
¼ tsp. ground ginger
2 tsp. minced garlic
½ cup sugar-free teriyaki sauce
2 lb. chicken wings
2 tsp. baking powder

Instructions
1.   In a small bowl, combine together the ginger, garlic, and teriyaki sauce. Place the chicken wings in a separate, larger bowl and pour the mixture over them. Toss to coat until the chicken is well covered.
2.   Refrigerate for at least an hour.
3.   Remove the marinated wings from the fridge and add the baking powder, tossing again to coat. Then place the chicken in the basket of your air fryer.
4.   Cook for 25 minutes at 400°F, giving the basket a shake intermittently throughout the cooking time.
5.   When the wings are 165°F and golden in color, remove from the fryer and serve immediately.

Chicken Pizza Crusts

Ingredients: Prep + Cook Time: 35 minutes | Servings: 1

Ingredients:
½ cup mozzarella, shredded
¼ cup parmesan cheese, grated
1 lb. ground chicken

Instructions
1.   In a large bowl, combine all the ingredients and then spread the mixture out, dividing it into four parts of equal size.
2.   Cut a sheet of parchment paper into four circles, roughly six inches in diameter, and put some of the chicken mixture onto the center of each piece, flattening the mixture to fill out the circle.
3.   Depending on the size of your fryer, cook either one or two circles at a time at 375°F for 25 minutes. Halfway through, turn the crust over to cook on the other side. Keep each batch warm while you move onto the next one.
4.   Once all the crusts are cooked, top with cheese and the toppings of your choice. If desired, cook the topped crusts for an additional five minutes.
5.   Serve hot, or freeze and save for later!

Crispy Chicken Thighs

Ingredients: Prep + Cook Time: 35 minutes | Servings: 1

Ingredients:
1 lb. chicken thighs
Salt and pepper
2 cups roasted pecans
1 cup water
1 cup flour

Instructions
1.   Pre-heat your fryer to 400°F.
2.   Season the chicken with salt and pepper, then set aside.
3.   Pulse the roasted pecans in a food processor until a flour-like consistency is achieved.
4.   Fill a dish with the water, another with the flour, and a third with the pecans.
5.   Coat the thighs with the flour. Mix the remaining flour with the processed pecans.
6.   Dredge the thighs in the water and then press into the -pecan mix, ensuring the chicken is completely covered.
7.   Cook the chicken in the fryer for twenty-two minutes, with an extra five minutes added if you would like the chicken a darker-brown color. Check the temperature has reached 165°F before serving.

Strawberry Turkey

Ingredients: Prep + Cook Time: 50 minutes | Servings: 2

Ingredients:
2 lb. turkey breast
1 tbsp. olive oil
Salt and pepper
1 cup fresh strawberries

Instructions
1.   Pre-heat your fryer to 375°F.
2.   Massage the turkey breast with olive oil, before seasoning with a generous amount of salt and pepper.
3.   Cook the turkey in the fryer for fifteen minutes. Flip the turkey and cook for a further fifteen minutes.
4.   During these last fifteen minutes, blend the strawberries in a food processor until a smooth consistency has been achieved.
5.   Heap the strawberries over the turkey, then cook for a final seven minutes and enjoy.

Chimichurri Turkey

Ingredients: Prep + Cook Time: 70 minutes | Servings: 1

Ingredients:
1 lb. turkey breast
½ cup chimichurri sauce
½ cup butter
¼ cup parmesan cheese, grated
¼ tsp. garlic powder

Instructions
1.   Massage the chimichurri sauce into the turkey breast, then refrigerate in an airtight container for at least a half hour.
2.   In the meantime, prepare the herbed butter. Mix together the butter, parmesan, and garlic powder, using a hand mixer if desired (this will make it extra creamy)

3.   Preheat your fryer at 350°F and place a rack inside. Remove the turkey from the refrigerator and allow to return to room temperature for roughly twenty minutes while the fryer warms.
4.   Place the turkey in the fryer and allow to cook for twenty minutes. Flip and cook on the other side for a further twenty minutes.
5.   Take care when removing the turkey from the fryer. Place it on a serving dish and enjoy with the herbed butter.

Betty's Baked Chicken

Ingredients: Prep + Cook Time: 70 minutes | Servings: 1

Ingredients:
½ cup butter
1 tsp. pepper
3 tbsp. garlic, minced
1 whole chicken

Instructions
1.   Pre-heat your fryer at 350°F.
2.   Allow the butter to soften at room temperature, then mix well in a small bowl with the pepper and garlic.
3.   Massage the butter into the chicken. Any remaining butter can go inside the chicken.
4.   Cook the chicken in the fryer for half an hour. Flip, then cook on the other side for another thirty minutes.
5.   Test the temperature of the chicken by sticking a meat thermometer into the fat of the thigh to make sure it has reached 165°F. Take care when removing the chicken from the fryer. Let sit for ten minutes before you carve it and serve.

Chicken Breasts & Spiced Tomatoes

Ingredients: Prep + Cook Time: 40 minutes | Servings: 1

Ingredients
1 lb. boneless chicken breast
Salt and pepper
1 cup butter
1 cup tomatoes, diced
1 ½ tsp. paprika
1 tsp. pumpkin pie spices

Instructions
1.   Preheat your fryer at 375°F.
2.   Cut the chicken into relatively thick slices and put them in the fryer. Sprinkle with salt and pepper to taste. Cook for fifteen minutes.
3.   In the meantime, melt the butter in a saucepan over medium heat, before adding the tomatoes, paprika, and pumpkin pie spices. Leave simmering while the chicken finishes cooking.
4.   When the chicken is cooked through, place it on a dish and pour the tomato mixture over. Serve hot.

Fennel Chicken

Ingredients: Prep + Cook Time: 40 minutes | Servings: 4

Ingredients
1 ½ cup coconut milk
2 tbsp. garam masala
1 ½ lb. chicken thighs
¾ tbsp. coconut oil, melted

Instructions
1. Combine the coconut oil and garam masala together in a bowl. Pour the mixture over the chicken thighs and leave to marinate for a half hour.
2. Pre-heat your fryer at 375°F.
3. Cook the chicken into the fryer for fifteen minutes.
4. Add in the coconut milk, giving it a good stir, then cook for an additional ten minutes.
5. Remove the chicken and place on a serving dish. Make sure to pour all of the coconut "gravy" over it and serve immediately.

Roasted Chicken

Ingredients: Prep + Cook Time: 90 minutes | Servings: 6

Ingredients
6 lb. whole chicken
1 tsp. olive oil
1 tbsp. minced garlic
1 white onion, peeled and halved
3 tbsp. butter

Instructions
1. Pre-heat the fryer at 360°F.
2. Massage the chicken with the olive oil and the minced garlic.
3. Place the peeled and halved onion, as well as the butter, inside of the chicken.
4. Cook the chicken in the fryer for seventy-five minutes.
5. Take care when removing the chicken from the fryer, then carve and serve.

Chicken & Honey Sauce

Prep + Cook Time: 20 minutes | Servings: 4

Ingredients
4 chicken sausages
2 tbsp. honey
¼ cup mayonnaise
2 tbsp. Dijon mustard
1 tbsp. balsamic vinegar
½ tsp. dried rosemary

Instructions
1. Pre-heat your Air Fryer at 350°F.
2. Place the sausages on the grill pan of your fryer and grill for about 13 minutes, flipping them halfway through the cooking time.
3. In the meantime, make the sauce by whisking together the rest of the ingredients.
4. Pour the sauce over the warm sausages before serving.

Penne Chicken Sausage Meatballs

Prep + Cook Time: 20 minutes | Servings: 4

Ingredients
1 cup chicken meat, ground
1 sweet red pepper, minced
¼ cup green onions, chopped
1 green garlic, minced
4 tbsp. friendly bread crumbs
½ tsp. cumin powder
1 tbsp. fresh coriander, minced
½ tsp. sea salt
¼ tsp. mixed peppercorns, ground
1 package penne pasta, cooked

Instructions
1. Pre-heat the Air Fryer at 350°F.
2. Put the chicken, red pepper, green onions, and garlic into a mixing bowl and stir together to combine.
3. Throw in the seasoned bread crumbs and all of the seasonings. Combine again.
4. Use your hands to mold equal amounts of the mixture into small balls, each one roughly the size of a golf ball.
5. Put them in the fryer and cook for 15 minutes. Shake once or twice throughout the cooking time for even results.
6. Serve with cooked penne pasta.

Tarragon Chicken

Prep + Cook Time: 40 minutes | Servings: 4

Ingredients
2 cups roasted vegetable broth
2 chicken breasts, cut into halves
¾ tsp. fine sea salt
¼ tsp. mixed peppercorns, freshly cracked
1 tsp. cumin powder
1 ½ teaspoons sesame oil
1 ½ tbsp. Worcester sauce
½ cup of spring onions, chopped
1 Serrano pepper, deveined and chopped
1 bell pepper, deveined and chopped
1 tbsp. tamari sauce
½ chopped fresh tarragon

Instructions
1. Cook the vegetable broth and chicken breasts in a large saucepan for 10 minutes.
2. Lower the heat and simmer for another 10 minutes.
3. Let the chicken cool briefly. Then tear the chicken into shreds with a stand mixer or two forks.
4. Coat the shredded chicken with the salt, cracked peppercorns, cumin, sesame oil and the Worcester sauce.
5. Transfer to the Air Fryer and air fry at 380°F for 18 minutes, or longer as needed.
6. In the meantime, cook the remaining ingredients over medium heat in a skillet, until the vegetables are tender and fragrant.
7. Take the skillet off the heat. Stir in the shredded chicken, incorporating all the ingredients well.
8. Serve immediately.

Pizza Stuffed Chicken

Prep + Cook Time: 20 minutes | Servings: 4

Ingredients

4 small boneless, skinless chicken breasts
¼ cup pizza sauce
½ cup Colby cheese, shredded
16 slices pepperoni
Salt and pepper, to taste
1 ½ tbsp. olive oil
1 ½ tbsp. dried oregano

Instructions

1. Pre-heat your Air Fryer at 370°F.
2. Flatten the chicken breasts with a rolling pin.
3. Top the chicken with equal amounts of each ingredients and roll the fillets around the stuffing. Secure with a small skewer or two toothpicks.
4. Roast in the fryer on the grill pan for 13 - 15 minutes.

Special Maple-Glazed Chicken

Prep + Cook Time: 20 minutes | Servings: 4

Ingredients

2 ½ tbsp. maple syrup
1 tbsp. tamari soy sauce
1 tbsp. oyster sauce
1 tsp. fresh lemon juice
1 tsp. minced fresh ginger
1 tsp. garlic puree
Seasoned salt and freshly ground pepper, to taste
2 boneless, skinless chicken breasts

Instructions

1. In a bowl, combine the maple syrup, tamari sauce, oyster sauce, lemon juice, fresh ginger and garlic puree. This is your marinade.
2. Sprinkle the chicken breasts with salt and pepper.
3. Coat the chicken breasts with the marinade. Place some foil over the bowl and refrigerate for 3 hours, or overnight if possible.
4. Remove the chicken from the marinade. Place it in the Air Fryer and fry for 15 minutes at 365°F, flipping each one once or twice throughout.
5. In the meantime, add the remaining marinade to a pan over medium heat. Allow the marinade to simmer for 3 - 5 minutes until it has reduced by half.
6. Pour over the cooked chicken and serve.

Turkey Quinoa Skewers

Prep + Cook Time: 15 minutes | Servings: 8

Ingredients

1 cup red quinoa, cooked
1 ½ cups water
14 oz. ground turkey
2 small eggs, beaten
1 tsp. ground ginger
2 ½ tbsp. vegetable oil
1 cup chopped fresh parsley
2 tbsp. seasoned friendly bread crumbs
¾ tsp. salt
1 heaped tsp. fresh rosemary, finely chopped
½ tsp. ground allspice

Instructions

1. In a bowl, combine all of the ingredients together using your hands, kneading the mixture well.
2. Mold equal amounts of the mixture into small balls.
3. Pre-heat your Air Fryer to 380°F.
4. Place the balls in the fryer basket and fry for 8 - 10 minutes.

5. Skewer them and serve with the dipping sauce of your choice.

Potato Cakes & Cajun Chicken Wings

Prep + Cook Time: 40 minutes | Servings: 4

Ingredients

4 large-sized chicken wings
1 tsp. Cajun seasoning
1 tsp. maple syrup
¾ tsp. sea salt flakes
¼ tsp. red pepper flakes, crushed
1 tsp. onion powder
1 tsp. porcini powder
½ tsp. celery seeds
1 small-seized head of cabbage, shredded
1 cup mashed potatoes
1 small-sized brown onion, coarsely grated
1 tsp. garlic puree
1 medium whole egg, well whisked
½ tsp. table salt
½ tsp. ground black pepper
1 ½ tbsp. flour
¾ tsp. baking powder
1 heaped tbsp. cilantro
1 tbsp. sesame oil

Instructions

1. Pre-heat your Air Fryer to 390°F.
2. Pat the chicken wings dry. Place them in the fryer and cook for 25 - 30 minutes, ensuring they are cooked through.
3. Make the rub by combining the Cajun seasoning, maple syrup, sea salt flakes, red pepper, onion powder, porcini powder, and celery seeds.
4. Mix together the shredded cabbage, potato, onion, garlic puree, egg, table salt, black pepper, flour, baking powder and cilantro.
5. Separate the cabbage mixture into 4 portions and use your hands to mold each one into a cabbage-potato cake.
6. Douse each cake with the sesame oil.
7. Bake the cabbage-potato cakes in the fryer for 10 minutes, turning them once through the cooking time. You will need to do this in multiple batches.
8. Serve the cakes and the chicken wings together.

Provençal Chicken

Prep + Cook Time: 25 minutes | Servings: 4

Ingredients

4 medium-sized skin-on chicken drumsticks
1 ½ tsp. herbs de Provence
Salt and pepper to taste
1 tbsp. rice vinegar
2 tbsp. olive oil
2 garlic cloves, crushed
12 oz. crushed canned tomatoes
1 small-size leek, thinly sliced
2 slices smoked bacon, chopped

Instructions

1. Season the chicken drumsticks with herbs de Provence, salt and pepper. Pour over a light drizzling of the rice vinegar and olive oil.
2. Cook in the baking pan at 360°F for 8 - 10 minutes.
3. Pause the fryer. Add in the rest of the ingredients, give them a stir, and resume cooking for 15 more minutes, checking them occasionally to ensure they don't overcook.
4. Serve with rice and lemon wedges.

Gourmet Chicken Omelet

Prep + Cook Time: 15 minutes | Servings: 2

Ingredients

4 eggs, whisked
4 oz. ground chicken
½ cup scallions, finely chopped
2 cloves garlic, finely minced
½ tsp. salt
½ tsp. ground black pepper
½ tsp. paprika
1 tsp. dried thyme
Dash of hot sauce

Instructions

1. Mix together all the ingredients in a bowl, ensuring to incorporate everything well.
2. Lightly grease two oven-safe ramekins with vegetable oil. Divide the mixture between them.
3. Transfer them to the Air Fryer, and air fry at 350°F for 13 minutes.
4. Ensure they are cooked through and serve immediately.

Peppery Turkey Sandwiches

Prep + Cook Time: 25 minutes | Servings: 4

Ingredients

1 cup leftover turkey, cut into bite-sized chunks
2 bell peppers, deveined and chopped
1 Serrano pepper, deveined and chopped
1 leek, sliced
½ cup sour cream
1 tsp. hot paprika
¾ tsp. kosher salt
½ tsp. ground black pepper
1 heaping tbsp. fresh cilantro, chopped
Dash of Tabasco sauce
4 hamburger buns

Instructions

1. Combine all of the ingredients except for the hamburger buns, ensuring to coat the turkey well.
2. Place in an Air Fryer baking pan and roast for 20 minutes at 385°F.
3. Top the hamburger buns with the turkey, and serve with mustard or sour cream as desired.

Chicken Wings & Piri Piri Sauce

Prep + Cook Time: 1 hr. 30 minutes | Servings: 6

Ingredients

12 chicken wings
1 ½ oz. butter, melted
1 tsp. onion powder
½ tsp. cumin powder
1 tsp. garlic paste
For the Sauce:
2 oz. piri piri peppers, stemmed and chopped
1 tbsp. pimiento, deveined and minced
1 garlic clove, chopped
2 tbsp. fresh lemon juice
⅓ tsp. sea salt
½ tsp. tarragon
¾ tsp. sugar

Instructions

1. Place the chicken wings in a steamer basket over a saucepan of boiling water. Lower the temperature and steam the chicken for 10 minutes over a medium heat.
2. Coat the wings with the butter, onion powder, cumin powder, and garlic paste.
3. Allow the chicken wings to cool slightly. Place them in the refrigerator for 45 - 50 minutes.
4. Pre-heat your Air Fryer at 330°F.
5. Roast the chicken wings in the fryer for 25 - 30 minutes, turning them once halfway through the cooking time.
6. In the meantime make the Piri Piri sauce. Blend together all of the sauce ingredients in a food processor.
7. Coat the chicken wings in the sauce before serving.

Marrod's Meatballs

Prep + Cook Time: 15 minutes | Servings: 6

Ingredients

1 lb. ground turkey
1 tbsp. fresh mint leaves, finely chopped
1 tsp. onion powder
1 ½ teaspoons garlic paste
1 tsp. crushed red pepper flakes
¼ cup melted butter
¾ tsp. fine sea salt
¼ cup grated Pecorino Romano

Instructions

1. In a bowl, combine all of the ingredients well. Using an ice cream scoop, mold the meat into balls.
2. Air fry the meatballs at 380°F for about 7 minutes, in batches if necessary. Shake the basket frequently throughout the cooking time for even results.
3. Serve with basil leaves and tomato sauce if desired.

Turmeric & Mustard Chicken Thighs

Prep + Cook Time: 20 minutes | Servings: 6

Ingredients

1 large egg, well whisked
2 tbsp. whole-grain Dijon mustard
¼ cup of mayonnaise
¼ cup of chili sauce
½ tsp. sugar
1 tsp. fine sea salt
½ tsp. ground black pepper, or more to taste
½ tsp. turmeric powder
10 chicken thighs
2 cups crushed saltines

Instructions

1. In a large bowl, combine the egg, mustard, mayonnaise, chili sauce, sugar, salt, pepper, and turmeric, incorporating everything well.
2. Coat the chicken thighs with the mixture. Place a layer of aluminum foil over the bowl, transfer it to the refrigerator and allow the chicken to marinate for at least 5 hours or overnight.
3. Pre-heat the Air Fryer to 360°F.
4. Separate the chicken from the marinade.
5. Put the crushed saltines into a shallow dish and use them to coat the chicken.
6. Place the chicken in the fryer and cook for 15 minutes, ensuring the thighs are cooked through.
7. Serve with the rest of the marinade as a sauce.

Roasted Turkey Thighs

Prep + Cook Time: 1 hr. 15 minute | Servings: 4

Ingredients

1 red onion, cut into wedges
1 carrot, trimmed and sliced
1 celery stalk, trimmed and sliced
1 cup Brussels sprouts, trimmed and halved
1 cup roasted vegetable broth
1 tbsp. apple cider vinegar
1 tsp. maple syrup
2 turkey thighs
½ tsp. mixed peppercorns, freshly cracked
1 tsp. fine sea salt
1 tsp. cayenne pepper
1 tsp. onion powder
½ tsp. garlic powder
⅓ tsp. mustard seeds

Instructions

1. Put the vegetables into a baking dish small enough to fit inside your Air Fryer and add in the roasted vegetable broth.
2. In a large bowl, pour in the rest of the ingredients, and set aside for 30 minutes.
3. Place them on the top of the vegetables.
4. Roast at 330°F for 40 - 45 minutes.

Vegetables & Italian Turkey Sausage

Prep + Cook Time: 40 minutes | Servings: 4

Ingredients

1 onion, cut into wedges
2 carrots, trimmed and sliced
1 parsnip, trimmed and sliced
2 potatoes, peeled and diced
1 tsp. dried thyme
½ tsp. dried marjoram
1 tsp. dried basil
½ tsp. celery seeds
Sea salt and ground black pepper to taste
1 tbsp. melted butter
¾ lb. sweet Italian turkey sausage

Instructions

1. Cover the vegetables with all of the seasonings and the melted butter.
2. Place the vegetables in the Air Fryer basket.
3. Add the sausage on top.
4. Roast at 360°F for 33 - 37 minutes, ensuring the sausages are no longer pink, giving the basket a good shake halfway through the cooking time. You may need to cook everything in batches.

Ricotta Wraps & Spring Chicken

Prep + Cook Time: 20 minutes | Servings: 12

Ingredients

2 large-sized chicken breasts, cooked and shredded
⅓ tsp. sea salt
¼ tsp. ground black pepper, or more to taste
2 spring onions, chopped
¼ cup soy sauce
1 tbsp. molasses
1 tbsp. rice vinegar
10 oz. Ricotta cheese
1 tsp. grated fresh ginger
50 wonton wrappers

Instructions

1. In a bowl, combine all of the ingredients, minus the wonton wrappers.
2. Unroll the wrappers and spritz with cooking spray.
3. Fill each of the wonton wrappers with equal amounts of the mixture.
4. Dampen the edges with a little water as an adhesive and roll up the wrappers, fully enclosing the filling.
5. Cook the rolls in the Air Fryer for 5 minutes at 375°F. You will need to do this step in batches.
6. Serve with your preferred sauce.

Cajun-Mustard Turkey Fingers

Prep + Cook Time: 20 minutes | Servings: 4

Ingredients

½ cup cornmeal mix
½ cup flour
1 ½ tbsp. Cajun seasoning
1 ½ tbsp. whole-grain mustard
1 ½ cups buttermilk
1 tsp. soy sauce
¾ lb. turkey tenderloins, cut into finger-sized strips
Salt and ground black pepper to taste

Instructions

1. In a bowl, combine the cornmeal, flour, and Cajun seasoning.
2. In a separate bowl, combine the whole-grain mustard, buttermilk and soy sauce.
3. Sprinkle some salt and pepper on the turkey fingers.
4. Dredge each finger in the buttermilk mixture, before coating them completely with the cornmeal mixture.
5. Place the prepared turkey fingers in the Air Fryer baking pan and cook for 15 minutes at 360°F.
6. Serve immediately, with ketchup if desired.

Honey Glazed Turkey Breast

Prep + Cook Time: 55 minutes | Servings: 6

Ingredients

2 tsp. butter, softened
1 tsp. dried sage
2 sprigs rosemary, chopped
1 tsp. salt
¼ tsp. freshly ground black pepper, or more if desired
1 whole turkey breast
2 tbsp. turkey broth
¼ cup honey
2 tbsp. whole-grain mustard
1 tbsp. butter

Instructions

1. Pre-heat your Air Fryer to 360°F.
2. Mix together the 2 tbsp. of butter, sage, rosemary, salt, and pepper.
3. Rub the turkey breast with this mixture.
4. Place the turkey in your fryer's cooking basket and roast for 20 minutes. Turn the turkey breast over and allow to cook for another 15 - 16 minutes.
5. Finally turn it once more and roast for another 12 minutes.
6. In the meantime, mix together the remaining ingredients in a saucepan using a whisk.
7. Coat the turkey breast with the glaze.
8. Place the turkey back in the Air Fryer and cook for an additional 5 minutes. Remove it from the fryer, let it rest, and carve before serving.

Chicken Curry

Prep + Cook Time: 60 minutes | Servings: 2

Ingredients
2 chicken thighs
1 small zucchini
2 cloves garlic
6 dried apricots
3 ½ oz. long turnip
6 basil leaves
1 tbsp. whole pistachios
1 tbsp. raisin soup
1 tbsp. olive oil
1 large pinch salt
Pinch of pepper
1 tsp. curry powder

Instructions
1.   Pre-heat Air Fryer at 320°F.
2.   Cut the chicken into 2 thin slices and chop up the vegetables into bite-sized pieces.
3.   In a dish, combine all of the ingredients, incorporating everything well.
4.   Place in the fryer and cook for a minimum of 30 minutes.
5.   Serve with rice if desired.

Marjoram Chicken

Prep + Cook Time: 1 hr. | Servings: 2

Ingredients
2 skinless, boneless small chicken breasts
2 tbsp. butter
1 tsp. sea salt
½ tsp. red pepper flakes, crushed
2 tsp. marjoram
¼ tsp. lemon pepper

Instructions
1.   In a bowl, coat the chicken breasts with all of the other ingredients. Set aside to marinate for 30 – 60 minutes.
2.   Pre-heat your Air Fryer to 390 degrees.
3.   Cook for 20 minutes, turning halfway through cooking time.
4.   Check for doneness using an instant-read thermometer. Serve over jasmine rice.

Hoisin Glazed Turkey Drumsticks

Prep + Cook Time: 40 minutes + marinating time | Servings: 4

Ingredients
2 turkey drumsticks
2 tbsp. balsamic vinegar
2 tbsp. dry white wine
1 tbsp. extra-virgin olive oil
1 sprig rosemary, chopped
Salt and ground black pepper, to taste
2 ½ tbsp. butter, melted
For the Hoisin Glaze:
2 tbsp. hoisin sauce
1 tbsp. honey
1 tbsp. honey mustard

Instructions
1.   In a bowl, coat the turkey drumsticks with the vinegar, wine, olive oil, and rosemary. Allow to marinate for 3 hours.
2.   Pre-heat the Air Fryer to 350°F.
3.   Sprinkle the turkey drumsticks with salt and black pepper. Cover the surface of each drumstick with the butter.
4.   Place the turkey in the fryer and cook at 350°F for 30 - 35 minutes, flipping it occasionally through the cooking time. You may have to do this in batches.
5.   In the meantime, make the Hoisin glaze by combining all the glaze ingredients.
6.   Pour the glaze over the turkey, and roast for another 5 minutes.
7.   Allow the drumsticks to rest for about 10 minutes before carving.

Turkey Sliders & Chive Mayonnaise

Prep + Cook Time: 20 minutes | Servings: 6

Ingredients
For the Turkey Sliders:
¾ lb. turkey mince
¼ cup pickled jalapeno, chopped
1 tbsp. oyster sauce
1 – 2 cloves garlic, minced
1 tbsp. chopped fresh cilantro
2 tbsp. chopped scallions
Sea salt and ground black pepper to taste
For the Chive Mayo:
1 cup mayonnaise
1 tbsp. chives
1 tsp. salt
Zest of 1 lime

Instructions
1.   In a bowl, combine together all of the ingredients for the turkey sliders. Use your hands to shape 6 equal amounts of the mixture into slider patties.
2.   Transfer the patties to the Air Fryer and fry them at 365°F for 15 minutes.
3.   In the meantime, prepare the Chive Mayo by combining the rest of the ingredients.
4.   Make sandwiches by placing each patty between two burger buns and serve with the mayo.

Thai Turkey Wings

Prep + Cook Time: 40 minutes| Servings: 4

Ingredients
¾ lb. turkey wings, cut into pieces
1 tsp. ginger powder
1 tsp. garlic powder
¾ tsp. paprika
2 tbsp. soy sauce
1 handful minced lemongrass
Sea salt flakes and ground black pepper to taste
2 tbsp. rice wine vinegar
¼ cup peanut butter
1 tbsp. sesame oil
½ cup Thai sweet chili sauce

Instructions
1.   Boil the turkey wings in a saucepan full of water for 20 minutes.
2.   Put the turkey wings in a large bowl and cover them with the remaining ingredients, minus the Thai sweet chili sauce.
3.   Transfer to the Air Fryer and fry for 20 minutes at 350°F, turning once halfway through the cooking time. Ensure they are cooked through before serving with the Thai sweet chili sauce, as well as some lemon wedges if desired.

Stuffed Turkey Roulade

Prep + Cook Time: 50 minutes | Servings: 4

Ingredients

1 turkey fillet
Salt and garlic pepper to taste
⅓ tsp. onion powder
½ tsp. dried basil
⅓ tsp. ground red chipotle pepper
1 ½ tbsp. mustard seeds
½ tsp. fennel seeds
2 tbsp. melted butter
3 tbsp. coriander, finely chopped
½ cup scallions, finely chopped
2 cloves garlic, finely minced

Instructions

1.   Flatten out the turkey fillets with a mallet, until they are about a half-inch thick.
2.   Season each one with salt, garlic pepper, and onion powder.
3.   In a small bowl, mix together the basil, chipotle pepper, mustard seeds, fennel seeds and butter.
4.   Use a pallet knife to spread the mixture over the fillets, leaving the edges uncovered.
5.   Add the coriander, scallions and garlic on top.
6.   Roll up the fillets into a log and wrap a piece of twine around them to hold them in place.
7.   Place them in the Air Fryer cooking basket.
8.   Roast at 350°F for about 50 minutes, flipping it at the halfway point. Cook for longer if necessary. Serve warm.

Mac's Chicken Nuggets

Prep + Cook Time: 40 minutes | Servings: 4

Ingredients

2 slices friendly breadcrumbs
9 oz. chicken breast, chopped
1 tsp. garlic, minced
1 tsp. tomato ketchup
2 medium egg
1 tbsp. olive oil
1 tsp. paprika
1 tsp. parsley
Salt and pepper to taste

Instructions

1.   Combine the breadcrumbs, paprika, salt, pepper and oil into a thick batter.
2.   Coat the chopped chicken with the parsley, one egg and ketchup.
3.   Shape the mixture into several nuggets and dredge each one in the other egg. Roll the nuggets into the breadcrumbs.
4.   Cook at 390°F for 10 minutes in the Air Fryer.
5.   Serve the nuggets with a side of mayo dip if desired.

Colby's Turkey Meatloaf

Prep + Cook Time: 50 minutes | Servings: 6

Ingredients

1 lb. turkey mince
½ cup scallions, finely chopped
2 garlic cloves, finely minced
1 tsp. dried thyme
½ tsp. dried basil
¾ cup Colby cheese, shredded
¾ cup crushed saltines
1 tbsp. tamari sauce
Salt and black pepper, to taste
¼ cup roasted red pepper tomato sauce
1 tsp. sugar
¾ tbsp. olive oil
1 medium egg, well beaten

Instructions

1.   Over a medium heat, fry up the turkey mince, scallions, garlic, thyme, and basil until soft and fragrant.
2.   Pre-heat the Air Fryer to 360°F.
3.   Combine the mixture with the cheese, saltines and tamari sauce, before shaping it into a loaf.
4.   Stir together the remaining items and top the meatloaf with them.
5.   Place in the Air Fryer baking pan and allow to cook for 45 - 47 minutes.

Chicken Drumsticks

Prep + Cook Time: 35 minutes | Servings: 4

Ingredients

8 chicken drumsticks
1 tsp. cayenne pepper
2 tbsp. mustard powder
2 tbsp. oregano
2 tbsp. thyme
3 tbsp. coconut milk
1 large egg, lightly beaten
⅓ cup cauliflower
⅓ cup oats
Pepper and salt to taste

Instructions

1.   Pre-heat the Air Fryer to 350°F.
2.   Sprinkle salt and pepper over the chicken drumsticks and massage the coconut milk into them.
3.   Put all the ingredients except the egg into the food processor and pulse to create a bread crumb-like mixture.
4.   Transfer to a bowl.
5.   In a separate bowl, put the beaten egg. Coat each chicken drumstick in the bread crumb mixture before dredging it in the egg. Roll it in the bread crumbs once more.
6.   Put the coated chicken drumsticks in Air Fryer basket and cook for 20 minutes. Serve hot.

Bacon-Wrapped Chicken

Prep + Cook Time: 20 minutes | Servings: 6

Ingredients

1 chicken breast, cut into 6 pieces
6 rashers back bacon
1 tbsp. soft cheese

Instructions

1.   Put the bacon rashers on a flat surface and cover one side with the soft cheese.
2.   Lay the chicken pieces on each bacon rasher. Wrap the bacon around the chicken and use a toothpick stick to hold each one in place. Put them in Air Fryer basket.
3.   Air fry at 350°F for 15 minutes.

Family Farm's Chicken Wings

Prep + Cook Time: 20 minutes | Servings: 6

Ingredients
6 chicken wings
1 tbsp. honey
2 cloves garlic, chopped
1 tsp. red chili flakes
2 tbsp. Worcestershire sauce
Pepper and salt to taste

Instructions
1. Place all the ingredients, except for the chicken wings, in a bowl and combine well.
2. Coat the chicken with the mixture and refrigerate for 1 hour.
3. Put the marinated chicken wings in the Air Fryer basket and spritz with cooking spray.
4. Air fry the chicken wings at 320°F for 8 minutes. Raise the temperature to 350°F and cook for an additional 4 minutes. Serve hot.

Chicken Surprise

Prep + Cook Time: 30 minutes | Servings: 2

Ingredients
2 chicken breasts, boneless and skinless
2 large eggs
½ cup skimmed milk
6 tbsp. soy sauce
1 cup flour
1 tsp. smoked paprika
1 tsp. salt
¼ tsp. black pepper
½ tsp. garlic powder
1 tbsp. olive oil
4 hamburger buns

Instructions
1. Slice the chicken breast into 2 – 3 pieces.
2. Place in a large bowl and drizzle with the soy sauce. Sprinkle on the smoked paprika, black pepper, salt, and garlic powder and mix well.
3. Allow to marinate for 30 – 40 minutes.
4. In the meantime, combine the eggs with the milk in a bowl. Put the flour in a separate bowl.
5. Dip the marinated chicken into the egg mixture before coating it with the flour. Cover each piece of chicken evenly.
6. Pre-heat the Air Fryer to 380°F.
7. Drizzle on the olive oil and put chicken pieces in the fryer.
8. Cook for 10 – 12 minutes. Flip the chicken once throughout the cooking process.
9. Toast the hamburger buns and put each slice of chicken between two buns to make a sandwich. Serve with ketchup or any other sauce of your choice.

Lemon & Garlic Chicken

Prep + Cook Time: 25 minutes | Servings: 1

Ingredients
1 chicken breast
1 tsp. garlic, minced
1 tbsp. chicken seasoning
1 lemon juice
Handful black peppercorns
Pepper and salt to taste

Instructions
1. Pre-heat the Air Fryer to 350°F.
2. Sprinkle the chicken with pepper and salt. Massage the chicken seasoning into the chicken breast, coating it well, and lay the seasoned chicken on a sheet of aluminum foil.

3. Top the chicken with the garlic, lemon juice, and black peppercorns. Wrap the foil to seal the chicken tightly.
4. Cook the chicken in the fryer basket for 15 minutes.

Cajun Seasoned Chicken

Prep + Cook Time: 15 minutes | Servings: 2

Ingredients
2 boneless chicken breasts
3 tbsp. Cajun spice

Instructions
1. Coat both sides of the chicken breasts with Cajun spice. Put the seasoned chicken in Air Fryer basket.
2. Air fry at 350°F for 10 minutes, ensuring they are cooked through before slicing up and serving.

Chicken Fillets

Prep + Cook Time: 30 minutes | Servings: 3

Ingredients
8 pieces of chicken fillet [approximately 3 x 1 x 1-inch dimensions]
1 egg
1 oz. salted butter, melted
1 cup friendly bread crumbs
1 tsp. garlic powder
½ cup parmesan cheese
1 tsp. Italian herbs

Instructions
1. Cover the chicken pieces in the whisked egg, melted butter, garlic powder, and Italian herbs. Allow to marinate for about 10 minutes.
2. In a bowl, mix together the Panko bread crumbs and parmesan. Use this mixture to coat the marinated chicken.
3. Put the aluminum foil in your Air Fryer basket.
4. Set the fryer to 390°F and briefly allow to warm. Line the basket with aluminum foil.
5. Place 4 pieces of the chicken in the basket. Cook for 6 minutes until golden brown. Don't turn the chicken over.
6. Repeat with the rest of the chicken pieces.
7. Serve the chicken fillets hot.

Chicken Nuggets

Prep + Cook Time: 30 minutes | Servings: 4

Ingredients
½ lb. chicken breast, cut into pieces
1 tsp. parsley
1 tsp. paprika
1 tbsp. olive oil
2 eggs, beaten
1 tsp. tomato ketchup
1 tsp. garlic, minced
½ cup friendly bread crumbs
Pepper and salt to taste

Instructions
1. In a bowl, combine the bread crumbs, olive oil, paprika, pepper, and salt.
2. Place the chicken, ketchup, one egg, garlic, and parsley in a food processor and pulse together.
3. Put the other egg in a bowl.
4. Shape equal amounts of the pureed chicken into nuggets. Dredge each one in the egg before coating it in bread crumbs.
5. Put the coated chicken nuggets in the Air Fryer basket and cook at 390°F for 10 minutes.
6. Serve the nuggets hot.

Cracked Chicken Tenders

Prep + Cook Time: 30 minutes | Servings: 4

Ingredients

2 lb. skinless and boneless chicken tenders
3 large eggs
6 tbsp. skimmed milk
½ cup flour
1 cup friendly bread crumbs
¼ tsp. black pepper
1 tsp. salt
2 tbsp. olive oil

Instructions

1.   In a large bowl, combine the bread crumbs and olive oil.
2.   In a separate bowl, stir together the eggs and milk using a whisk. Sprinkle in the salt and black pepper.
3.   Put the flour in a third bowl.
4.   Slice up the chicken tenders into 1-inch strips. Coat each piece of chicken in the flour, before dipping it into the egg mixture, followed by the bread crumbs.
5.   Pre-heat the Air Fryer to 380°F.
6.   Cook the coated chicken tenders for about 13 – 15 minutes, shaking the basket a few times to ensure they turn crispy. Serve hot, with mashed potatoes and a dipping sauce if desired.

Randy's Roasted Chicken

Prep + Cook Time: 55 minutes | Servings: 4

Ingredients

5 – 7 lb. whole chicken with skin
1 tsp. garlic powder
1 tsp. onion powder
½ tsp. dried thyme
½ tsp. dried basil
½ tsp. dried rosemary
½ tsp. black pepper
2 tsp. salt
2 tbsp. extra virgin olive oil

Instructions

1.   Massage the salt, pepper, herbs, and olive oil into the chicken. Allow to marinade for a minimum of 20 – 30 minutes.
2.   In the meantime, pre-heat the Air Fryer to 340 F.
3.   Place the chicken in the fryer and cook for 18 – 20 minutes.
4.   Flip the chicken over and cook for an additional 20 minutes.
5.   Leave the chicken to rest for about 10 minutes before carving and serving.

Herbed Chicken

Prep + Cook Time: 40 minutes | Servings: 6

Ingredients

4 lb. chicken wings
6 tbsp. red wine vinegar
6 tbsp. lime juice
1 tsp. fresh ginger, minced
1 tbsp. sugar
1 tsp. thyme, chopped
½ tsp. white pepper
¼ tsp. ground cinnamon
1 habanero pepper, chopped
6 garlic cloves, chopped
2 tbsp. soy sauce
2 ½ tbsp. olive oil
¼ tsp. salt

Instructions

1.   Place all of the ingredients in a bowl and combine well, ensuring to coat the chicken entirely.
2.   Put the chicken in the refrigerator to marinate for 1 hour.
3.   Pre-heat the Air Fryer to 390°F.
4.   Put half of the marinated chicken in the fryer basket and cook for 15 minutes, shaking the basket once throughout the cooking process.
5.   Repeat with the other half of the chicken.
6.   Serve hot.

Rosemary Chicken

Prep + Cook Time: 30 minutes | Servings: 2

Ingredients

¾ lb. chicken
½ tbsp. olive oil
1 tbsp. soy sauce
1 tsp. fresh ginger, minced
1 tbsp. oyster sauce
3 tbsp. sugar
1 tbsp. fresh rosemary, chopped
½ fresh lemon, cut into wedges

Instructions

1.   In a bowl, combine the chicken, oil, soy sauce, and ginger, coating the chicken well.
2.   Refrigerate for 30 minutes.
3.   Pre-heat the Air Fryer to 390°F for 3 minutes.
4.   Place the chicken in the baking pan, transfer to the fryer and cook for 6 minutes.
5.   In the meantime, put the rosemary, sugar, and oyster sauce in a bowl and mix together.
6.   Add the rosemary mixture in the fryer over the chicken and top the chicken with the lemon wedges.
7.   Resume cooking for another 13 minutes, turning the chicken halfway through.

Chicken Strips

Prep + Cook Time: 25 minutes | Servings: 2

Ingredients

1 chicken breast, cut into strips
1 egg, beaten
¼ cup flour
¾ cup friendly bread crumbs
1 tsp. mix spice
1 tbsp. plain oats
1 tbsp. desiccated coconut
Pepper and salt to taste

Instructions

1.   In a bowl, mix together the bread crumbs, mix spice, oats, coconut, pepper, and salt.
2.   Put the beaten egg in a separate bowl. Pour the flour into a shallow dish.
3.   Roll the chicken strips in the flour. Dredge each one in the egg and coat with the bread crumb mixture. Put the coated chicken strips in the Air Fryer basket and air fry at 350°F for 8 minutes.
4.   Reduce the heat to 320°F and cook for another 4 minutes. Serve hot.

Grandma's Chicken

Prep + Cook Time: 20 minutes | Servings: 4

Ingredients
12 oz. chicken breast, diced
6 oz. general Tso sauce
½ tsp. white pepper
¼ cup milk
1 cup cornstarch

Instructions
1. Place the chicken and milk in a bowl.
2. Separate the milk from the chicken and coat the chicken with cornstarch.
3. Put the chicken in the Air Fryer basket and air fry at 350°F for 12 minutes.
4. Plate up the chicken and season with the white pepper.
5. Pour the Tso sauce over the chicken before serving.

=

Worcestershire Chicken Wings

Prep + Cook Time: 40 minutes | Servings: 6

Ingredients
6 chicken wings
1 ½ tbsp. Worcestershire sauce
1 tbsp. sugar
Juice and zest of 1 orange
½ tsp. thyme, dried
½ tsp. sage
1 tsp. mint
1 tsp. basil
½ tsp. oregano
1 tsp. parsley
1 tsp. rosemary
Salt and pepper to taste

Instructions
1. Combine all of the ingredients in a bowl, coating the chicken wings well with the other ingredients.
2. Refrigerate the marinated chicken for 30 minutes.
3. Pre-heat the Air Fryer to 350°F.
4. Wrap the marinated chicken in a sheet of aluminum foil, ensuring to seal with the juices. Put the wrapped chicken in Air Fryer basket and cook at 350°F for 20 minutes.
5. Unfold the foil, remove the orange zest and air fry the chicken wings at 350°F for a further 15 minutes. Serve hot.

Lime & Honey Chicken Wings

Prep + Cook Time: 7 hours | Servings: 2

Ingredients
16 winglets
½ tsp. sea salt
2 tbsp. light soya sauce
¼ tsp. white pepper powder
½ crush black pepper

2 tbsp. honey
2 tbsp. lime juice

Instructions
1. Place all of the ingredients in a glass dish. Coat the winglets well and allow to marinate in the refrigerator for a minimum of 6 hours.
2. Allow to return to room temperature for 30 minutes.
3. Put the wings in the Air Fryer and air fry at 355°F for 6 minutes. Turn each wing over before cooking for another 6 minutes.
4. Allow the chicken to cool before serving with a wedge of lemon.

Chicken Kebabs

Prep + Cook Time: 30 minutes | Servings: 3

Ingredients
1 lb. chicken breasts, diced
5 tbsp. honey
½ cup soy sauce
6 large mushrooms, cut in halves
3 medium bell peppers, cut
1 small zucchini, cut into rings
2 medium tomatoes, cut into rings
Salt and pepper to taste
¼ cup sesame seeds
1 tbsp. olive oil

Instructions
1. Cube the chicken breasts and place them in a large bowl.
2. Season with some salt and pepper. Drizzle over one tablespoon of olive oil and mix well.
3. Pour in the honey and soy sauce, and add in the sesame seeds.
4. Leave to marinate for 15 – 30 minutes.
5. Slice up the vegetables.
6. Thread the chicken and vegetables on wooden skewers, in alternating patterns.
7. Pre-heat the Air Fryer to 340°F
8. Put the chicken kebabs into the fryer basket.
9. Cook for about 15 minutes, flipping once during cooking. Serve once crispy and brown.

Chicken Tenderloins

Prep + Cook Time: 25 minutes | Servings: 4

Ingredients
8 chicken tenderloins
1 egg, beaten
2 tbsp. olive oil
1 cup friendly bread crumbs
Pepper and salt to taste

Instructions
1. Pre-heat the Air Fryer to 350°F.
2. Combine the friendly bread crumbs, olive oil, pepper, and salt in a shallow dish.
3. Put the beaten egg in separate dish.
4. Dip the chicken tenderloins into the egg before rolling them in the bread crumbs.
5. Transfer to the Air Fryer basket. Air fry the chicken for 12 minutes.

Buffalo Wings

Prep + Cook Time: 35 min. + [2 - 12 hours marinate] | Servings: 4

Ingredients

2 lb. chicken wings, without the wing tips
¼ cup + ¼ cup hot sauce, separately
3 + 3 tbsp. melted butter, separately
Sea salt to taste
Blue cheese, optional
Celery sticks, optional

Instructions

1. Prepare the chicken wings by separating the drumettes from the wingettes and put them into a bowl.
2. In a separate bowl, thoroughly combine 3 tablespoons of melted butter and ¼ cup of hot sauce.
3. Use this mixture to coat the chicken and marinate for 2 hours or overnight if possible.
4. Briefly pre-heat the Air Fryer to 400°F.
5. Divide the chicken into 2 batches. Put the first batch in the Air Fryer and cook for about 12 minutes. Give the basket a good shake at the halfway point. Repeat with the second batch.
6. Combine the cooked batches and return them to the Air Fryer, cooking for an additional 2 minutes.
7. In the meantime, make the sauce by stirring together the remaining 3 tablespoons of butter and ¼ cup of hot sauce.
8. Coat the cooked wings in the sauce before serving with a side of celery sticks and blue cheese if desired.

Moroccan Chicken

Prep + Cook Time: 25 minutes | Servings: 2

Ingredients

½ lb. shredded chicken
1 cup broth
1 carrot
1 broccoli, chopped
Pinch of cinnamon
Pinch of cumin
Pinch of red pepper
Pinch of sea salt

Instructions

1. In a bowl, cover the shredded chicken with cumin, red pepper, sea salt and cinnamon.
2. Chop up the carrots into small pieces. Put the carrot and broccoli into the bowl with the chicken.
3. Add the broth and stir everything well. Set aside for about 30 minutes.
4. Transfer to the Air Fryer. Cook for about 15 minutes at 390°F. Serve hot.

Chinese Chicken Wings

Prep + Cook Time: 45 minutes | Servings: 4

Ingredients

8 chicken wings
2 tbsp. five spice
2 tbsp. soy sauce
1 tbsp. mixed spices
Salt and pepper to taste

Instructions

1. In a bowl, mix together all of the ingredients.
2. Cover the base of the fryer with an aluminum foil and pre-heat the fryer to 360°F.
3. Add in some oil and pour in the mixture. Cook for 15 minutes.

4. Turn up the heat to 390°F, turn the chicken wings and cook for another 5 minutes. Serve with mayo dip if desired.

Chicken & Potatoes

Prep + Cook Time: 45 minutes | Servings: 6

Ingredients

1 lb. potatoes
2 lb. chicken
2 tbsp. olive oil
Pepper and salt to taste

Instructions

1. Pre-heat the Air Fryer to 350°F.
2. Place the chicken in Air Fryer basket along with the potatoes. Sprinkle on the pepper and salt.
3. Add a drizzling of the olive oil, making sure to cover the chicken and potatoes well.
4. Cook for 40 minutes.

Chicken Tenders

Prep + Cook Time: 30 minutes | Servings: 4

Ingredients

1 lb. chicken tenders
1 tsp. ginger, minced
4 garlic cloves, minced
2 tbsp. sesame oil
6 tbsp. pineapple juice
2 tbsp. soy sauce
½ tsp. pepper

Instructions

1. Put all of the ingredients, except for the chicken, in a bowl and combine well.
2. Thread the chicken onto skewers and coat with the seasonings. Allow to marinate for 2 hours.
3. Pre-heat the Air Fryer to 350°F.
4. Put the marinated chicken in fryer basket and cook for 18 minutes. Serve hot.

Lime Dijon Chicken

Prep + Cook Time: 20 minutes | Servings: 6

Ingredients

8 chicken drumsticks
1 lime juice
1 lime zest
Kosher salt to taste
1 tbsp. light mayonnaise
¾ tsp. black pepper
1 clove garlic, crushed
3 tbsp. Dijon mustard
1 tsp. dried parsley

Instructions

1. Pre-heat the Air Fryer to 375°F.
2. Remove the chicken skin and sprinkle the chicken with the salt.
3. In a bowl, mix the Dijon mustard with the lime juice, before stirring in the lime zest, pepper, parsley and garlic.
4. Cover the chicken with the lime mixture. Allow it to marinate for roughly 10 - 15 minutes.
5. Drizzle some oil in the bottom of your Air Fryer. Transfer the chicken drumsticks inside and cook for 5 minutes.
6. Give the basket a shake and fry for an additional 5 minutes.
7. Serve immediately, with a side of mayo.

Fried Chicken Thighs

Prep + Cook Time: 35 minutes | Servings: 4

Ingredients

4 chicken thighs
1 ½ tbsp. Cajun seasoning
1 egg, beaten
½ cup flour
1 tsp. seasoning salt

Instructions

1. Pre-heat the Air Fryer to 350°F.
2. In a bowl combine the flour, Cajun seasoning, and seasoning salt.
3. Place the beaten egg in another bowl.
4. Coat the chicken with the flour before dredging it in the egg. Roll once more in the flour.
5. Put the chicken in the Air Fryer and cook for 25 minutes. Serve hot.

Fried Wings

Prep + Cook Time: 35 minutes | Servings: 6

Ingredients

4 Lb. chicken wings
1 tbsp. sugar
1 tbsp. Worcestershire sauce
½ cup butter, melted
½ cup hot sauce
½ tsp. salt

Instructions

1. In a bowl, combine the sugar, Worcestershire sauce, butter, salt, and hot sauce.
2. Place the chicken wings in the Air Fryer basket and air fry at 380°F for 25 minutes, giving the basket a good shake halfway through the cooking time.
3. Raise the temperature to 400°F and continue to cook for another 5 minutes.
4. Place the air fried chicken wings in the bowl with the sugar mixture and toss to coat. Serve right away.

Teriyaki Chicken

Prep + Cook Time: 30 minutes | Servings: 2

Ingredients

2 boneless chicken drumsticks
1 tsp. ginger, grated
1 tbsp. cooking wine
3 tbsp. teriyaki sauce

Instructions

1. Combine all of the ingredients in a bowl. Refrigerate for half an hour.
2. Place the chicken in the Air Fryer baking pan and fry at 350°F for 8 minutes. Turn the chicken over and raise the temperature to 380°F. Allow to cook for another 6 minutes. Serve hot.

Asian Style Chicken

Prep + Cook Time: 25 minutes | Servings: 3

Ingredients

1 lb. skinless and boneless chicken breasts
3 garlic cloves, minced
1 tbsp. grated ginger
¼ tsp. ground black pepper
½ cup soy sauce
½ cup pineapple juice
1 tbsp. olive oil
2 tbsp. sesame seeds

Instructions

1. Mix together all of the ingredients except for the chicken in a large bowl.
2. Slice up the chicken breasts and coat in the mixture. Allow to marinade for at least 30 – 40 minutes.
3. Transfer the marinated chicken to the Air Fryer and cook at 380°F for about 10 – 15 minutes.
4. Top with sesame seeds before serving.

Whole Chicken

Prep + Cook Time: 30 minutes | Servings: 2

Ingredients

1 lb. whole chicken
1 lemon, juiced
1 tsp. lemon zest
1 tbsp. soy sauce
1 ½ tbsp. honey

Instructions

1. Place all of the ingredients in a bowl and combine well. Refrigerate for 1 hour.
2. Put the marinated chicken in the Air Fryer baking pan. Air fry at 320°F for 18 minutes.
3. Raise the heat to 350°F and cook for another 10 minutes or until chicken has turned light brown.

Honey & Garlic Chicken Wings

Prep + Cook Time: 25 minutes | Servings: 4

Ingredients

16 chicken wings
½ tsp. salt
¾ cup potato starch
¼ cup butter, melted
4 cloves garlic, minced
¼ cup honey

Instructions

1. Pre-heat your Air Fryer to 370°F.
2. Put the chicken wings in a bowl and cover them well with the potato starch.
3. Spritz a baking dish with cooking spray.
4. Transfer the wings to the dish, place inside the fryer and cook for 5 minutes.
5. In the meantime, mix together the rest of the ingredients with a whisk.
6. Top the chicken with this mixture and allow to cook for another 10 minutes before serving.

Buffalo Chicken Wings

Prep + Cook Time: 37 minutes | Servings: 3

Ingredients

2 lb. chicken wings
1 tsp. salt
¼ tsp. black pepper
1 cup buffalo sauce

Instructions

1. Wash the chicken wings and pat them dry with clean kitchen towels.
2. Place the chicken wings in a large bowl and sprinkle on salt and pepper.
3. Pre-heat the Air Fryer to 380°F.
4. Place the wings in the fryer and cook for 15 minutes, giving them an occasional stir throughout.
5. Place the wings in a bowl. Pour over the buffalo sauce and toss well to coat.
6. Put the chicken back in the Air Fryer and cook for a final 5 – 6 minutes.

Chicken Meatballs

Prep + Cook Time: 20 minutes | Servings: 10

Ingredients

2 chicken breasts
1 tbsp. mustard powder
1 tbsp. cumin
1 tbsp. basil
1 tbsp. thyme
1 tsp. chili powder
3 tbsp. soy sauce
2 tbsp. honey
1 onion, diced
Pepper and salt to taste

Instructions

1. Blend the chicken in your food processor to make a mince. Place the rest of the ingredients in the processor and pulse to combine well.
2. Shape the mixture into several small meatballs and place each one in the basket of the Air Fryer.
3. Air fry at 350°F for 15 minutes. Serve hot.

Chicken Legs

Prep + Cook Time: 35 minutes | Servings: 4

Ingredients

3 chicken legs, bone-in, with ski
3 chicken thighs, bone-in, with skin
2 cups flour
1 cup buttermilk
1 tsp. salt
1 tsp. ground black pepper
1 tsp. garlic powder
1 tsp. onion powder
1 tsp. ground cumin
2 tbsp. extra virgin olive oil

Instructions

1. Wash the chicken, dry it, and place it in a large bowl.
2. Pour the buttermilk over the chicken and refrigerate for 2 hours.
3. In a separate bowl, combine the flour with all of the seasonings.
4. Dip the chicken into the flour mixture. Dredge it the buttermilk before rolling it in the flour again.
5. Pre-heat the Air Fryer to 360°F
6. Put the chicken legs and thighs in the fryer basket. Drizzle on the olive oil and cook for roughly 20 minutes, flipping each piece of chicken a few times throughout the cooking time, until cooked through and crisped up.

Beastly BBQ Drumsticks

Prep + Cook Time: 45 minutes | Servings: 4

Ingredients

4 chicken drumsticks
½ tbsp. mustard
1 clove garlic, crushed
1 tsp. chili powder
2 tsp. sugar
1 tbsp. olive oil

Freshly ground black pepper

Instructions

1. Pre-heat the Air Fryer to 390°F.
2. Mix together the garlic, sugar, mustard, a pinch of salt, freshly ground pepper, chili powder and oil.
3. Massage this mixture into the drumsticks and leave to marinate for a minimum of 20 minutes.
4. Put the drumsticks in the fryer basket and cook for 10 minutes.
5. Bring the temperature down to 300°F and continue to cook the drumsticks for a further 10 minutes. When cooked through, serve with bread and corn salad.

Turkey Loaf

Prep + Cook Time: 50 minutes | Servings: 4

Ingredients

2/3 cup of finely chopped walnuts
1 egg
1 tbsp. organic tomato paste
1 ½ lb. turkey breast, diced
1 tbsp. Dijon mustard
½ tsp. dried savory or dill
1 tbsp. onion flakes
½ tsp. ground allspice
1 small garlic clove, minced
½ tsp. sea salt
¼ tsp. black pepper
1 tbsp. liquid aminos
2 tbsp. grated parmesan cheese

Instructions

1. Pre-heat Air Fryer to 375°F.
2. Coat the inside of a baking dish with a little oil.
3. Mix together the egg, dill, tomato paste, liquid aminos, mustard, salt, dill, garlic, pepper and allspice using a whisk. Stir in the diced turkey, followed by the walnuts, cheese and onion flakes.
4. Transfer the mixture to the greased baking dish and bake in the Air Fryer for 40 minutes.
5. Serve hot.

Charcoal Chicken

Prep + Cook Time: 20 minutes | Servings: 2

Ingredients

2 medium skinless, boneless chicken breasts
½ tsp. salt
3 tbsp. Cajun spice
1 tbsp. olive oil

Instructions

1. Massage the salt and Cajun spice into the chicken breasts. Drizzle with olive oil.
2. Pre-heat the Air Fryer to 370°F.
3. Place the chicken in the fryer and cook for 7 minutes.
4. Flip both chicken breasts over and cook for an additional 3 – 4 minutes.
5. Slice up before serving.

Battered Chicken Thighs

Prep + Cook Time: 4 hours 45 minutes | Servings: 4

Ingredients
2 cups buttermilk
3 tsp. salt
1 tsp. cayenne pepper
1 tbsp. paprika
1 ½ lb. chicken thighs
2 tsp. black pepper
2 cups flour
1 tbsp. garlic powder
1 tbsp. baking powder

Instructions
1. Put the chicken thighs in a large bowl.
2. In a separate bowl, combine the buttermilk, salt, cayenne, and black pepper.
3. Coat the thighs with the buttermilk mixture. Place a sheet of aluminum foil over the bowl and set in the refrigerator for 4 hours.
4. Pre-heat your Air Fryer to 400°F.
5. Combine together the flour, baking powder, and paprika in a shallow bowl. Cover a baking dish with a layer of parchment paper.
6. Coat the chicken thighs in the flour mixture and bake in the fryer for 10 minutes. Turn the thighs over and air fry for another 8 minutes. You will have to do this in two batches.

Chicken Bites

Prep + Cook Time: 30 minutes | Servings: 4

Ingredients
1 lb. skinless, boneless chicken breasts
¼ cup blue cheese salad dressing
¼ cup blue cheese, crumbled
½ cup sour cream
1 cup friendly bread crumbs
1 tbsp. olive oil
½ tsp. salt
¼ tsp. black pepper

Instructions
1. In a large bowl, combine the salad dressing, sour cream, and blue cheese.
2. In a separate bowl, combine the bread crumbs, olive oil, salt and pepper.
3. Chop the chicken breast into 1 - 2-inch pieces and coat in the bread crumbs.
4. Pre-heat the Air Fryer to 380°F.
5. Place the chicken bites in your fryer's basket.
6. Cook for 12 – 15 minutes. When cooked through and crispy, serve with the sauce of your choice.

Coconut Chicken

Prep + Cook Time: 45 minutes | Servings: 2 – 4

Ingredients
3 pcs whole chicken leg [skinless or with skin, it's up to you]
1.8 oz. pure coconut paste [alternatively, 1.8 oz. coconut milk]
4 – 5 tsp. ground turmeric
1.8 oz. old ginger
1.8 oz. galangal [a.k.a. lengkuas]
¾ tbsp. salt

Instructions
1. Mix together all of the ingredients, except for the chicken.

2. Slice a few slits into the chicken leg, mainly around the thick parts. This will help the chicken absorb the marinade.
3. Coat the chicken in the mixture and set aside to absorb.
4. Pre-heat the Air Fryer at 375°F.
5. Air fry the chicken for 20 – 25 minutes, turning it once halfway through, until golden brown.

Simple Turkey Breasts

Prep + Cook Time: 35 minutes | Servings: 5

Ingredients
6 – 7 lb. skinless, boneless turkey breast
2 tsp. salt
1 tsp. black pepper
½ tsp. dried cumin
2 tbsp. olive oil

Instructions
1. Massage all of the other ingredients into the turkey breast.
2. Pre-heat the Air Fryer to 340°F,
3. Cook the turkey breast for 15 minutes. Turn it over and cook for an additional 10 – 15 minutes, until cooked through and crispy.
4. Slice and serve the turkey with rice or fresh vegetables.

Chicken Wrapped in Bacon

Prep + Cook Time: 25 minutes | Servings: 6

Ingredients
6 rashers unsmoked back bacon
1 small chicken breast
1 tbsp. garlic soft cheese

Instructions
1. Cut the chicken breast into six bite-sized pieces.
2. Spread the soft cheese across one side of each slice of bacon.
3. Put the chicken on top of the cheese and wrap the bacon around it, holding it in place with a toothpick.
4. Transfer the wrapped chicken pieces to the Air Fryer and cook for 15 minutes at 350°F.

Chicken, Rice & Vegetables

Prep + Cook Time: 30 minutes | Servings: 4

Ingredients
1 lb. skinless, boneless chicken breasts
½ lb. button mushrooms, sliced
1 medium onion, chopped
1 package [10 oz.] Alfredo sauce
2 cups cooked rice
½ tsp. dried thyme
1 tbsp. olive oil
Salt and black pepper to taste

Instructions
1. Slice up the chicken breasts into 1-inch cubes.
2. In a large bowl, combine all of the ingredients. Sprinkle on salt and dried thyme and mix again.
3. Pre-heat the Air Fryer to 370°F and drizzle the basket with the olive oil.
4. Place the chicken and vegetables in the fryer and cook for 10 – 12 minutes. Stir the contents now and again.
5. Pour in the Alfredo sauce and allow to cook for an additional 3 – 4 minutes.
6. Serve with rice if desired.

Breadcrumb Turkey Breasts

Prep + Cook Time: 25 minutes | Servings: 6

Ingredients
6 turkey breasts
1 stick butter, melted
1 tsp. salt
2 cups friendly breadcrumbs
½ tsp. cayenne pepper
½ tsp. black pepper

Instructions
1. Put the breadcrumbs, half a teaspoon of the salt, a quarter teaspoon of the pepper, and the cayenne pepper in a large bowl. Combine well.
2. In a separate bowl, sprinkle the melted butter with the rest of the salt and pepper.
3. Coat the turkey breasts with the butter using a brush. Roll the turkey in the bread crumbs and transfer to a lined baking dish. Place in the Air Fryer.
4. Air fry at 390°F for 15 minutes.

Chicken Escallops

Prep + Cook Time: 45 minutes | Servings: 4

Ingredients
4 skinless chicken breasts
6 sage leaves
¼ cup friendly bread crumbs
2 eggs, beaten
½ cup flour
¼ cup parmesan cheese
Cooking spray

Instructions
1. Cut the chicken breasts into thin slices.
2. In a bowl, combine the sage and parmesan. Add in the flour, beaten eggs, salt and pepper and mix well.
3. Cover the chicken in the mixture before rolling it in the bread crumbs.
4. Grease the pan with the cooking spray.
5. Pre-heat your Air Fryer to 390°F and cook the chicken for 20 minutes, until it turns golden. Serve with rice.

Turkey & Maple Mustard

Prep + Cook Time: 70 minutes | Servings: 6

Ingredients
5 lb. whole turkey breast
1 tbsp. olive oil
1 tsp. dried thyme
½ tsp. smoked paprika
½ tsp. dried sage
1 tsp. sea salt
½ tsp. black pepper
1 tbsp. unsalted butter, melted
2 tbsp. Dijon mustard
¼ cup maple syrup

Instructions
1. Pre-heat the fryer to 350°F.
2. Brush the turkey breast with the olive oil.
3. Mix together the thyme, paprika, sage, salt, and pepper. Coat the turkey breast all over with this mixture.
4. Put the turkey breast in the Air Fryer basket and allow to cook for 25 minutes.
5. Flip it over and cook on the other side for a further 12 minutes.
6. Turn it once again and cook for another 12 minutes.
7. Check the temperature with a meat thermometer and ensure it has reached 165°F before removing it from the fryer.

8. In the meantime, combine the maple syrup, mustard, and melted butter in a saucepan over a medium heat. Stir continuously until a smooth consistency is achieved.
9. Pour the sauce over the cooked turkey in the fryer.
10. Cook for a final 5 minutes, ensuring the turkey turns brown and crispy.
11. Allow the turkey to rest, under a layer of aluminum foil, before carving up and serving.

Chicken Wings

Prep + Cook Time: 55 minutes | Servings: 4

Ingredients
3 lb. bone-in chicken wings
¾ cup flour
1 tbsp. old bay seasoning
4 tbsp. butter
Couple fresh lemons

Instructions
1. In a bowl, combine the all-purpose flour and Old Bay seasoning.
2. Toss the chicken wings with the mixture to coat each one well.
3. Pre-heat the Air Fryer to 375°F.
4. Give the wings a shake to shed any excess flour and place each one in the Air Fryer. You may have to do this in multiple batches, so as to not overlap any.
5. Cook for 30 – 40 minutes, shaking the basket frequently, until the wings are cooked through and crispy.
6. In the meantime, melt the butter in a frying pan over a low heat. Squeeze one or two lemons and add the juice to the pan. Mix well.
7. Serve the wings topped with the sauce.

Mozzarella Turkey Rolls

Prep + Cook Time: 20 minutes | Servings: 4

Ingredients
4 slices turkey breast
1 cup sliced fresh mozzarella
1 tomato, sliced
½ cup fresh basil
4 chive shoots

Instructions
1. Pre-heat your Air Fryer to 390°F.
2. Lay the slices of mozzarella, tomato and basil on top of each turkey slice.
3. Roll the turkey up, enclosing the filling well, and secure by tying a chive shoot around each one.
4. Put in the Air Fryer and cook for 10 minutes. Serve with a salad if desired.

Sage & Onion Turkey Balls

Prep + Cook Time: 40 minutes | Servings: 2

Ingredients
3.5 oz. turkey mince
½ small onion, diced
1 medium egg
1 tsp. sage
½ tsp. garlic, pureed
3 tbsp. friendly bread crumbs
Salt to taste
Pepper to taste

Instructions
1. Put all of the ingredients in a bowl and mix together well.
2. Take equal portions of the mixture and mold each one into a small ball. Transfer to the Air Fryer and cook for 15 minutes at 350°F.
3. Serve with tartar sauce and mashed potatoes.

Marinated Flank Steak

Prep + Cook Time: 15 minutes | Servings: 4

Ingredients

¾ lb. flank steak
1 ½ tbsp. sake
1 tbsp. brown miso paste
1 tsp. honey
2 cloves garlic, pressed
1 tbsp. olive oil

Instructions

1.   Put all of the ingredients in a Ziploc bag. Shake to cover the steak well with the seasonings and refrigerate for at least 1 hour.
2.   Coat all sides of the steak with cooking spray.
3.   Put the steak in the Air Fryer baking pan.
4.   Cook at 400°F for 12 minutes, turning the steak twice during the cooking time, then serve immediately.

Fried Steak

Prep + Cook Time: 15 minutes | Servings: 1

Ingredients

3 cm-thick beef steak
Pepper and salt to taste

Instructions

1.   Pre-heat the Air Fryer 400°F for 5 minutes.
2.   Place the beef steak in the baking tray and sprinkle on pepper and salt.
3.   Spritz the steak with cooking spray.
4.   Allow to cook for 3 minutes. Turn the steak over and cook on the other side for 3 more minutes. Serve hot.

Homemade Meatballs

Prep + Cook Time: 20 minutes | Servings: 4

Ingredients

1 lb. ground beef
1 tsp. red Thai curry paste
½ lime, rind and juice
1 tsp. Chinese spice
2 tsp. lemongrass, finely chopped
1 tbsp. sesame oil

Instructions

1.   Mix all of the ingredients in a bowl, combining well.
2.   Take 24 equal amounts of the mixture and shape each one into a meatball. Put them in the Air Fryer cooking basket.
3.   Cook at 380°F for 10 minutes.
4.   Turn them over and cook for a further 5 minutes on the other side, ensuring they are well-cooked before serving with your favorite dipping sauce.

Crumbed Filet Mignon

Prep + Cook Time: 20 minutes | Servings: 4

Ingredients

½ lb. filet mignon
Sea salt and ground black pepper, to taste
½ tsp. cayenne pepper
1 tsp. dried basil
1 tsp. dried rosemary
1 tsp. dried thyme

1 tbsp. sesame oil
1 small-sized egg, well-whisked
½ cup friendly breadcrumbs

Instructions

1.   Cover the filet mignon with the salt, black pepper, cayenne pepper, basil, rosemary, and thyme. Coat with a light brushing of sesame oil.
2.   Put the egg in a shallow plate.
3.   Pour the friendly breadcrumbs in another plate.
4.   Dip the filet mignon into the egg. Roll it into the crumbs.
5.   Transfer the steak to the Air Fryer and cook for 10 to 13 minutes at 360°F or until it turns golden.
6.   Serve with a salad.

Grilled Beef Ribs

Prep + Cook Time: 20 minutes + marinating time | Servings: 4

Ingredients

1 lb. meaty beef ribs
3 tbsp. apple cider vinegar
1 cup coriander, finely chopped
1 heaped tbsp. fresh basil leaves, chopped
2 garlic cloves, finely chopped
1 chipotle powder
1 tsp. fennel seeds
1 tsp. hot paprika
Kosher salt and black pepper, to taste
½ cup vegetable oil

Instructions

1.   Wash and dry the ribs.
2.   Coat the ribs with the rest of the ingredients and refrigerate for a minimum of 3 hours.
3.   Separate the ribs from the marinade and put them on an Air Fryer grill pan.
4.   Cook at 360°F for 8 minutes, or longer as needed.
5.   Pour the remaining marinade over the ribs before serving immediately.

London Broil

Prep + Cook Time: 30 minutes + marinating time | Servings: 8

Ingredients

2 lb. London broil
3 large garlic cloves, minced
3 tbsp. balsamic vinegar
3 tbsp. whole-grain mustard
2 tbsp. olive oil
Sea salt and ground black pepper, to taste
½ tsp. dried hot red pepper flakes

Instructions

1.   Wash and dry the London broil. Score its sides with a knife.
2.   Mix together the rest of the ingredients. Rub this mixture into the broil, coating it well. Allow to marinate for a minimum of 3 hours.
3.   Cook the meat at 400°F for 15 minutes.
4.   Turn it over and cook for an additional 10 - 12 minutes before serving.

Smoked Beef Roast

Prep + Cook Time: 45 minutes | Servings: 8

Ingredients
2 lb. roast beef, at room temperature
2 tbsp. extra-virgin olive oil
1 tsp. sea salt flakes
1 tsp. black pepper, preferably freshly ground
1 tsp. smoked paprika
Few dashes of liquid smoke
2 jalapeño peppers, thinly sliced

Instructions
1.   Pre-heat the Air Fryer to 330°F.
2.   With kitchen towels, pat the beef dry.
3.   Massage the extra-virgin olive oil and seasonings into the meat. Cover with liquid smoke.
4.   Place the beef in the Air Fryer and roast for 30 minutes. Flip the roast over and allow to cook for another 15 minutes.
5.   When cooked through, serve topped with sliced jalapeños.

Vegetables & Beef Cubes

Prep + Cook Time: 20 minutes + marinating time | Servings: 4

Ingredients
1 lb. top round steak, cut into cubes
2 tbsp. olive oil
1 tbsp. apple cider vinegar
1 tsp. fine sea salt
½ tsp. ground black pepper
1 tsp. shallot powder
¾ tsp. smoked cayenne pepper
½ tsp. garlic powder
¼ tsp. ground cumin
¼ lb. broccoli, cut into florets
¼ lb. mushrooms, sliced
1 tsp. dried basil
1 tsp. celery seeds

Instructions
1.   Massage the olive oil, vinegar, salt, black pepper, shallot powder, cayenne pepper, garlic powder, and cumin into the cubed steak, ensuring to coat each piece evenly.
2.   Allow to marinate for a minimum of 3 hours.
3.   Put the beef cubes in the Air Fryer cooking basket and allow to cook at 365°F for 12 minutes.
4.   When the steak is cooked through, place it in a bowl.
5.   Wipe the grease from the cooking basket and pour in the vegetables. Season them with basil and celery seeds.
6.   Cook at 400°F for 5 to 6 minutes. When the vegetables are hot, serve them with the steak.

Beef & Kale Omelet

Prep + Cook Time: 20 minutes | Servings: 4

Ingredients
Cooking spray
½ lb. leftover beef, coarsely chopped
2 garlic cloves, pressed
1 cup kale, torn into pieces and wilted
1 tomato, chopped
¼ tsp. sugar
4 eggs, beaten
4 tbsp. heavy cream
½ tsp. turmeric powder
Salt and ground black pepper to taste

1/8 tsp. ground allspice

Instructions
1.   Grease four ramekins with cooking spray.
2.   Place equal amounts of each of the ingredients into each ramekin and mix well.
3.   Air-fry at 360°F for 16 minutes, or longer if necessary. Serve immediately.

Cheeseburgers

Prep + Cook Time: 15 minutes | Servings: 4

Ingredients
¾ lb. ground chuck
1 envelope onion soup mix
Kosher salt and freshly ground black pepper, to taste
1 tsp. paprika
4 slices Monterey-Jack cheese
4 ciabatta rolls
Mustard and pickled salad, to serve

Instructions
1.   In a bowl, stir together the ground chuck, onion soup mix, salt, black pepper, and paprika to combine well.
2.   Pre-heat your Air Fryer at 385°F.
3.   Take four equal portions of the mixture and mold each one into a patty. Transfer to the fryer and air fry for 10 minutes.
4.   Put the slices of cheese on the top of the burgers.
5.   Cook for another minute before serving on ciabatta rolls along with mustard and the pickled salad of your choosing.

Simple Beef

Prep + Cook Time: 25 minutes | Servings: 1

Ingredients
1 thin beef schnitzel
1 egg, beaten
½ cup friendly bread crumbs
2 tbsp. olive oil
Pepper and salt to taste

Instructions
1.   Pre-heat the Air Fryer to 350°F.
2.   In a shallow dish, combine the bread crumbs, oil, pepper, and salt.
3.   In a second shallow dish, place the beaten egg.
4.   Dredge the schnitzel in the egg before rolling it in the bread crumbs.
5.   Put the coated schnitzel in the fryer basket and air fry for 12 minutes.

Meatloaf

Prep + Cook Time: 30 minutes | Servings: 4

Ingredients
1 lb. ground beef
1 egg, beaten
1 mushrooms, sliced
1 tbsp. thyme
1 small onion, chopped
3 tbsp. friendly breadcrumbs
Pepper to taste

Instructions
1.   Pre-heat the Air Fryer at 400°F.
2.   Place all the ingredients into a large bowl and combine entirely.
3.   Transfer the meatloaf mixture into the loaf pan, and move it to the Air Fryer basket.
4.   Cook for 25 minutes. Slice up before serving.

Beef Burgers

Prep + Cook Time: 65 minutes | Servings: 4

Ingredients

10.5 oz. beef, minced
1 onion, diced
1 tsp. garlic, minced or pureed
1 tsp. tomato, pureed
1 tsp. mustard
1 tsp. basil
1 tsp. mixed herbs
Salt to taste
Pepper to taste
1 oz. cheddar cheese
4 buns
Salad leaves

Instructions

1. Drizzle the Air Fryer with one teaspoon of olive oil and allow it to warm up.
2. Place the diced onion in the fryer and fry until they turn golden brown.
3. Mix in all of the seasoning and cook for 25 minutes at 390°F.
4. Lay 2 – 3 onion rings and pureed tomato on two of the buns. Place one slice of cheese and the layer of beef on top. Top with salad leaves and any other condiments you desire before closing off the sandwich with the other buns.
5. Serve with ketchup, cold drink and French fries.

Brussels Sprouts & Tender Beef Chuck

Prep + Cook Time: 25 minutes + marinating time | Servings: 4

Ingredients

1 lb. beef chuck shoulder steak
2 tbsp. vegetable oil
1 tbsp. red wine vinegar
1 tsp. fine sea salt
½ tsp. ground black pepper
1 tsp. smoked paprika
1 tsp. onion powder
½ tsp. garlic powder
½ lb. Brussels sprouts, cleaned and halved
½ tsp. fennel seeds
1 tsp. dried basil
1 tsp. dried sage

Instructions

1. Massage the beef with the vegetable oil, wine vinegar, salt, black pepper, paprika, onion powder, and garlic powder, coating it well.
2. Allow to marinate for a minimum of 3 hours.
3. Air fry at 390°F for 10 minutes.
4. Put the prepared Brussels sprouts in the fryer along with the fennel seeds, basil, and sage.
5. Lower the heat to 380°F and cook everything for another 5 minutes.
6. Pause the machine and give the contents a good stir. Cook for an additional 10 minutes.
7. Take out the beef and allow the vegetables too cook for a few more minutes if necessary or desired.
8. Serve everything together with the sauce of your choice.

Swedish Meatballs

Prep + Cook Time: 25 minutes | Servings: 8

Ingredients

1 lb. ground beef
2 friendly bread slices, crumbled
1 small onion, minced
½ tsp. garlic salt
1 cup tomato sauce
2 cups pasta sauce
1 egg, beaten
2 carrots, shredded
Pepper and salt to taste

Instructions

1. Pre-heat Air Fryer to 400°F.
2. In a bowl, combine the ground beef, egg, carrots, crumbled bread, onion, garlic salt, pepper and salt.
3. Divide the mixture into equal amounts and shape each one into a small meatball.
4. Put them in the Air Fryer basket and cook for 7 minutes.
5. Transfer the meatballs to an oven-safe dish and top with the tomato sauce.
6. Set the dish into the Air Fryer basket and allow to cook at 320°F for 5 more minutes. Serve hot.

German Schnitzel

Prep + Cook Time: 15 minutes | Servings: 4

Ingredients

4 thin beef schnitzel
1 tbsp. sesame seeds
2 tbsp. paprika
3 tbsp. olive oil
4 tbsp. flour
2 eggs, beaten
1 cup friendly bread crumbs
Pepper and salt to taste

Instructions

1. Pre-heat the Air Fryer at 350°F.
2. Sprinkle the pepper and salt on the schnitzel.
3. In a shallow dish, combine the paprika, flour, and salt
4. In a second shallow dish, mix the bread crumbs with the sesame seeds.
5. Place the beaten eggs in a bowl.
6. Coat the schnitzel in the flour mixture. Dip it into the egg before rolling it in the bread crumbs.
7. Put the coated schnitzel in the Air Fryer basket and allow to cook for 12 minutes before serving hot.

Steak Total

Prep + Cook Time: 30 minutes | Servings: 4

Ingredients

2 lb. rib eye steak
1 tbsp. olive oil
1 tbsp. steak rub

Instructions

1. Set the Air Fryer to 400°F and allow to warm for 4 minutes.
2. Massage the olive oil and steak rub into both sides of the steak.
3. Put the steak in the fryer's basket and cook for 14 minutes. Turn the steak over and cook on the other side for another 7 minutes.
4. Serve hot.

Betty's Beef Roast

Prep + Cook Time: 65 minutes | Servings: 6

Ingredients

2 lb. beef
1 tbsp. olive oil
1 tsp. dried rosemary
1 tsp. dried thyme
½ tsp. black pepper
½ tsp. oregano
½ tsp. garlic powder
1 tsp. salt
1 tsp. onion powder

Instructions

1. Preheat the Air Fryer to 330°F.
2. In a small bowl, mix together all of the spices.
3. Coat the beef with a brushing of olive oil.
4. Massage the spice mixture into the beef.
5. Transfer the meat to the Air Fryer and cook for 30 minutes. Turn it over and cook on the other side for another 25 minutes.

Beef Meatloaf

Prep + Cook Time: 30 minutes | Servings: 4

Ingredients

¾ lb. ground chuck
¼ lb. ground pork sausage
1 cup shallots, finely chopped
2 eggs, well beaten
3 tbsp. plain milk
1 tbsp. oyster sauce
1 tsp. porcini mushrooms
½ tsp. cumin powder
1 tsp. garlic paste
1 tbsp. fresh parsley
Seasoned salt and crushed red pepper flakes to taste
1 cup crushed saltines

Instructions

1. Mix together all of the ingredients in a large bowl, combining everything well.
2. Transfer to the Air Fryer baking dish and cook at 360°F for 25 minutes.
3. Serve hot.

Stuffed Bell Pepper

Prep + Cook Time: 25 minutes | Servings: 4

Ingredients

4 bell peppers, cut top of bell pepper
16 oz. ground beef
2/3 cup cheese, shredded
½ cup rice, cooked
1 tsp. basil, dried
½ tsp. chili powder
1 tsp. black pepper
1 tsp. garlic salt
2 tsp. Worcestershire sauce
8 oz. tomato sauce
2 garlic cloves, minced
1 small onion, chopped

Instructions

1. Grease a frying pan with cooking spray and fry the onion and garlic over a medium heat.
2. Stir in the beef, basil, chili powder, black pepper, and garlic salt, combining everything well. Allow to cook until the beef is nicely browned, before taking the pan off the heat.
3. Add in half of the cheese, the rice, Worcestershire sauce, and tomato sauce and stir to combine.
4. Spoon equal amounts of the beef mixture into the four bell peppers, filling them entirely.
5. Pre-heat the Air Fryer at 400°F.
6. Spritz the Air Fryer basket with cooking spray.
7. Put the stuffed bell peppers in the basket and allow to cook for 11 minutes.
8. Add the remaining cheese on top of each bell pepper with remaining cheese and cook for a further 2 minutes. When the cheese is melted and the bell peppers are piping hot, serve immediately.

Asian Beef Burgers

Prep + Cook Time: 20 minutes | Servings: 4

Ingredients

¾ lb. lean ground beef
1 tbsp. soy sauce
1 tsp. Dijon mustard
Few dashes of liquid smoke
1 tsp. shallot powder
1 clove garlic, minced
½ tsp. cumin powder
¼ cup scallions, minced
⅓ tsp. sea salt flakes
⅓ tsp. freshly cracked mixed peppercorns
1 tsp. celery seeds
1 tsp. parsley flakes

Instructions

1. Mix together all of the ingredients in a bowl using your hands, combining everything well.
2. Take four equal amounts of the mixture and mold each one into a patty.
3. Use the back of a spoon to create a shallow dip in the center of each patty. This will prevent them from puffing up during the cooking process.
4. Lightly coat all sides of the patties with cooking spray.
5. Place each one in the Air Fryer and cook for roughly 12 minutes at 360°F.
6. Test with a meat thermometer – the patties are ready once they have reached 160°F. Serve them on top of butter rolls with any sauces and toppings you desire.

Burger Patties

Prep + Cook Time: 15 minutes | Servings: 6

Ingredients

1 lb. ground beef
6 cheddar cheese slices
Pepper and salt to taste

Instructions

1. Pre-heat the Air Fryer to 350°F.
2. Sprinkle the salt and pepper on the ground beef.
3. Shape six equal portions of the ground beef into patties and put each one in the Air Fryer basket.
4. Air fry the patties for 10 minutes.
5. Top the patties with the cheese slices and air fry for one more minute.
6. Serve the patties on top of dinner rolls.

Beef Rolls

Prep + Cook Time: 30 minutes | Servings: 2

Ingredients

2 lb. beef flank steak
3 tsp. pesto
1 tsp. black pepper
6 slices of provolone cheese
3 oz. roasted red bell peppers
¾ cup baby spinach
1 tsp. sea salt

Instructions

1.   Spoon equal amounts of the pesto onto each flank steak and spread it across evenly.
2.   Place the cheese, roasted red peppers and spinach on top of the meat, about three-quarters of the way down.
3.   Roll the steak up, holding it in place with toothpicks. Sprinkle on the sea salt and pepper.
4.   Place inside the Air Fryer and cook for 14 minutes at 400°F, turning halfway through the cooking time.
5.   Allow the beef to rest for 10 minutes before slicing up and serving.

Spring Rolls

Prep + Cook Time: 35 minutes | Servings: 20

Ingredients

⅓ cup noodles
1 cup beef minced
2 tbsp. cold water
1 packet spring roll sheets
1 tsp. soy sauce
1 cup fresh mix vegetables
3 garlic cloves, minced
1 small onion, diced
1 tbsp. sesame oil

Instructions

1.   Cook the noodle in hot water to soften them up, drain them and snip them to make them shorter.
2.   In a frying pan over medium heat, cook the minced beef, soy sauce, mixed vegetables, garlic, and onion in a little oil until the beef minced is cooked through. Take the pan off the heat and throw in the noodles. Mix well to incorporate everything.
3.   Unroll a spring roll sheet and lay it flat. Scatter the filling diagonally across it and roll it up, brushing the edges lightly with water to act as an adhesive. Repeat until you have used up all of the sheets and the filling.
4.   Pre-heat the Air Fryer to 350°F.
5.   Coat each spring roll with a light brushing of oil and transfer to the fryer.
6.   Cook for 8 minutes and serve hot.

Cheesy Schnitzel

Prep + Cook Time: 30 minutes | Servings: 1

Ingredients

1 thin beef schnitzel
1 egg, beaten
½ cup friendly bread crumbs
2 tbsp. olive oil
3 tbsp. pasta sauce
¼ cup parmesan cheese, grated
Pepper and salt to taste

Instructions

1.   Pre-heat the Air Fryer to 350°F.
2.   In a shallow dish, combine the bread crumbs, olive oil, pepper, and salt. In another shallow dish, put the beaten egg.
3.   Cover the schnitzel in the egg before press it into the breadcrumb mixture and placing it in the Air Fryer basket. Cook for 15 minutes.
4.   Pour the pasta sauce over the schnitzel and top with the grated cheese. Cook for an additional 5 minutes until the cheese melts. Serve hot.

Beef Schnitzel

Prep + Cook Time: 30 minutes | Servings: 1

Ingredients

1 egg
1 thin beef schnitzel
3 tbsp. friendly bread crumbs
2 tbsp. olive oil
1 parsley, roughly chopped
½ lemon, cut in wedges

Instructions:

1.   Pre-heat your Air Fryer to the 360°F.
2.   In a bowl combine the bread crumbs and olive oil to form a loose, crumbly mixture.
3.   Beat the egg with a whisk.
4.   Coat the schnitzel first in the egg and then in the bread crumbs, ensuring to cover it fully.
5.   Place the schnitzel in the Air Fryer and cook for 12 – 14 minutes. Garnish the schnitzel with the lemon wedges and parsley before serving.

Mighty Meatballs

Prep + Cook Time: 20 minutes | Servings: 4

Ingredients

1 egg
½ lb. beef minced
½ cup friendly breadcrumbs
1 tbsp. parsley, chopped
2 tbsp. raisins
1 cup onion, chopped and fried
½ tbsp. pepper
½ tsp. salt

Instructions

1.   Place all of the ingredients in a bowl and combine well.
2.   Use your hands to shape equal amounts of the mixture into small balls. Place each one in the Air Fryer basket.
3.   Air fry the meatballs at 350°F for 15 minutes. Serve with the sauce of your choice.

Bjorn's Beef Steak

Prep + Cook Time: 15 minutes | Servings: 1

Ingredients

1 steak, 1-inch thick
1 tbsp. olive oil
Black pepper to taste
Sea salt to taste

Instructions

1. Place the baking tray inside the Air Fryer and pre-heat for about 5 minutes at 390°F.
2. Brush or spray both sides of the steak with the oil.
3. Season both sides with salt and pepper.
4. Take care when placing the steak in the baking tray and allow to cook for 3 minutes. Flip the meat over, and cook for an additional 3 minutes.
5. Take it out of the fryer and allow to sit for roughly 3 minutes before serving.

Beef & Broccoli

Prep + Cook Time: 25 minutes | Servings: 4

Ingredients

1 lb. broccoli, cut into florets
¾ lb. round steak, cut into strips
1 garlic clove, minced
1 tsp. ginger, minced
1 tbsp. olive oil
1 tsp. cornstarch
1 tsp. sugar
1 tsp. soy sauce
⅓ cup sherry wine
2 tsp. sesame oil
⅓ cup oyster sauce

Instructions

1. In a bowl, combine the sugar, soy sauce, sherry wine, cornstarch, sesame oil, and oyster sauce.
2. Place the steak strips in the bowl, coat each one with the mixture and allow to marinate for 45 minutes.
3. Put the broccoli in the Air Fryer and lay the steak on top.
4. Top with the olive oil, garlic and ginger.
5. Cook at 350°F for 12 minutes. Serve hot with rice if desired.

Beef & Mushrooms

Prep + Cook Time: 3 hours 15 minutes | Servings: 1

Ingredients

6 oz. beef
¼ onion, diced
½ cup mushroom slices
2 tbsp. favorite marinade [preferably bulgogi]

Instructions

1. Slice or cube the beef and put it in a bowl.
2. Cover the meat with the marinade, place a layer of aluminum foil or saran wrap over the bowl, and place the bowl in the refrigerator for 3 hours.
3. Put the meat in a baking dish along with the onion and mushrooms
4. Air Fry at 350°F for 10 minutes. Serve hot.

Max's Meatloaf

Prep + Cook Time: 35 minutes | Servings: 4

Ingredients

1 large onion, peeled and diced
2 kg. minced beef
1 tsp. Worcester sauce
3 tbsp. tomato ketchup
1 tbsp. basil
1 tbsp. oregano
1 tbsp. mixed herbs
1 tbsp. friendly bread crumbs
Salt & pepper to taste

Instructions

1. In a large bowl, combine the mince with the herbs, Worcester sauce, onion and tomato ketchup, incorporating every component well.
2. Pour in the breadcrumbs and give it another stir.
3. Transfer the mixture to a small dish and cook for 25 minutes in the Air Fryer at 350°F.

VEGAN & VEGETARIAN

Parmesan Artichokes

Prep + Cook Time: 35 minutes | Servings: 4

Ingredients

2 medium artichokes, trimmed and quartered, with the centers removed
2 tbsp. coconut oil, melted
1 egg, beaten
½ cup parmesan cheese, grated
¼ cup blanched, finely ground flour

Instructions

1.   Place the artichokes in a bowl with the coconut oil and toss to coat, then dip the artichokes into a bowl of beaten egg.
2.   In a separate bowl, mix together the parmesan cheese and the flour. Combine with the pieces of artichoke, making sure to coat each piece well. Transfer the artichoke to the fryer.
3.   Cook at 400°F for ten minutes, shaking occasionally throughout the cooking time. Serve hot.

Cheese Pizza with Broccoli Crust

Prep + Cook Time: 30 minutes | Servings: 1

Ingredients

3 cups broccoli rice, steamed
½ cup parmesan cheese, grated
1 egg
3 tbsp. low-carb Alfredo sauce
½ cup parmesan cheese, grated

Instructions

1.   Drain the broccoli rice and combine with the parmesan cheese and egg in a bowl, mixing well.
2.   Cut a piece of parchment paper roughly the size of the base of the fryer's basket. Spoon four equal-sized amounts of the broccoli mixture onto the paper and press each portion into the shape of a pizza crust. You may have to complete this part in two batches. Transfer the parchment to the fryer.
3.   Cook at 370°F for five minutes. When the crust is firm, flip it over and cook for an additional two minutes.
4.   Add the Alfredo sauce and mozzarella cheese on top of the crusts and cook for an additional seven minutes. The crusts are ready when the sauce and cheese have melted. Serve hot.

Stuffed Eggplant

Prep + Cook Time: 35 minutes | Servings: 2

Ingredients

large eggplant
¼ medium yellow onion, diced
2 tbsp. red bell pepper, diced
1 cup spinach
¼ cup artichoke hearts, chopped

Instructions

1.   Cut the eggplant lengthwise into slices and spoon out the flesh, leaving a shell about a half-inch thick. Chop it up and set aside.
2.   Set a skillet over a medium heat and spritz with cooking spray. Cook the onions for about three to five minutes to soften. Then add the pepper, spinach, artichokes, and the flesh of eggplant. Fry for a further five minutes, then remove from the heat.
3.   Scoop this mixture in equal parts into the eggplant shells and place each one in the fryer.

4.   Cook for twenty minutes at 320°F until the eggplant shells are soft. Serve warm.

Broccoli Salad

Prep + Cook Time: 15 minutes | Servings: 2

Ingredients

3 cups fresh broccoli florets
2 tbsp. coconut oil, melted
¼ cup sliced s
½ medium lemon, juiced

Instructions

1.   Take a six-inch baking dish and fill with the broccoli florets. Pour the melted coconut oil over the broccoli and add in the sliced s. Toss together. Put the dish in the air fryer.
2.   Cook at 380°F for seven minutes, stirring at the halfway point.
3.   Place the broccoli in a bowl and drizzle the lemon juice over it.

Roasted Cauliflower

Prep + Cook Time: 20 minutes | Servings: 2

Ingredients

medium head cauliflower
2 tbsp. salted butter, melted
1 medium lemon
1 tsp. dried parsley
½ tsp. garlic powder

Instructions

1.   Having removed the leaves from the cauliflower head, brush it with the melted butter. Grate the rind of the lemon over it and then drizzle some juice. Finally add the parsley and garlic powder on top.
2.   Transfer the cauliflower to the basket of the fryer.
3.   Cook for fifteen minutes at 350°F, checking regularly to ensure it doesn't overcook. The cauliflower is ready when it is hot and fork tender.
4.   Take care when removing it from the fryer, cut up and serve.

Mushroom Loaf

Prep + Cook Time: 20 minutes | Servings: 2

Ingredients

2 cups mushrooms, chopped
½ cups cheddar cheese, shredded
¾ cup flour
2 tbsp. butter, melted
2 eggs

Instructions

1.   In a food processor, pulse together the mushrooms, cheese, flour, melted butter, and eggs, along with some salt and pepper if desired, until a uniform consistency is achieved.
2.   Transfer into a silicone loaf pan, spreading and levelling with a palette knife.
3.   Pre-heat the fryer at 375°F and put the rack inside.
4.   Set the loaf pan on the rack and cook for fifteen minutes.
5.   Take care when removing the pan from the fryer and leave it to cool. Then slice and serve.

Green Bean Casserole

Prep + Cook Time: 10 minutes | Servings: 2

Ingredients

tbsp. butter, melted
1 cup green beans
6 oz. cheddar cheese, shredded
7 oz. parmesan cheese, shredded
¼ cup heavy cream

Instructions

1. Pre-heat your fryer at 400°F.
2. Take a baking dish small enough to fit inside the fryer and cover the bottom with melted butter. Throw in the green beans, cheddar cheese, and any seasoning as desired, then give it a stir. Add the parmesan on top and finally the heavy cream.
3. Cook in the fryer for six minutes. Allow to cool before serving.

Cabbage Steaks

Prep + Cook Time: 5 minutes | Servings: 2

Ingredients

small head cabbage
1 tsp. butter, butter
1 tsp. paprika
1 tsp. olive oil

Instructions

1. Halve the cabbage.
2. In a bowl, mix together the melted butter, paprika, and olive oil. Massage into the cabbage slices, making sure to coat it well. Season as desired with salt and pepper or any other seasonings of your choosing.
3. Pre-heat the fryer at 400°F and set the rack inside.
4. Put the cabbage in the fryer and cook for three minutes. Flip it and cook on the other side for another two minutes. Enjoy!

Zucchini Gratin

Prep + Cook Time: 15 minutes | Servings: 2

Ingredients

5 oz. parmesan cheese, shredded
1 tbsp. coconut flour
1 tbsp. dried parsley
2 zucchinis
1 tsp. butter, melted

Instructions

1. Mix the parmesan and coconut flour together in a bowl, seasoning with parsley to taste.
2. Cut the zucchini in half lengthwise and chop the halves into four slices.
3. Pre-heat the fryer at 400°F.
4. Pour the melted butter over the zucchini and then dip the zucchini into the parmesan-flour mixture, coating it all over. Cook the zucchini in the fryer for thirteen minutes.

Cheesy Kale

Prep + Cook Time: 15 minutes | Servings: 2

Ingredients

lb. kale
8 oz. parmesan cheese, shredded
1 onion, diced
1 tsp. butter
1 cup heavy cream

Instructions

1. Dice up the kale, discarding any hard stems. In a baking dish small enough to fit inside the fryer, combine the kale with the parmesan, onion, butter and cream.
2. Pre-heat the fryer at 250°F.
3. Set the baking dish in the fryer and cook for twelve minutes. Make sure to give it a good stir before serving.

Spaghetti Squash

Prep + Cook Time: 45 minutes | Servings: 2

Ingredients

spaghetti squash
1 tsp. olive oil
Salt and pepper
4 tbsp. heavy cream
1 tsp. butter

Instructions

1. Pre-heat your fryer at 360°F.
2. Cut and de-seed the spaghetti squash. Brush with the olive oil and season with salt and pepper to taste.
3. Put the squash inside the fryer, placing it cut-side-down. Cook for thirty minutes. Halfway through cooking, fluff the spaghetti inside the squash with a fork.
4. When the squash is ready, fluff the spaghetti some more, then pour some heavy cream and butter over it and give it a good stir. Serve with the low-carb tomato sauce of your choice.

SNACKS & SIDE DISHES

Chipotle Jicama Hash

Prep + Cook Time: 15 minutes | Servings: 2

Ingredients
4 slices bacon, chopped
12 oz jicama, peeled and diced
4 oz purple onion, chopped
1 oz green bell pepper (or poblano), seeded and chopped
4 tbsp Chipotle mayonnaise

Instructions
1. Using a skillet, brown the bacon on a high heat.
2. Remove and place on a towel to drain the grease.
3. Use the remaining grease to fry the onions and jicama until brown.
4. When ready, add the bell pepper and cook the hash until tender.
5. Transfer the hash onto two plates and serve each plate with 4 tablespoons of Chipotle mayonnaise.

Fried Queso Blanco

Prep + Cook Time: 170 minutes | Servings: 4

Ingredients
5 oz queso blanco
1 ½ tbsp olive oil
3 oz cheese
2 oz olives
1 pinch red pepper flakes

Instructions
1. Cube some cheese and freeze it for 1-2 hours.
2. Pour the oil in a skillet and heat to boil over a medium temperature.
3. Add the cheese cubes and heat till brown.
4. Combine the cheese together using a spatula and flatten.
5. Cook the cheese on both sides, flipping regularly.
6. While flipping, fold the cheese into itself to form crispy layers.
7. Use a spatula to roll it into a block.
8. Remove it from the pan, allow it to cool, cut it into small cubes, and serve.

Spinach with Bacon & Shallots

Prep + Cook Time: 30 minutes | Servings: 4

Ingredients
16 oz raw spinach
½ cup chopped white onion
½ cup chopped shallot
½ pound raw bacon slices
2 tbsp butter

Instructions
1. Slice the bacon strips into small narrow pieces.
2. In a skillet, heat the butter and add the chopped onion, shallots and bacon.
3. Sauté for 15-20 minutes or until the onions start to caramelize and the bacon is cooked.

4. Add the spinach and sauté on a medium heat. Stir frequently to ensure the leaves touch the skillet while cooking.
5. Cover and steam for around 5 minutes, stir and continue until wilted.
6. Serve!

Bacon-Wrapped Sausage Skewers

Prep + Cook Time: 8 minutes | Servings: 2

Ingredients
5 Italian chicken sausages
10 slices bacon

Instructions
1. Preheat your air fryer to 370°F/190°C.
2. Cut the sausage into four pieces.
3. Slice the bacon in half.
4. Wrap the bacon over the sausage.
5. Skewer the sausage.
6. Fry for 4-5 minutes until browned.

Roasted Brussels Sprouts & Bacon

Prep + Cook Time: 45 minutes | Servings: 2

Ingredients
24 oz brussels sprouts
¼ cup fish sauce
¼ cup bacon grease
6 strips bacon
Pepper to taste

Instructions
1. De-stem and quarter the brussels sprouts.
2. Mix them with the bacon grease and fish sauce.
3. Slice the bacon into small strips and cook.
4. Add the bacon and pepper to the sprouts.
5. Spread onto a greased pan and cook at 450°F/230°C for 35 minutes.
6. Stir every 5 minute or so.
7. Broil for a few more minutes and serve.

Ham & Cheese Rolls

Prep + Cook Time: 5 minutes | Servings: 4

Ingredients
16 slices ham
1 package chive and onion cream cheese (8 oz)
16 slices thin Swiss cheese

Instructions
1. Place the ham on a chopping board.
2. Dry the slices with a paper towel.
3. Thinly spread 2 teaspoons of Swiss cheese over each slice of ham.
4. On the clean section of ham, add a half inch slice of cheese.
5. On the cheese side, fold the ham over the cheese and roll it up.
6. Leave it as is, or slice into smaller rolls.

Hillbilly Cheese Surprise

Prep + Cook Time: 40 minutes | Servings: 6

Ingredients

4 cups broccoli florets
¼ cup ranch dressing
½ cup sharp cheddar cheese, shredded
¼ cup heavy whipping cream
Kosher salt and pepper to taste

Instructions

1. Preheat your fryer to 375°F/190°C.
2. In a bowl, combine all of the ingredients until the broccoli is well-covered.
3. In a casserole dish, spread out the broccoli mixture.
4. Bake for 30 minutes.
5. Take out of your fryer and mix.
6. If the florets are not tender, bake for another 5 minutes until tender.
7. Serve!

Parmesan & Garlic Cauliflower

Prep + Cook Time: 40 minutes | Servings: 4

Ingredients

3/4 cup cauliflower florets
2 tbsp butter
1 clove garlic, sliced thinly
2 tbsp shredded parmesan
1 pinch of salt

Instructions

1. Preheat your fryer to 350°F/175°C.
2. On a low heat, melt the butter with the garlic for 5-10 minutes.
3. Strain the garlic in a sieve.
4. Add the cauliflower, parmesan and salt.
5. Bake for 20 minutes or until golden.

Jalapeño Guacamole

Prep + Cook Time: 30 minutes | Servings: 4

Ingredients

2 Hass avocados, ripe
¼ red onion
1 jalapeño
1 tbsp fresh lime juice
Sea salt

Instructions

1. Spoon the avocado innings into a bowl.
2. Dice the jalapeño and onion.
3. Mash the avocado to the desired consistency.
4. Add in the onion, jalapeño and lime juice.
5. Sprinkle with salt.

Green Beans & s

Prep + Cook Time: 15 minutes | Servings: 4

Ingredients

1 lb fresh green beans, trimmed
2 tbsp butter
¼ cup sliced s
2 tsp lemon pepper

Instructions

1. Steam the green beans for 8 minutes, until tender, then drain.
2. On a medium heat, melt the butter in a skillet.
3. Sauté the s until browned.
4. Sprinkle with salt and pepper.
5. Mix in the green beans.

Sugar Snap Bacon

Prep + Cook Time: 10 minutes | Servings: 4

Ingredients

3 cups sugar snap peas
½ tbsp lemon juice
2 tbsp bacon fat
2 tsp garlic
½ tsp red pepper flakes

Instructions

1. In a skillet, cook the bacon fat until it begins to smoke.
2. Add the garlic and cook for 2 minutes.
3. Add the sugar peas and lemon juice.
4. Cook for 2-3 minutes.
5. Remove and sprinkle with red pepper flakes and lemon zest.
6. Serve!

Flax Cheese Chips

Prep + Cook Time: 20 minutes | Servings: 2

Ingredients

1 ½ cup cheddar cheese
4 tbsp ground flaxseed meal
Seasonings of your choice

Instructions

1. Preheat your fryer to 425°F/220°C.
2. Spoon 2 tablespoons of cheddar cheese into a mound, onto a non-stick pad.
3. Spread out a pinch of flax seed on each chip.
4. Season and bake for 10-15 minutes.

Country Style Chard

Prep + Cook Time: 5 minutes | Servings: 2

Ingredients

4 slices bacon, chopped
2 tbsp butter
2 tbsp fresh lemon juice
½ tsp garlic paste
1 bunch Swiss chard, stems removed, leaves cut into 1-inch pieces

Instructions

1. On a medium heat, cook the bacon in a skillet until the fat begins to brown.
2. Melt the butter in the skillet and add the lemon juice and garlic paste.
3. Add the chard leaves and cook until they begin to wilt.
4. Cover and turn up the heat to high.
5. Cook for 3 minutes.
6. Mix well, sprinkle with salt and serve.

Baked Tortillas

Prep + Cook Time: 30 minutes | Servings: 4

Ingredients

1 large head of cauliflower divided into florets.
4 large eggs
2 garlic cloves (minced)
1 ½ tsp herbs (whatever your favorite is - basil, oregano, thyme)
½ tsp salt

Instructions

1. Preheat your fryer to 375°F/190°C.
2. Put parchment paper on two baking sheets.
3. In a food processor, break down the cauliflower into rice.
4. Add ¼ cup water and the riced cauliflower to a saucepan.
5. Cook on a medium high heat until tender for 10 minutes. Drain.
6. Dry with a clean kitchen towel.
7. Mix the cauliflower, eggs, garlic, herbs and salt.
8. Make 4 thin circles on the parchment paper.
9. Bake for 20 minutes, until dry.

Homemade Mayonnaise

Prep + Cook Time: 30 minutes | Servings: 4

Ingredients

1 large egg
Juice from 1 lemon.
1 tsp dry mustard
½ tsp black pepper
1 cup avocado oil

Instructions

1. Combine the egg and lemon juice in a container and let sit for 20 minutes.
2. Add the dry mustard, pepper, and avocado oil.
3. Insert an electric whisk into the container.
4. Blend for 30 seconds.
5. Transfer to a sealed container and store in your refrigerator.

Hollandaise Sauce

Prep + Cook Time: 2 minutes | Servings: 8

Ingredients

8 large egg yolks
½ tsp salt
2 tbsp fresh lemon juice
1 cup unsalted butter

Instructions

1. Combine the egg yolks, salt, and lemon juice in a blender until smooth.
2. Put the butter in your microwave for around 60 seconds, until melted and hot.
3. Turn the blender on a low speed and slowly pour in the butter until the sauce begins to thicken.
4. Serve!

Granny's Green Beans

Prep + Cook Time: 10 minutes | Servings: 4

Ingredients

1 lb green beans, trimmed
1 cup butter
2 cloves garlic, minced
1 cup toasted pine nuts

Instructions

1. Boil a pot of water.
2. Add the green beans and cook until tender for 5 minutes.
3. Heat the butter in a large skillet over a high heat. Add the garlic and pine nuts and sauté for 2 minutes or until the pine nuts are lightly browned.
4. Transfer the green beans to the skillet and turn until coated.
5. Serve!

Mini Pepper Poppers

Prep + Cook Time: 10 minutes | Servings: 4

Ingredients

8 mini sweet peppers
¼ cup pepper jack cheese, shredded
4 slices sugar-free bacon, cooked and crumbled
4 oz. full-fat cream cheese, softened

Instructions

1. Prepare the peppers by cutting off the tops and halving them lengthwise. Then take out the membrane and the seeds.
2. In a small bowl, combine the pepper jack cheese, bacon, and cream cheese, making sure to incorporate everything well
3. Spoon equal-sized portions of the cheese-bacon mixture into each of the pepper halves.
4. Place the peppers inside your fryer and cook for eight minutes at 400°F. Take care when removing them from the fryer and enjoy warm.

Bacon-Wrapped Jalapeno Popper

Prep + Cook Time: 20 minutes | Servings: 4

Ingredients

6 jalapenos
1/3 cup medium cheddar cheese, shredded
¼ tsp. garlic powder
3 oz. full-fat cream cheese
12 slices sugar-free bacon

Instructions

1. Prepare the jalapenos by slicing off the tops and halving each one lengthwise. Take care when removing the seeds and membranes, wearing gloves if necessary.
2. In a microwavable bowl, combine the cheddar cheese, garlic powder, and cream cheese. Microwave for half a minute and mix again, before spoon equal parts of this mixture into each of the jalapeno halves.
3. Take a slice of bacon and wrap it around one of the jalapeno halves, covering it entirely. Place it in the basket of your fryer. Repeat with the rest of the bacon and jalapenos.
4. Cook at 400°F for twelve minutes, flipping the peppers halfway through in order to ensure the bacon gets crispy. Make sure not to let any of the contents spill out of the jalapeno halves when turning them.
5. Eat the peppers hot or at room temperature.

Cheesy Bacon Bread

Prep + Cook Time: 25 minutes | Servings: 2

Ingredients

4 slices sugar-free bacon, cooked and chopped
2 eggs
¼ cup pickled jalapenos, chopped
¼ cup parmesan cheese, grated
2 cups mozzarella cheese, shredded

Instructions

1. Add all of the ingredients together in a bowl and mix together.
2. Cut out a piece of parchment paper that will fit the base of your fryer's basket. Place it inside the fryer
3. With slightly wet hands, roll the mixture into a circle. You may have to form two circles to cook in separate batches, depending on the size of your fryer.
4. Place the circle on top of the parchment paper inside your fryer. Cook at 320°F for ten minutes.
5. Turn the bread over and cook for another five minutes.
6. The bread is ready when it is golden and cooked all the way through. Slice and serve warm.

Mozzarella Sticks

Prep + Cook Time: 60 minutes | Servings: 4

Ingredients

6 x 1-oz. mozzarella string cheese sticks
1 tsp. dried parsley
½ oz. pork rinds, finely ground
½ cup parmesan cheese, grated
2 eggs

Instructions

1. Halve the mozzarella sticks and freeze for forty-five minutes. Optionally you can leave them longer and place in a Ziploc bag to prevent them from becoming freezer burned.
2. In a small bowl, combine the dried parsley, pork rinds, and parmesan cheese.
3. In a separate bowl, beat the eggs with a fork.
4. Take a frozen mozzarella stick and dip it into the eggs, then into the pork rind mixture, making sure to coat it all over. Proceed with the rest of the cheese sticks, placing each coated stick in the basket of your air fryer.
5. Cook at 400°F for ten minutes, until they are golden brown.
6. Serve hot, with some homemade marinara sauce if desired.

Beef Jerky

Prep + Cook Time: 250 minutes | Servings: 4

Ingredients

¼ tsp. garlic powder
¼ tsp. onion powder
¼ cup soy sauce
2 tsp. Worcestershire sauce
1 lb. flat iron steak, thinly sliced

Instructions

1. In a bowl, combine the garlic powder, onion powder, soy sauce, and Worcestershire sauce. Marinade the beef slices with the mixture in an airtight bag, shaking it well to ensure the beef is well-coated. Leave to marinate for at least two hours
2. Place the meat in the basket of your air fryer, making sure it is evenly spaced. Cook the beef slices in more than one batch if necessary.
3. Cook for four hours at 160°F.
4. Allow to cool before serving. You can keep the jerky in an airtight container for up to a week, if you can resist it that long.

Bacon-Wrapped Brie

Prep + Cook Time: 15 minutes | Servings: 1

Ingredients

4 slices sugar-free bacon
8 oz. brie cheese

Instructions

1. On a cutting board, lay out the slices of bacon across each other in a star shape (two Xs overlaid). Then place the entire round of brie in the center of this star.
2. Lift each slice of bacon to wrap it over the brie and use toothpicks to hold everything in place. Cut up a piece of parchment paper to fit in your fryer's basket and place it inside, followed by the wrapped brie, setting it in the center of the sheet of parchment.
3. Cook at 400°F for seven minutes. Turn the brie over and cook for a further three minutes.
4. It is ready once the bacon is crispy and cheese is melted on the inside.
5. Slice up the brie and enjoy hot.

Crust-less Meaty Pizza

Prep + Cook Time: 15 minutes | Servings: 1

Ingredients

½ cup mozzarella cheese, shredded
2 slices sugar-free bacon, cooked and crumbled
¼ cup ground sausage, cooked
7 slices pepperoni
1 tbsp. parmesan cheese, grated

Instructions

1. Spread the mozzarella across the bottom of a six-inch cake pan. Throw on the bacon, sausage, and pepperoni, then add a sprinkle of the parmesan cheese on top. Place the pan inside your air fryer.
2. Cook at 400°F for five minutes. The cheese is ready once brown in color and bubbly. Take care when removing the pan from the fryer and serve.

Radish Chips

Prep + Cook Time: 15 minutes | Servings: 1

Ingredients

2 cups water
1 lb. radishes
½ tsp. garlic powder
¼ tsp. onion powder
2 tbsp. coconut oil, melted

Instructions

1. Boil the water over the stove.
2. In the meantime, prepare the radish chips. Slice off the tops and bottoms and, using a mandolin, shave into thin slices of equal size. Alternatively, this step can be completed using your food processor if it has a slicing blade.
3. Put the radish chips in the pot of boiling water and allow to cook for five minutes, ensuring they become translucent. Take care when removing from the water and place them on a paper towel to dry.
4. Add the radish chips, garlic powder, onion powder, and melted coconut oil into a bowl and toss to coat. Transfer the chips to your fryer.
5. Cook at 320°F for five minutes, occasionally giving the basket a good shake to ensure even cooking. The chips are done when cooked through and crispy. Serve immediately.

Parmesan Zucchini Chips

Prep + Cook Time: 10 minutes | Servings: 1

Ingredients

2 medium zucchini
1 oz. pork rinds, finely ground
½ cup parmesan cheese, grated
1 egg

Instructions

1.   Cut the zucchini into slices about a quarter-inch thick. Lay on a paper towel to dry.
2.   In a bowl, combine the ground pork rinds and the grated parmesan.
3.   In a separate bowl, beat the egg with a fork.
4.   Take a zucchini slice and dip it into the egg, then into the pork rind-parmesan mixture, making sure to coat it evenly. Repeat with the rest of the slices. Lay them in the basket of your fryer, taking care not to overlap. This step may need to be completed in more than one batch.
5.   Cook at 320°F for five minutes. Turn the chips over and allow to cook for another five minutes.
6.   Allow to cool to achieve a crispier texture or serve warm. Enjoy!

Buffalo Cauliflower

Prep + Cook Time: 10 minutes | Servings: 1

Ingredients

½ packet dry ranch seasoning
2 tbsp. salted butter, melted
Cauliflower florets
¼ cup buffalo sauce

Instructions

1.   In a bowl, combine the dry ranch seasoning and butter. Toss with the cauliflower florets to coat and transfer them to the fryer.
2.   Cook at 400°F for five minutes, shaking the basket occasionally to ensure the florets cook evenly.
3.   Remove the cauliflower from the fryer, pour the buffalo sauce over it, and enjoy.

Zesty Cilantro Roasted Cauliflower

Prep + Cook Time: 10 minutes | Servings: 2

Ingredients

2 cups cauliflower florets, chopped
2 tbsp. coconut oil, melted
2 ½ tsp. taco seasoning mix
1 medium lime
2 tbsp. cilantro, chopped

Instructions

1.   Mix the cauliflower with the melted coconut oil and the taco seasoning, ensuring to coat the florets all over.
2.   Cook at 350°F for seven minutes, shaking the basket a few times through the cooking time. Then transfer the cauliflower to a bowl.
3.   Squeeze the lime juice over the cauliflower and season with the cilantro. Toss once more to coat and enjoy.

Fried Green Tomatoes

Prep + Cook Time: 10 minutes | Servings: 2

Ingredients

2 medium green tomatoes
1 egg
¼ cup blanched finely ground flour
1/3 cup parmesan cheese, grated

Instructions

1.   Slice the tomatoes about a half-inch thick.
2.   Crack the egg into a bowl and beat it with a whisk. In a separate bowl, mix together the flour and parmesan cheese.
3.   Dredge the tomato slices in egg, then dip them into the flour-cheese mixture to coat. Place each slice into the fryer basket. They may need to be cooked in multiple batches.
4.   Cook at 400°F for seven minutes, turning them halfway through the cooking time, and then serve warm.

Avocado Sticks

Prep + Cook Time: 10 minutes | Servings: 2

Ingredients

2 avocados
4 egg yolks
1 ½ tbsp. water
Salt and pepper
1 cup flour
1 cup herbed butter

Instructions

1.   Halve the avocados, twist to open, and take out the pits. Cut each half into three equal slices.
2.   In a bowl, combine the egg yolks and water. Season with salt and pepper to taste and whisk together.
3.   Pour the flour into a shallow bowl.
4.   Coat each slice of avocado in the flour, then in the egg, before dipping it in the flour again. Ensure the flour coats the avocado well and firmly.
5.   Pre-heat the fryer at 400°F. When it is warm, put the avocados inside and cook for eight minutes.
6.   Take care when removing the avocados from the fryer and enjoy with a side of the herbed butter.

Cheesy Cauliflower Bites

Prep + Cook Time: 20 minutes | Servings: 3

Ingredients

2 cup cauliflower florets
¾ cup cheddar cheese, shredded
½ cup onion, chopped
1 tsp. seasoning salt
2 tbsp. butter, melted
2 cloves garlic, minced

Instructions

1.   Pulse the cauliflower florets in the food processor until they become crumbly. Use a cheesecloth to remove all the moisture from the cauliflower.
2.   In a bowl, combine the cauliflower with the cheese, onion, seasoning salt, and melted butter. With your hands, roll the mixture into balls.
3.   Pre-heat the fryer at 400°F.
4.   Fry the balls for fourteen minutes, leaving them in the fryer for an additional two minutes if you like them browner. Serve hot.

Brussels Sprouts with Cheese Sauce

Prep + Cook Time: 10 minutes | Servings: 2

Ingredients

¾ cups Brussels sprouts
1 tbsp. extra virgin olive oil
¼ tsp. salt
¼ cup mozzarella cheese, shredded

Instructions

1. Halve the Brussels sprouts and drizzle with the olive oil. Season with salt and toss to coat.
2. Pre-heat your fryer at 375°F. When warm, transfer the Brussels sprouts inside and add the shredded mozzarella on top.
3. Cook for five minutes, serving when the cheese is melted.

Vegetable Mix

Prep + Cook Time: 45 minutes | Servings: 4

Ingredients

3.5 oz. radish
½ tsp. parsley
3.5 oz. celeriac
1 yellow carrot
1 orange carrot
1 red onion
3.5 oz. pumpkin
3.5 oz. parsnips
Salt to taste
Epaulette pepper to taste
1 tbsp. olive oil
4 cloves garlic, unpeeled

Instructions

1. Peel and slice up all the vegetables into 2- to 3-cm pieces.
2. Pre-heat your Air Fryer to 390°F.
3. Pour in the oil and allow it to warm before placing the vegetables in the fryer, followed by the garlic, salt and pepper.
4. Roast for 18 – 20 minutes.
5. Top with parsley and serve hot with rice if desired.

Potato Chips

Prep + Cook Time: 45 minutes | Servings: 4

Ingredients

2 large potatoes, peel and sliced
1 tbsp. rosemary
3.5 oz. sour cream
¼ tsp. salt

Instructions

1. Place the potato slices in water and allow to absorb for 30 minutes.
2. Drain the potato slices and transfer to a large bowl. Toss with the rosemary, sour cream, and salt.
3. Pre-heat the Air Fryer to 320°F
4. Put the coated potato slices in the fryer's basket and cook for 35 minutes. Serve hot.

Brussels Sprouts

Prep + Cook Time: 15 minutes | Servings: 2

Ingredients

2 cups Brussels sprouts, sliced in half
1 tbsp. balsamic vinegar
1 tbsp. olive oil
¼ tsp. salt

Instructions

1. Toss all of the ingredients together in a bowl, coating the Brussels sprouts well.
2. Place the sprouts in the Air Fryer basket and air fry at 400°F for 10 minutes, shaking the basket at the halfway point.

Garlic Potatoes

Prep + Cook Time: 40 minutes | Servings: 4

Ingredients

1 lb. russet baking potatoes
1 tbsp. garlic powder
1 tbsp. freshly chopped parsley
½ tsp. salt
¼ tsp. black pepper
1 – 2 tbsp. olive oil

Instructions

1. Wash the potatoes and pat them dry with clean paper towels.
2. Pierce each potato several times with a fork.
3. Place the potatoes in a large bowl and season with the garlic powder, salt and pepper.
4. Pour over the olive oil and mix well.
5. Pre-heat the Air Fryer to 360°F.
6. Place the potatoes in the fryer and cook for about 30 minutes, shaking the basket a few times throughout the cooking time.
7. Garnish the potatoes with the chopped parsley and serve with butter, sour cream or another dipping sauce if desired.

Zucchini Rolls

Prep + Cook Time: 15 minutes | Servings: 2 – 4

Ingredients

3 zucchinis, sliced thinly lengthwise with a mandolin or very sharp knife
1 tbsp. olive oil
1 cup goat cheese
¼ tsp. black pepper

Instructions

1. Preheat your Air Fryer to 390°F.
2. Coat each zucchini strip with a light brushing of olive oil.
3. Combine the sea salt, black pepper and goat cheese.
4. Scoop a small, equal amount of the goat cheese onto the center of each strip of zucchini. Roll up the strips and secure with a toothpick.
5. Transfer to the Air Fryer and cook for 5 minutes until the cheese is warm and the zucchini slightly crispy. If desired, add some tomato sauce on top.

Asparagus

Prep + Cook Time: 15 minutes | Servings: 4

Ingredients

10 asparagus spears, woody end cut off
1 clove garlic, minced
4 tbsp. olive oil
Pepper to taste
Salt to taste

Instructions

1. Set the Air Fryer to 400°F and allow to heat for 5 minutes.
2. In a bowl, combine the garlic and oil.
3. Cover the asparagus with this mixture and put it in the fryer basket. Sprinkle over some pepper and salt.
4. Cook for 10 minutes and serve hot.

Zucchini Chips

Prep + Cook Time: 30 minutes | Servings: 2

Ingredients

3 medium zucchini, sliced
1 tsp. parsley, chopped
3 tbsp. parmesan cheese, grated
Pepper to taste
Salt to taste

Instructions

1. Pre-heat the Air Fryer to 425°F.
2. Put the sliced zucchini on a sheet of baking paper and spritz with cooking spray.
3. Combine the cheese, pepper, parsley, and salt. Use this mixture to sprinkle over the zucchini.
4. Transfer to the Air Fryer and cook for 25 minutes, ensuring the zucchini slices have crisped up nicely before serving.

Sweet Potato Wedges

Prep + Cook Time: 25 minutes | Servings: 2

Ingredients

2 large sweet potatoes, cut into wedges
1 tbsp. olive oil
1 tsp. chili powder
1 tsp. mustard powder
1 tsp. cumin
1 tbsp. Mexican seasoning
Pepper to taste
Salt to taste

Instructions

1. Pre-heat the Air Fryer at 350°F.
2. Place all of the ingredients into a bowl and combine well to coat the sweet potatoes entirely.
3. Place the wedges in the Air Fryer basket and air fry for 20 minutes, shaking the basket at 5-minute intervals.

Potato Wedges

Prep + Cook Time: 30 minutes | Servings: 4

Ingredients

4 medium potatoes, cut into wedges
1 tbsp. Cajun spice
1 tbsp. olive oil
Pepper to taste
Salt to taste

Instructions

1. Place the potato wedges in the Air Fryer basket and pour in the olive oil.
2. Cook wedges at 370°F for 25 minutes, shaking the basket twice throughout the cooking time.
3. Put the cooked wedges in a bowl and coat them with the Cajun spice, pepper, and salt. Serve warm.

Banana Chips

Prep + Cook Time: 20 minutes | Servings: 3

Ingredients

2 large raw bananas, peel and sliced
½ tsp. red chili powder
1 tsp. olive oil
¼ tsp. turmeric powder
1 tsp. salt

Instructions

1. Put some water in a bowl along with the turmeric powder and salt.
2. Place the sliced bananas in the bowl and allow to soak for 10 minutes.
3. Dump the contents into a sieve to strain the banana slices before drying them with a paper towel.
4. Pre-heat the Air Fryer to 350°F.
5. Put the banana slices in a bowl and coat them with the olive oil, chili powder and salt.
6. Transfer the chips to the fryer basket and air fry for 15 minutes.

Honey Carrots

Prep + Cook Time: 20 minutes | Servings: 4

Ingredients

1 tbsp. honey
3 cups baby carrots or carrots, cut into bite-size pieces
1 tbsp. olive oil
Sea salt to taste
Ground black pepper to taste

Instructions

1. In a bowl, combine the carrots, honey, and olive oil, coating the carrots completely. Sprinkle on some salt and ground black pepper.
2. Transfer the carrots to the Air Fryer and cook at 390°F for 12 minutes. Serve immediately.

Potato Totes

Prep + Cook Time: 20 minutes | Servings: 2

Ingredients

1 large potato, diced
1 tsp. onion, minced
1 tsp. olive oil
Pepper to taste
Salt to taste

Instructions

1. Boil the potatoes in a saucepan of water over a medium-high heat.
2. Strain the potatoes, transfer them to bowl, and mash them thoroughly.
3. Combine with the olive oil, onion, pepper and salt in mashed potato.
4. Shape equal amounts of the mixture into small tots and place each one in the Air Fryer basket. Cook at 380°F for 8 minutes.
5. Give the basket a good shake and cook for an additional 5 minutes before serving.

Zucchini

Prep + Cook Time: 30 minutes | Servings: 6

Ingredients

6 medium zucchini, cut into sticks
4 tbsp. parmesan cheese, grated
4 egg whites, beaten
½ tsp. garlic powder
1 cup friendly bread crumbs
Pepper to taste
Salt to taste

Instructions

1. Pre-heat the Air Fryer to 400°F.
2. In a bowl, mix the beaten egg whites with some salt and pepper.
3. In a separate bowl, combine the bread crumbs, garlic powder, and parmesan cheese.
4. Dredge each zucchini stick in the egg whites before rolling in the bread crumbs.
5. Place the coated zucchini in the fryer basket and allow to cook for 20 minutes.

Carrots & Cumin

Prep + Cook Time: 25 minutes | Servings: 4

Ingredients

2 cups carrots, peeled and chopped
1 tsp. cumin seeds
1 tbsp. olive oil
¼ cup coriander

Instructions

1. Cover the carrots with the cumin and oil.
2. Transfer to the Air Fryer and cook at 390°F for 12 minutes.
3. Season with the coriander before serving.

Cheese Sticks

Prep + Cook Time: 15 minutes | Servings: 4

Ingredients

1 lb. mozzarella cheese
2 eggs, beaten
1 tsp. cayenne pepper
1 cup friendly bread crumbs
1 tsp. onion powder
1 tsp. garlic powder
1 cup flour
½ tsp. salt

Instructions

1. Slice the mozzarella cheese into 3- x ½-inch sticks.
2. Put the beaten eggs in a bowl.
3. Pour the flour into a shallow dish.
4. In a second bowl combine the bread crumbs, cayenne pepper, onion powder, garlic powder, and salt.
5. Dredge the mozzarella strips in the beaten egg before coating it in the flour. Dip it in the egg again. Lastly, press it into the bread crumbs.
6. Refrigerate for 20 minutes.
7. Pre-heat the Air Fryer to 400°F.
8. Spritz the Air Fryer basket with cooking spray.
9. Put the coated cheese sticks in the Air Fryer basket and cook for 5 minutes. Serve immediately.

Onion Rings

Prep + Cook Time: 25 minutes | Servings: 2

Ingredients

1 large onion, cut into slices
1 egg, beaten
¾ cup friendly bread crumbs

1 cup milk
1 tsp. baking powder
1 ¼ cup flour
1 tsp. salt

Instructions

1. Pre-heat the Air Fryer for 5 minutes.
2. In a small bowl, combine the baking powder, flour, and salt
3. In a second bowl, stir together the milk and egg using a whisk.
4. Put the bread crumbs in a shallow dish.
5. Coat each slice of onion with the flour, then dredge it in the egg mixture. Lastly, press it into the breadcrumbs.
6. Transfer the coated onion rings to the Air Fryer basket and cook at
7. 350°F for 10 minutes.

Vegan Veggie Dish

Prep + Cook Time: 30 minutes | Servings: 4

Ingredients

1 large zucchini, sliced
3 – 4 cherry tomatoes on the vine
1 medium carrot, peeled and cubed
1 large parsnip, peeled and cubed
1 green pepper, sliced
1 tsp. mustard
1 tsp. mixed herbs
2 cloves garlic, crushed
2 tbsp. honey
3+3 tbsp. olive oil, separately
Sea salt to taste
Black pepper to taste

Instructions

1. Place the slices of zucchini, green pepper, parsnip, carrot and cherry tomatoes inside the Air Fryer.
2. Pour 3 tablespoons of oil over the vegetables and cook at 360°F for 15 minutes.
3. In the meantime, make the marinade by mixing together all of the other ingredients in the Air Fryer baking dish.
4. Transfer the cooked vegetables to the baking dish and coat it completely with the marinade. Season with pepper and salt as desired.
5. Return to the fryer and cook at 390°F for 5 minutes. Serve hot.

Tofu

Prep + Cook Time: 20 minutes | Servings: 4

Ingredients

15 oz. extra firm tofu, drained and cut into cubes
1 tsp. chili flakes
¾ cup cornstarch
¼ cup cornmeal
Pepper to taste
Salt to taste

Instructions

1. In a bowl, combine the cornmeal, cornstarch, chili flakes, pepper, and salt.
2. Coat the tofu cubes completely with the mixture.
3. Pre-heat your Air Fryer at 350°F.
4. Spritz the basket with cooking spray.
5. Transfer the coated tofu to the basket and air fry for 8 minutes, shaking the basket at the 4-minute mark.

Friday's Fries

Prep + Cook Time: 25 minutes | Servings: 2

Ingredients
1 large eggplant, cut into 3-inch slices
¼ cup water
1 tbsp. olive oil
¼ cup cornstarch
¼ tsp. salt

Instructions
1. Pre-heat the Air Fryer to 400°F.
2. In a bowl, combine the water, olive oil, cornstarch, and salt.
3. Coat the sliced eggplant with the mixture.
4. Put the coated eggplant slices in the Air Fryer basket and cook for 20 minutes.

Sweet Potato Bites

Prep + Cook Time: 30 minutes | Servings: 2

Ingredients
2 sweet potatoes, diced into 1-inch cubes
1 tsp. red chili flakes
2 tsp. cinnamon
2 tbsp. olive oil
2 tbsp. honey
½ cup fresh parsley, chopped

Instructions
1. Pre-heat the Air Fryer at 350°F.
2. Place all of the ingredients in a bowl and stir well to coat the sweet potato cubes entirely.
3. Put the sweet potato mixture into the Air Fryer basket and cook for 15 minutes.

Kale Chips

Prep + Cook Time: 15 minutes | Servings: 2

Ingredients
1 head kale
1 tbsp. olive oil
1 tsp. soy sauce

Instructions
1. De-stem the head of kale and shred each leaf into a 1 ½" piece. Wash and dry well.
2. Toss the kale with the olive oil and soy sauce to coat it completely.
3. Transfer to the Air Fryer and cook at 390°F for 2 to 3 minutes, giving the leaves a good toss at the halfway mark.

Stuffed Tomatoes

Prep + Cook Time: 30 minutes | Servings: 4

Ingredients
4 large tomatoes, without tops, seeds, or pith
1 clove garlic, crushed
1 onion, cubed
1 cup frozen peas
2 cups cooked rice, cold
1 tbsp. soy sauce
1 carrot, cubed
1 tbsp. olive oil
Parsley to taste, roughly chopped
Cooking spray

Instructions
1. Fry up the rice in a pan with the olive oil over a low heat.
2. Add in the cubed onion, carrots, crushed garlic, and frozen peas and allow to cook for 2 minutes, stirring occasionally.
3. Pour in the soy sauce and toss to coat. Remove the pan from the heat.
4. Pre-heat the Air Fryer to 360°F.
5. Stuff each tomato with the rice and vegetables
6. Put the tomatoes in the Air Fryer and cook for 20 minutes.
7. Garnish the cooked tomatoes with the chopped parsley and serve.

Mix Nuts

Prep + Cook Time: 15 minutes | Servings: 8

Ingredients
2 cup mixed nuts
1 tsp. chipotle chili powder
1 tsp. ground cumin
1 tbsp. butter, melted
1 tsp. pepper
1 tsp. salt

Instructions
1. In a bowl, combine all of the ingredients, coating the nuts well.
2. Set your Air Fryer to 350°F and allow to heat for 5 minutes.
3. Place the mixed nuts in the fryer basket and roast for 4 minutes, shaking the basket halfway through the cooking time.

Cheesy Potatoes

Prep + Cook Time: 20 minutes | Servings: 4

Ingredients
11 oz. potatoes, diced and boiled
1 egg yolk
2 tbsp. flour
3 tbsp. parmesan cheese
3 tbsp. friendly bread crumbs, tossed with a little oil
Pepper to taste
Nutmeg to taste
Salt to taste

Instructions
1. Pre-heat Air Fryer at 390°F.
2. Mash up the potatoes and combine with all of the ingredients, minus the bread crumbs.
3. Shape equal amounts of the mixture into medium-sized balls and roll each one in the bread crumbs.
4. Place the potato balls in the fryer and cook for 4 minutes.

Baked Potatoes

Prep + Cook Time: 45 minutes | Servings: 3

Ingredients
3 Idaho or russet baking potatoes, washed
2 cloves garlic, crushed
1 tbsp. olive oil
1 tbsp. sea salt
Parsley, roughly chopped
Sour cream to taste

Instructions
1. Pierce each potato several times with a fork.
2. Sprinkle the potatoes with salt and coat with the garlic puree and olive oil.
3. Place the potatoes in the Air Fryer basket and cook at 390°F for 35 - 40 minutes until soft. Serve with parsley and sour cream, or whatever toppings you desire.

Baby Corn

Prep + Cook Time: 20 minutes | Servings: 4

Ingredients

8 oz. baby corns, boiled
1 cup flour
1 tsp. garlic powder
½ tsp. carom seeds
¼ tsp. chili powder
Pinch of baking soda
Salt to taste

Instructions

1.   In a bowl, combine the flour, chili powder, garlic powder, cooking soda, salt and carom seed. Add in a little water to create a batter-like consistency.
2.   Coat each baby corn in the batter.
3.   Pre-heat the Air Fryer at 350°F.
4.   Cover the Air Fryer basket with aluminum foil before laying the coated baby corns on top of the foil.
5.   Cook for 10 minutes.

French Fries

Prep + Cook Time: 25 minutes | Servings: 4

Ingredients

1 lb. russet potatoes
1 tsp. salt
½ tsp. black pepper
1 tbsp. olive oil

Instructions

1.   In a pot filled with water, blanch the potatoes until softened.
2.   Remove from the heat and allow to cool. Slice the potatoes into matchstick shapes.
3.   Place them in a large bowl and coat with the olive oil, salt and pepper.
4.   Pre-heat the Air Fryer to 390°F.
5.   Cook the French fries for about 15 minutes, giving the basket a shake now and again throughout the cooking time. Serve with freshly chopped herbs if desired.

Roasted Corn

Prep + Cook Time: 15 minutes | Servings: 8

Ingredients

4 fresh ears of corn
2 to 3 tsp. vegetable oil
Salt and pepper to taste

Instructions

1.   Remove the husks from the corn, before washing and drying the corn. Slice up the corn to fit your Air Fryer basket if necessary.
2.   Pour a drizzling of vegetable oil over the corn, coating it well. Sprinkle on salt and pepper.
3.   Place in the fryer and cook at 400°F for about 10 minutes.

Roasted Carrots

Prep + Cook Time: 20 minutes | Servings: 2

Ingredients

1 tbsp. olive oil
3 cups baby carrots or carrots, cut into large chunks
1 tbsp. honey
Salt and pepper to taste

Instructions

1.   In a bowl, coat the carrots with the honey and olive oil before sprinkling on some salt and pepper.
2.   Place into the Air Fryer and cook at 390°F for 12 minutes. Serve hot.

Fried Kale Chips

Prep + Cook Time: 10 minutes | Servings: 2

Ingredients

1 head kale, torn into 1 ½-inch pieces
1 tbsp. olive oil
1 tsp. soy sauce

Instructions

1.   Wash and dry the kale pieces.
2.   Transfer the kale to a bowl and coat with the soy sauce and oil.
3.   Place it in the Air Fryer and cook at 400°F for 3 minutes, tossing it halfway through the cooking process.

Orange Cauliflower

Prep + Cook Time: 30 minutes | Servings: 2

Ingredients

½ lemon, juiced
1 head cauliflower
½ tbsp. olive oil
1 tsp. curry powder
Sea salt to taste
Ground black pepper to taste

Instructions

1.   Wash the cauliflower. Cut out the leaves and core.
2.   Chop the cauliflower into equally-sized florets.
3.   Coat the inside of the Air Fryer with the oil and allow it to warm up for about 2 minutes at 390°F.
4.   In a bowl, mix together the fresh lemon juice and curry powder. Add in the cauliflower florets. Sprinkle in the pepper and salt and mix again, coating the florets well.
5.   Transfer to the fryer, cook for 20 minutes, and serve warm.

Lemon Green Beans

Prep + Cook Time: 20 minutes | Servings: 4

Ingredients

1 lemon, juiced
1 lb. green beans, washed and destemmed
¼ tsp. extra virgin olive oil
Sea salt to taste
Black pepper to taste

Instructions

1.   Pre-heat the Air Fryer to 400°F.
2.   Put the green beans in your Air Fryer basket and drizzle the lemon juice over them.
3.   Sprinkle on the pepper and salt. Pour in the oil, and toss to coat the green beans well.
4.   Cook for 10 – 12 minutes and serve warm.

Broccoli Florets

Prep + Cook Time: 20 minutes | Servings: 4

Ingredients

1 lb. broccoli, cut into florets
1 tbsp. lemon juice
1 tbsp. olive oil
1 tbsp. sesame seeds
3 garlic cloves, minced

Instructions

1. In a bowl, combine all of the ingredients, coating the broccoli well.
2. Transfer to the Air Fryer basket and air fry at 400°F for 13 minutes.

Avocado Fries

Prep + Cook Time: 20 minutes | Servings: 4

Ingredients

½ cup panko
½ tsp. salt
1 whole avocado
1 oz. aquafaba

Instructions

1. In a shallow bowl, stir together the panko and salt.
2. In a separate shallow bowl, add the aquafaba.
3. Dip the avocado slices into the aquafaba, before coating each one in the panko.
4. Place the slices in your Air Fryer basket, taking care not to overlap any. Air fry for 10 minutes at 390°F.

Oriental Spinach Samosa

Prep + Cook Time: 45 minutes | Servings: 2

Ingredients

¾ cup boiled and blended spinach puree
¼ cup green peas
½ tsp. sesame seeds
Ajwain, salt, chaat masala, chili powder to taste
2 tsp. olive oil
1 tsp. chopped fresh coriander leaves
1 tsp. garam masala
¼ cup boiled and cut potatoes
½ 1 cup flour
½ tsp. cooking soda

Instructions

1. In a bowl, combine the Ajwain, flour, cooking soda and salt to form a dough-like consistency. Pour in one teaspoon of the oil and the spinach puree. Continue to mix the dough, ensuring it is smooth.
2. Refrigerate for 20 minutes. Add another teaspoon of oil to a saucepan and sauté the potatoes and peas for 5 minutes.
3. Stir in the sesame seeds, coriander, and any other spices you desire.
4. Use your hands to shape equal sized amounts of the dough into small balls. Mold these balls into cone-shapes.
5. Fill each cone with the potatoes and peas mixture and seal.
6. Pre-heat your Air Fryer to 390°F.

7. Put the samosas in the basket and cook for 10 minutes.
8. Serve the samosas with the sauce of your choice.

Tomatoes & Herbs

Prep + Cook Time: 30 minutes | Servings: 2

Ingredients

2 large tomatoes, washed and cut into halves
Herbs, such as oregano, basil, thyme, rosemary, sage to taste
Cooking spray
Pepper to taste
Parmesan, grated [optional]
Parsley, minced [optional]

Instructions

1. Spritz both sides of each tomato half with a small amount of cooking spray.
2. Coat the tomatoes with a light sprinkling of pepper and the herbs of your choice.
3. Place the tomatoes in the basket, cut-side-up. Cook at 320°F for 20 minutes, or longer if necessary.
4. Serve hot, at room temperature, or chilled as a refreshing summer snack. Optionally, you can garnish them with grated Parmesan and minced parsley before serving.

Vegetable Fritters

Prep + Cook Time: 15 minutes | Servings: 4

Ingredients

1 cup bell peppers, deveined and chopped
1 tsp. sea salt flakes
1 tsp. cumin
¼ tsp. paprika
½ cup shallots, chopped
2 cloves garlic, minced
1 ½ tbsp. fresh chopped cilantro
1 egg, whisked
¾ cup Cheddar cheese, grated
¼ cup cooked quinoa
¼ cup flour

Instructions

1. In a bowl, combine all of the ingredients well.
2. Divide the mixture into equal portions and shape each one into a ball. Use your palm to flatten each ball very slightly to form patties.
3. Lightly coat the patties with a cooking spray.
4. Put the patties in your Air Fryer cooking basket, taking care not to overlap them.
5. Cook at 340°F for 10 minutes, turning them over halfway through.

DESSERTS

Cheesecake Cups

Prep + Cook Time: 10 minutes | Servings: 4

Ingredients
8 oz cream cheese, softened
2 oz heavy cream
1 tsp Sugar Glycerite
1 tsp Splenda
1 tsp vanilla flavoring (Frontier Organic)

Instructions
1. Combine all the ingredients.
2. Whip until a pudding consistency is achieved.
3. Divide in cups.
4. Refrigerate until served!

Strawberry Shake

Prep + Cook Time: 5 minutes | Servings: 1

Ingredients
3/4 cup coconut milk (from the carton)
¼ cup heavy cream
7 ice cubes
2 tbsp sugar-free strawberry Torani syrup
¼ tsp Xanthan Gum

Instructions
1. Combine all the ingredients into blender.
2. Blend for 1-2 minutes.
3. Serve!

Raspberry Pudding Surprise

Prep + Cook Time: 40 minutes | Servings: 1

Ingredients
3 tbsp chia seeds
½ cup unsweetened milk
1 scoop chocolate protein powder
¼ cup raspberries, fresh or frozen
1 tsp honey

Instructions
1. Combine the milk, protein powder and chia seeds together.
2. Let rest for 5 minutes before stirring.
3. Refrigerate for 30 minutes.
4. Top with raspberries.
5. Serve!

Vanilla Bean Dream

Prep + Cook Time: 35 minutes | Servings: 1

Ingredients
½ cup extra virgin coconut oil, softened
½ cup coconut butter, softened
Juice of 1 lemon
Seeds from ½ a vanilla bean

Instructions
1. Whisk the ingredients in an easy-to-pour cup.
2. Pour into a lined cupcake or loaf pan.
3. Refrigerate for 20 minutes. Top with lemon zest.
4. Serve!

White Chocolate Berry Cheesecake

Prep + Cook Time: 5-10 minutes | Servings: 4

Ingredients
8 oz cream cheese, softened
2 oz heavy cream
½ tsp Splenda
1 tsp raspberries
1 tbsp Da Vinci Sugar-Free syrup, white chocolate flavor

Instructions
1. Whip together the ingredients to a thick consistency.
2. Divide in cups.
3. Refrigerate.
4. Serve!

Coconut Pillow

Prep + Cook Time: 1-2 days | Servings: 4

Ingredients
1 can unsweetened coconut milk
Berries of choice
Dark chocolate

Instructions
1. Refrigerate the coconut milk for 24 hours.
2. Remove it from your refrigerator and whip for 2-3 minutes.
3. Fold in the berries.
4. Season with the chocolate shavings.
5. Serve!

Coffee Surprise

Prep + Cook Time: 5 minutes | Servings: 1

Ingredients
2 heaped tbsp flaxseed, ground
100ml cooking cream 35% fat
½ tsp cocoa powder, dark and unsweetened
1 tbsp goji berries
Freshly brewed coffee

Instructions
1. Mix together the flaxseeds, cream and cocoa and coffee.
2. Season with goji berries.
3. Serve!

Chocolate Cheesecake

Prep + Cook Time: 60 minutes | Servings: 4

Ingredients
4 oz cream cheese
½ oz heavy cream
1 tsp Sugar Glycerite
1 tsp Splenda
1 oz Enjoy Life mini chocolate chips

Instructions
1. Combine all the ingredients except the chocolate to a thick consistency.
2. Fold in the chocolate chips.
3. Refrigerate in serving cups.
4. Serve!

Crusty

Prep + Cook Time: 60 minutes | Servings: 3

Ingredients
2 cups flour
4 tsp melted butter
2 large eggs
½ tsp salt

Instructions
1.   Mix together the flour and butter.
2.   Add in the eggs and salt and combine well to form a dough ball.
3.   Place the dough between two pieces of parchment paper. Roll out to 10" by 16" and ¼ inch thick.
4.   Serve!

Chocolate Peanut Butter Cups

Prep + Cook Time: 70 minutes | Servings: 2

Ingredients
1 stick unsalted butter
1 oz / 1 cube unsweetened chocolate
5 packets Sugar in the Raw
1 tbsp heavy cream
4 tbsp peanut butter

Instructions
1.   In a microwave, melt the butter and chocolate.
2.   Add the Sugar.
3.   Stir in the cream and peanut butter.
4.   Line the muffin tins. Fill the muffin cups.
5.   Freeze for 60 minutes.
6.   Serve!

Macaroon Bites

Prep + Cook Time: 30 minutes | Servings: 2

Ingredients
4 egg whites
½ tsp vanilla
½ tsp EZ-Sweet (or equivalent of 1 cup artificial sweetener)
4½ tsp water
1 cup unsweetened coconut

Instructions
1.   Preheat your fryer to 375°F/190°C.
2.   Combine the egg whites, liquids and coconut.
3.   Put into the fryer and reduce the heat to 325°F/160°C.
4.   Bake for 15 minutes.
5.   Serve!

Choco-berry Fudge Sauce

Prep + Cook Time: 30 minutes | Servings: 2

Ingredients
4 oz cream cheese, softened
1-3.5 oz 90% chocolate Lindt bar, chopped
¼ cup powdered erythritol
¼ cup heavy cream
1 tbsp Monin sugar-free raspberry syrup

Instructions
1.   In a large skillet, melt together the cream cheese and chocolate.
2.   Stir in the sweetener.
3.   Remove from the heat and allow to cool.
4.   Once cool, mix in the cream and syrup.
5.   Serve!

Choco-Coconut Puddin

Prep + Cook Time: 65 minutes | Servings: 1

Ingredients
1 cup coconut milk
2 tbsp cacao powder or organic cocoa
½ tsp Sugar powder extract or 2 tbsp honey/maple syrup
½ tbsp quality gelatin
1 tbsp water

Instructions
1.   On a medium heat, combine the coconut milk, cocoa and sweetener.
2.   In a separate bowl, mix in the gelatin and water.
3.   Add to the pan and stir until fully dissolved.
4.   Pour into small dishes and refrigerate for 1 hour.
5.   Serve!

Strawberry Frozen Dessert

Prep + Cook Time: 45 minutes | Servings: 1

Ingredients
½ cup sugar-free strawberry preserves
½ cup Sugar in the Raw or Splenda
2 cups Fage Total 0% Greek Yogurt
Ice cream maker

Instructions
1.   In a food processor, purée the strawberries. Add the strawberry preserves.
2.   Add the Greek yogurt and fully mix.
3.   Put into the ice cream maker for 25-30 minute.
4.   Serve!

Berry Layer Cake

Prep + Cook Time: 8 minutes | Servings: 1

Ingredients
¼ lemon pound cake
¼ cup whipping cream
½ tsp Truvia
1/8 tsp orange flavor
1 cup of mixed berries

Instructions
1.   Using a sharp knife, divide the lemon cake into small cubes.
2.   Dice the strawberries.
3.   Combine the whipping cream, Truvia, and orange flavor.
4.   Layer the fruit, cake and cream in a glass.
5.   Serve!

Chocolate Pudding

Prep + Cook Time: 50 minutes | Servings: 1

Ingredients
3 tbsp chia seeds
1 cup unsweetened milk
1 scoop cocoa powder
¼ cup fresh raspberries
½ tsp honey

Instructions
1.   Mix together all of the ingredients in a large bowl.
2.   Let rest for 15 minutes but stir halfway through.
3.   Stir again and refrigerate for 30 minutes. Garnish with raspberries.
4.   Serve!

Cranberry Cream Surprise

Prep + Cook Time: 30 minutes | Servings: 1

Ingredients

1 cup mashed cranberries
½ cup Confectioner's Style Swerve
2 tsp natural cherry flavoring
2 tsp natural rum flavoring
1 cup organic heavy cream

Instructions

1. Combine the mashed cranberries, sweetener, cherry and rum flavorings.
2. Cover and refrigerate for 20 minutes.
3. Whip the heavy cream until soft peaks form.
4. Layer the whipped cream and cranberry mixture.
5. Top with fresh cranberries, mint leaves or grated dark chocolate.
6. Serve!

Banana Chocolate Cake

Prep + Cook Time: 30 minutes | Servings: 10

Ingredients

1 stick softened butter
½ cup sugar
1 egg
1 bananas, mashed
2 tbsp. maple syrup
2 cups flour
¼ tsp. anise star, ground
¼ tsp. ground mace
¼ tsp. ground cinnamon
¼ tsp. crystallized ginger
½ tsp. vanilla paste
Pinch of kosher salt
½ cup cocoa powder

Instructions

1. Beat together the softened butter and sugar to combine well.
2. Mix together the egg, mashed banana and maple syrup using a whisk.
3. Combine the two mixtures, stirring well until pale and creamy.
4. Add in the flour, anise star, mace, cinnamon, crystallized ginger, vanilla paste, salt, and cocoa powder. Mix well to form the batter.
5. Grease two cake pans with cooking spray.
6. Transfer the batter into the cake pans and place them in the Air Fryer.
7. Cook at 330°F for 30 minutes. Frost with chocolate glaze if desired

Lemon Butter Pound Cake

Prep + Cook Time: 2 hours 20 minutes | Servings: 8

Ingredients

1 stick softened butter
1 cup sugar
1 medium egg
1 ¼ cups flour
1 tsp. butter flavoring
1 tsp. vanilla essence
Pinch of salt
¾ cup milk
Grated zest of 1 medium-sized lemon
For the Glaze:
2 tbsp. freshly squeezed lemon juice

Instructions:

1. In a large bowl, use a creamer to mix together the butter and sugar. Fold in the egg and continue to stir.
2. Add in the flour, butter flavoring, vanilla essence, and salt, combining everything well.
3. Pour in the milk, followed by the lemon zest, and continue to mix.
4. Lightly brush the inside of a cake pan with the melted butter.
5. Pour the cake batter into the cake pan.
6. Place the pan in the Air Fryer and bake at 350°F for 15 minutes.
7. After removing it from the fryer, run a knife around the edges of the cake to loosen it from the pan and transfer it to a serving plate.
8. Leave it to cool completely.
9. In the meantime, make the glaze by combining with the lemon juice.
10. Pour the glaze over the cake and let it sit for a further 2 hours before serving.

Fried Pineapple Rings

Prep + Cook Time: 10 minutes | Servings: 6

Ingredients

2/3 cup flour
½ tsp. baking powder
½ tsp. baking soda
Pinch of kosher salt
½ cup water
1 cup rice milk
½ tsp. ground cinnamon
¼ tsp. ground anise star
½ tsp. vanilla essence
4 tbsp. sugar
¼ cup unsweetened flaked coconut
1 medium pineapple, peeled and sliced

Instructions

1. Mix together all of the ingredients, minus the pineapple.
2. Cover the pineapple slices with the batter.
3. Place the slices in the Air Fryer and cook at 380°F for 6 - 8 minutes.
4. Pour a drizzling of maple syrup over the pineapple and serve with a side of vanilla ice cream.

Hazelnut Brownie Cups

Prep + Cook Time: 30 minutes | Servings: 12

Ingredients

6 oz. semisweet chocolate chips
1 stick butter, at room temperature
1 cup sugar
2 large eggs
¼ cup red wine
¼ tsp. hazelnut extract
1 tsp. pure vanilla extract
¾ cup flour
2 tbsp. cocoa powder
½ cup ground hazelnuts
Pinch of kosher salt

Instructions

1. Melt the butter and chocolate chips in the microwave.
2. In a large bowl, combine the sugar, eggs, red wine, hazelnut and vanilla extract with a whisk. Pour in the chocolate mix.
3. Add in the flour, cocoa powder, ground hazelnuts, and a pinch of kosher salt, continuing to stir until a creamy, smooth consistency is achieved.
4. Take a muffin tin and place a cupcake liner in each cup. Spoon an equal amount of the batter into each one.
5. Air bake at 360°F for 28 - 30 minutes, cooking in batches if necessary.
6. Serve with a topping of ganache if desired.

Swirled German Cake

Prep + Cook Time: 25 minutes | Servings: 8

Ingredients
1 cup flour
1 tsp. baking powder
1 cup sugar
1/8 tsp. kosher salt
¼ tsp. ground cinnamon
¼ tsp. grated nutmeg
1 tsp. orange zest
1 stick butter, melted
2 eggs
1 tsp. pure vanilla extract
¼ cup milk
2 tbsp. unsweetened cocoa powder

Instructions:
1.   Take a round pan that is small enough to fit inside your Air Fryer and lightly grease the inside with oil.
2.   In a bowl, use an electric mixer to combine the flour, baking powder, sugar, salt, cinnamon, nutmeg, and orange zest.
3.   Fold in the butter, eggs, vanilla, and milk, incorporating everything well.
4.   Spoon a quarter-cup of the batter to the baking pan.
5.   Stir the cocoa powder into the rest of the batter.
6.   Use a spoon to drop small amounts of the brown batter into the white batter. Swirl them together with a knife.
7.   Place the pan in the Air Fryer and cook at 360°F for about 15 minutes.
8.   Remove the pan from the fryer and leave to cool for roughly 10 minutes.

Oatmeal Apple & Plum Crumble

Prep + Cook Time: 20 minutes | Servings: 6

Ingredients
¼ lb. plums, pitted and chopped
¼ lb. Braeburn apples, cored and chopped
1 tbsp. fresh lemon juice
2 ½ oz. sugar
1 tbsp. honey
½ tsp. ground mace
½ tsp. vanilla paste
1 cup fresh cranberries
⅓ cup oats
2/3 cup flour
½ stick butter, chilled
1 tbsp. cold water

Instructions
1.   Coat the plums and apples with the lemon juice, sugar, honey, and ground mace.
2.   Lightly coat the inside of a cake pan with cooking spray.
3.   Pour the fruit mixture into the pan.
4.   In a bowl, mix together all of the other ingredients, combining everything well.
5.   Use a palette knife to spread this mixture evenly over the fruit.
6.   Place the pan in the Air Fryer and air bake at 390°F for 20 minutes. Ensure the crumble is cooked through before serving.

Chocolate Chip Cookies

Prep + Cook Time: 25 minutes | Servings: 9

Ingredients
1 ¼ cup flour
2/3 cup chocolate chips, or any kind of baker's chocolate
⅓ cup sugar
½ cup butter
4 tbsp. honey
1 tbsp. milk
High quality cooking spray

Instructions
1.   Set your Air Fryer to 320°F and allow to warm up for about 10 minutes.
2.   In the meantime, in a large bowl, cream the butter to soften it.
3.   Add in the sugar and combine to form a light and fluffy consistency.
4.   Stir in the honey.
5.   Gradually fold in the flour, incorporating it well.
6.   If you are using baker's chocolate, use a rolling pin or a mallet to break it up and create chocolate chips.
7.   Throw the chocolate into the bowl and mix well to ensure the chips are evenly distributed throughout the dough.
8.   Finally, add in the milk and combine well.
9.   Lightly spritz your Air Fryer basket with the cooking spray.
10.   Transfer the cookie dough into the fryer and cook for 20 minutes.
11.   Slice into 9 cookies. Serve immediately. Alternatively, the cookies can be stored in an airtight container for up to 3 days.

Homemade Coconut Banana Treat

Prep + Cook Time: 20 minutes | Servings: 6

Ingredients
2 tbsp. coconut oil
¾ cup friendly bread crumbs
2 tbsp. sugar
½ tsp. cinnamon powder
¼ tsp. ground cloves
6 ripe bananas, peeled and halved
⅓ cup flour
1 large egg, beaten

Instructions
1.   Heat a skillet over a medium heat. Add in the coconut oil and the bread crumbs, and mix together for approximately 4 minutes.
2.   Take the skillet off of the heat.
3.   Add in the sugar, cinnamon, and cloves.
4.   Cover all sides of the banana halves with the rice flour.
5.   Dip each one in the beaten egg before coating them in the bread crumb mix.
6.   Place the banana halves in the Air Fryer basket, taking care not to overlap them. Cook at 290°F for 10 minutes. You may need to complete this step in multiple batches.
7.   Serve hot or at room temperature, topped with a sprinkling of flaked coconut if desired.

Mini Strawberry Pies

Prep + Cook Time: 15 minutes | Servings: 8

Ingredients

1 cup sugar
¼ tsp. ground cloves
1/8 tsp. cinnamon powder
1 tsp. vanilla extract
1 [12-oz.] can biscuit dough
12 oz. strawberry pie filling
¼ cup butter, melted

Instructions

1. In a bowl, mix together the sugar, cloves, cinnamon, and vanilla.
2. With a rolling pin, roll each piece of the biscuit dough into a flat, round circle.
3. Spoon an equal amount of the strawberry pie filling onto the center of each biscuit.
4. Roll up the dough. Dip the biscuits into the melted butter and coat them with the sugar mixture.
5. Coat with a light brushing of non-stick cooking spray on all sides.
6. Transfer the cookies to the Air Fryer and bake them at 340°F for roughly 10 minutes, or until a golden-brown color is achieved.
7. Allow to cool for 5 minutes before serving.

Coconut Brownies

Prep + Cook Time: 15 minutes | Servings: 8

Ingredients

½ cup coconut oil
2 oz. dark chocolate
1 cup sugar
2 ½ tbsp. water
4 whisked eggs
¼ tsp. ground cinnamon
½ tsp. ground anise star
¼ tsp. coconut extract
½ tsp. vanilla extract
1 tbsp. honey
½ cup flour
½ cup desiccated coconut
sugar, to dust

Instructions

1. Melt the coconut oil and dark chocolate in the microwave.
2. Combine with the sugar, water, eggs, cinnamon, anise, coconut extract, vanilla, and honey in a large bowl.
3. Stir in the flour and desiccated coconut. Incorporate everything well.
4. Lightly grease a baking dish with butter. Transfer the mixture to the dish.
5. Place the dish in the Air Fryer and bake at 355°F for 15 minutes.
6. Remove from the fryer and allow to cool slightly.
7. Take care when taking it out of the baking dish. Slice it into squares.
8. Dust with sugar before serving.

Banana & Vanilla Pastry Puffs

Prep + Cook Time: 15 minutes | Servings: 8

Ingredients

1 package [8-oz.] crescent dinner rolls, refrigerated
1 cup milk
4 oz. instant vanilla pudding
4 oz. cream cheese, softened
2 bananas, peeled and sliced
1 egg, lightly beaten

Instructions

1. Roll out the crescent dinner rolls and slice each one into 8 squares.
2. Mix together the milk, pudding, and cream cheese using a whisk.
3. Scoop equal amounts of the mixture into the pastry squares. Add the banana slices on top.
4. Fold the squares around the filling, pressing down on the edges to seal them.
5. Apply a light brushing of the egg to each pastry puff before placing them in the Air Fryer.
6. Air bake at 355°F for 10 minutes.

Double Chocolate Cake

Prep + Cook Time: 45 minutes | Servings: 8

Ingredients

½ cup sugar
1 ¼ cups flour
1 tsp. baking powder
⅓ cup cocoa powder
¼ tsp. ground cloves
1/8 tsp. freshly grated nutmeg
Pinch of table salt
1 egg
¼ cup soda of your choice
¼ cup milk
½ stick butter, melted
2 oz. bittersweet chocolate, melted
½ cup hot water

Instructions

1. In a bowl, thoroughly combine the dry ingredients.
2. In another bowl, mix together the egg, soda, milk, butter, and chocolate.
3. Combine the two mixtures. Add in the water and stir well.
4. Take a cake pan that is small enough to fit inside your Air Fryer and transfer the mixture to the pan.
5. Place a sheet of foil on top and bake at 320°F for 35 minutes.
6. Take off the foil and bake for further 10 minutes.
7. Frost the cake with buttercream if desired before serving.

Banana Oatmeal Cookies

Prep + Cook Time: 20 minutes | Servings: 6

Ingredients

2 cups quick oats
¼ cup milk
4 ripe bananas, mashed
¼ cup coconut, shredded

Instructions

1. Pre-heat the Air Fryer to 350°F.
2. Combine all of the ingredients in a bowl.
3. Scoop equal amounts of the cookie dough onto a baking sheet and put it in the Air Fryer basket.
4. Bake the cookies for 15 minutes.

Sugar Butter Fritters

Prep + Cook Time: 30 minutes | Servings: 16

Ingredients

For the dough:

4 cups flour

1 tsp. kosher salt

1 tsp. sugar

3 tbsp. butter, at room temperature

1 packet instant yeast

1 ¼ cups lukewarm water

For the Cakes

1 cup sugar

Pinch of cardamom

1 tsp. cinnamon powder

1 stick butter, melted

Instructions

1. Place all of the ingredients in a large bowl and combine well.
2. Add in the lukewarm water and mix until a soft, elastic dough forms.
3. Place the dough on a lightly floured surface and lay a greased sheet of aluminum foil on top of the dough. Refrigerate for 5 to 10 minutes.
4. Remove it from the refrigerator and divide it in two. Mold each half into a log and slice it into 20 pieces.
5. In a shallow bowl, combine the sugar, cardamom and cinnamon.
6. Coat the slices with a light brushing of melted butter and the sugar.
7. Spritz Air Fryer basket with cooking spray.
8. Transfer the slices to the fryer and air fry at 360°F for roughly 10 minutes. Turn each slice once during the baking time.
9. Dust each slice with the sugar before serving.

Pear & Apple Crisp with Walnuts

Prep + Cook Time: 25 minutes | Servings: 6

Ingredients

½ lb. apples, cored and chopped

½ lb. pears, cored and chopped

1 cup flour

1 cup sugar

1 tbsp. butter

1 tsp. ground cinnamon

¼ tsp. ground cloves

1 tsp. vanilla extract

¼ cup chopped walnuts

Whipped cream, to serve

Instructions

1. Lightly grease a baking dish and place the apples and pears inside.
2. Combine the rest of the ingredients, minus the walnuts and the whipped cream, until a coarse, crumbly texture is achieved.
3. Pour the mixture over the fruits and spread it evenly. Top with the chopped walnuts.
4. Air bake at 340°F for 20 minutes or until the top turns golden brown.
5. When cooked through, serve at room temperature with whipped cream.

Sweet & Crisp Bananas

Prep + Cook Time: 20 minutes | Servings: 4

Ingredients

4 ripe bananas, peeled and halved

1 tbsp. meal

1 tbsp. cashew, crushed

1 egg, beaten

1 ½ tbsp. coconut oil

¼ cup flour

1 ½ tbsp. sugar

½ cup friendly bread crumbs

Instructions

1. Put the coconut oil in a saucepan and heat over a medium heat. Stir in the bread crumbs and cook, stirring continuously, for 4 minutes.
2. Transfer the bread crumbs to a bowl.
3. Add in the meal and crushed cashew. Mix well.
4. Coat each of the banana halves in the corn flour, before dipping it in the beaten egg and lastly coating it with the bread crumbs.
5. Put the coated banana halves in the Air Fryer basket. Season with the sugar.
6. Air fry at 350°F for 10 minutes.

Shortbread Fingers

Prep + Cook Time: 20 minutes | Servings: 10

Ingredients

1 ½ cups butter

1 cup flour

¾ cup sugar

Cooking spray

Instructions

1. Pre-heat your Air Fryer to 350°F.
2. In a bowl, combine the flour and sugar.
3. Cut each stick of butter into small chunks. Add the chunks into the flour and the sugar.
4. Blend the butter into the mixture to combine everything well.
5. Use your hands to knead the mixture, forming a smooth consistency.
6. Shape the mixture into 10 equal-sized finger shapes, marking them with the tines of a fork for decoration if desired.
7. Lightly spritz the Air Fryer basket with the cooking spray. Place the cookies inside, spacing them out well.
8. Bake the cookies for 12 minutes.
9. Let cool slightly before serving. Alternatively, you can store the cookies in an airtight container for up to 3 days.

Coconut & Banana Cake

Prep + Cook Time: 1 hour 15 minutes | Servings: 5

Ingredients

2/3 cup sugar, shaved
2/3 cup unsalted butter
3 eggs
1 ¼ cup flour
1 ripe banana, mashed
½ tsp. vanilla extract
1/8 tsp. baking soda
Sea salt to taste

Topping Ingredients

sugar to taste, shaved
Walnuts to taste, roughly chopped
Bananas to taste, sliced

Instructions

1. Pre-heat the Air Fryer to 360°F.
2. Mix together the flour, baking soda, and a pinch of sea salt.
3. In a separate bowl, combine the butter, vanilla extract and sugar using an electrical mixer or a blender, to achieve a fluffy consistency. Beat in the eggs one at a time.
4. Throw in half of the flour mixture and stir thoroughly. Add in the mashed banana and continue to mix. Lastly, throw in the remaining half of the flour mixture and combine until a smooth batter is formed.
5. Transfer the batter to a baking tray and top with the banana slices.
6. Scatter the chopped walnuts on top before dusting with the sugar
7. Place a sheet of foil over the tray and pierce several holes in it.
8. Put the covered tray in the Air Fryer. Cook for 48 minutes.
9. Decrease the temperature to 320°F, take off the foil, and allow to cook for an additional 10 minutes until golden brown.
10. Insert a skewer or toothpick in the center of the cake. If it comes out clean, the cake is ready.

Roasted Pumpkin Seeds & Cinnamon

Prep + Cook Time: 35 minutes | Servings: 2

Ingredients

1 cup pumpkin raw seeds
1 tbsp. ground cinnamon
2 tbsp. sugar
1 cup water
1 tbsp. olive oil

Instructions

1. In a frying pan, combine the pumpkin seeds, cinnamon and water.
2. Boil the mixture over a high heat for 2 - 3 minutes.
3. Pour out the water and place the seeds on a clean kitchen towel, allowing them to dry for 20 - 30 minutes.
4. In a bowl, mix together the sugar, dried seeds, a pinch of cinnamon and one tablespoon of olive oil.
5. Pre-heat the Air Fryer to 340°F.
6. Place the seed mixture in the fryer basket and allow to cook for 15 minutes, shaking the basket periodically throughout.

Pineapple Sticks

Prep + Cook Time: 20 minutes | Servings: 4

Ingredients

½ fresh pineapple, cut into sticks
¼ cup desiccated coconut

Instructions

1. Pre-heat the Air Fryer to 400°F.
2. Coat the pineapple sticks in the desiccated coconut and put each one in the Air Fryer basket.
3. Air fry for 10 minutes.

Sponge Cake

Prep + Cook Time: 50 minutes | Servings: 8

Ingredients

For the Cake:
9 oz. sugar
9 oz. butter
3 eggs
9 oz. flour
1 tsp. vanilla extract
Zest of 1 lemon
1 tsp. baking powder

For the Frosting

Juice of 1 lemon
Zest of 1 lemon
1 tsp. yellow food coloring
7 oz. sugar
4 egg whites

Instructions

1. Pre-heat your Air Fryer to 320°F.
2. Use an electric mixer to combine all of the cake ingredients.
3. Grease the insides of two round cake pans.
4. Pour an equal amount of the batter into each pan.
5. Place one pan in the fryer and cook for 15 minutes, before repeating with the second pan.
6. In the meantime, mix together all of the frosting ingredients.
7. Allow the cakes to cool. Spread the frosting on top of one cake and stack the other cake on top.

Apple Wedges

Prep + Cook Time: 25 minutes | Servings: 4

Ingredients

4 large apples
2 tbsp. olive oil
½ cup dried apricots, chopped
1 - 2 tbsp. sugar
½ tsp. ground cinnamon

Instructions

1. Peel the apples and slice them into eight wedges. Throw away the cores.
2. Coat the apple wedges with the oil.
3. Place each wedge in the Air Fryer and cook for 12 - 15 minutes at 350°F.
4. Add in the apricots and allow to cook for a further 3 minutes.
5. Stir together the sugar and cinnamon. Sprinkle this mixture over the cooked apples before serving.

Chocolate Lava Cake

Prep + Cook Time: 20 minutes | Servings: 4

Ingredients

1 cup dark cocoa candy melts
1 stick butter
2 eggs
4 tbsp. sugar
1 tbsp. honey
4 tbsp. flour
Pinch of kosher salt
Pinch of ground cloves
¼ tsp. grated nutmeg
¼ tsp. cinnamon powder

Instructions

1.   Spritz the insides of four custard cups with cooking spray.
2.   Melt the cocoa candy melts and butter in the microwave for 30 seconds to 1 minute.
3.   In a large bowl, combine the eggs, sugar and honey with a whisk until frothy. Pour in the melted chocolate mix.
4.   Throw in the rest of the ingredients and combine well with an electric mixer or a manual whisk.
5.   Transfer equal portions of the mixture into the prepared custard cups.
6.   Place in the Air Fryer and air bake at 350°F for 12 minutes.
7.   Remove from the Air Fryer and allow to cool for 5 to 6 minutes.
8.   Place each cup upside-down on a dessert plate and let the cake slide out. Serve with fruits and chocolate syrup if desired.

English Lemon Tarts

Prep + Cook Time: 30 minutes | Servings: 4

Ingredients

½ cup butter
½ lb. flour
2 tbsp. sugar
1 large lemon, juiced and zested
2 tbsp. lemon curd
Pinch of nutmeg

Instructions

1.   In a large bowl, combine the butter, flour and sugar until a crumbly consistency is achieved.
2.   Add in the lemon zest and juice, followed by a pinch of nutmeg. Continue to combine. If necessary, add a couple tablespoons of water to soften the dough.
3.   Sprinkle the insides of a few small pastry tins with flour. Pour equal portions of the dough into each one and add sugar or lemon zest on top.
4.   Pre-heat the Air Fryer to 360°F.
5.   Place the lemon tarts inside the fryer and allow to cook for 15 minutes.

Blueberry Pancakes

Prep + Cook Time: 20 minutes | Servings: 4

Ingredients

½ tsp. vanilla extract
2 tbsp. honey
½ cup blueberries
½ cup sugar
2 cups + 2 tbsp. flour
3 eggs, beaten
1 cup milk
1 tsp. baking powder
Pinch of salt

Instructions

1.   Pre-heat the Air Fryer to 390°F.
2.   In a bowl, mix together all of the dry ingredients.
3.   Pour in the wet ingredients and combine with a whisk, ensuring the mixture becomes smooth.
4.   Roll each blueberry in some flour to lightly coat it before folding it into the mixture. This is to ensure they do not change the color of the batter.
5.   Coat the inside of a baking dish with a little oil or butter.
6.   Spoon several equal amounts of the batter onto the baking dish, spreading them into pancake-shapes and ensuring to space them out well. This may have to be completed in two batches.
7.   Place the dish in the fryer and bake for about 10 minutes.

New England Pumpkin Cake

Prep + Cook Time: 50 minutes | Servings: 4

Ingredients

1 large egg
½ cup skimmed milk
7 oz. flour
2 tbsp. sugar
5 oz. pumpkin puree
Pinch of salt
Pinch of cinnamon [if desired]
Cooking spray

Instructions

1.   Stir together the pumpkin puree and sugar in a bowl. Crack in the egg and combine using a whisk until smooth.
2.   Add in the flour and salt, stirring constantly. Pour in the milk, ensuring to combine everything well.
3.   Spritz a baking tin with cooking spray.
4.   Transfer the batter to the baking tin.
5.   Pre-heat the Air Fryer to 350°F.
6.   Put the tin in the Air Fryer basket and bake for 15 minutes.

Mixed Berry Puffed Pastry

Prep + Cook Time: 20 minutes | Servings: 3

Ingredients

3 pastry dough sheets
½ cup mixed berries, mashed
1 tbsp. honey
2 tbsp. cream cheese
3 tbsp. chopped walnuts
¼ tsp. vanilla extract

Instructions

1.   Pre-heat your Air Fryer to 375°F.
2.   Roll out the pastry sheets and spread the cream cheese over each one.
3.   In a bowl, combine the berries, vanilla extract and honey.
4.   Cover a baking sheet with parchment paper.
5.   Spoon equal amounts of the berry mixture into the center of each sheet of pastry. Scatter the chopped walnuts on top.
6.   Fold up the pastry around the filling and press down the edges with the back of a fork to seal them.
7.   Transfer the baking sheet to the Air Fryer and cook for approximately 15 minutes.

Cherry Pie

Prep + Cook Time: 35 minutes | Servings: 8

Ingredients
1 tbsp. milk
2 ready-made pie crusts
21 oz. cherry pie filling
1 egg yolk

Instructions
1.   Pre-heat the Air Fryer to 310°F.
2.   Coat the inside of a pie pan with a little oil or butter and lay one of the pie crusts inside. Use a fork to pierce a few holes in the pastry.
3.   Spread the pie filling evenly over the crust.
4.   Slice the other crust into strips and place them on top of the pie filling to make the pie look more homemade.
5.   Place in the Air Fryer and cook for 15 minutes.

Apple Pie

Prep + Cook Time: 25 minutes | Servings: 7

Ingredients
2 large apples
½ cup flour
2 tbsp. unsalted butter
1 tbsp. sugar
½ tsp. cinnamon

Instructions
1.   Pre-heat the Air Fryer to 360°F.
2.   In a large bowl, combine the flour and butter. Pour in the sugar, continuing to mix.
3.   Add in a few tablespoons of water and combine everything to create a smooth dough.
4.   Grease the insides of a few small pastry tins with butter. Divide the dough between each tin and lay each portion flat inside.
5.   Peel, core and dice up the apples. Put the diced apples on top of the pastry and top with a sprinkling of sugar and cinnamon.
6.   Place the pastry tins in your Air Fryer and cook for 15 - 17 minutes.
7.   Serve with whipped cream or ice cream if desired.

Chocolate Molten Lava Cake

Prep + Cook Time: 25 minutes | Servings: 4

Ingredients
3 ½ oz. butter, melted
3 ½ tbsp. sugar
3 ½ oz. chocolate, melted
1 ½ tbsp. flour
2 eggs

Instructions
1.   Pre-heat the Air Fryer to 375°F.
2.   Grease four ramekins with a little butter.
3.   Rigorously combine the eggs and butter before stirring in the melted chocolate.
4.   Slowly fold in the flour.
5.   Spoon an equal amount of the mixture into each ramekin.
6.   Put them in the Air Fryer and cook for 10 minutes
7.   Place the ramekins upside-down on plates and let the cakes fall out. Serve hot.

Pineapple Cake

Prep + Cook Time: 40 minutes | Servings: 4

Ingredients
2 cups flour
¼ lb. butter
¼ cup sugar
½ lb. pineapple, chopped
½ cup pineapple juice
1 oz. dark chocolate, grated
1 large egg
2 tbsp. skimmed milk

Instructions
1.   Pre-heat the Air Fryer to 370°F.
2.   Grease a cake tin with a little oil or butter.
3.   In a bowl, combine the butter and flour to create a crumbly consistency.
4.   Add in the sugar, diced pineapple, juice, and crushed dark chocolate and mix well.
5.   In a separate bowl, combine the egg and milk. Add this mixture to the flour and stir well until a soft dough forms.
6.   Pour the mixture into the cake tin and transfer to the Air Fryer.
7.   Cook for 35 - 40 minutes.

Glazed Donuts

Prep + Cook Time: 25 minutes | Servings: 2 – 4

Ingredients
1 can [8 oz.] refrigerated croissant dough
Cooking spray
1 can [16 oz.] vanilla frosting

Instructions
1.   Cut the croissant dough into 1-inch-round slices. Make a hole in the center of each one to create a donut.
2.   Put the donuts in the Air Fryer basket, taking care not to overlap any, and spritz with cooking spray. You may need to cook everything in multiple batches.
3.   Cook at 400°F for 2 minutes. Turn the donuts over and cook for another 3 minutes.
4.   Place the rolls on a paper plate.
5.   Microwave a half-cup of frosting for 30 seconds and pour a drizzling of the frosting over the donuts before serving.

Apple Dumplings

Prep + Cook Time: 40 minutes | Servings: 2

Ingredients
2 tbsp. sultanas
2 sheets puff pastry
2 tbsp. butter, melted
2 small apples
1 tbsp. sugar

Instructions
1.   Pre-heat your Air Fryer to 350°F
2.   Peel the apples and remove the cores.
3.   In a bowl, stir together the sugar and the sultanas.
4.   Lay one apple on top of each pastry sheet and stuff the sugar and sultanas into the holes where the cores used to be.
5.   Wrap the pastry around the apples, covering them completely.
6.   Put them on a sheet of aluminum foil and coat each dumpling with a light brushing of melted butter
7.   Transfer to the Air Fryer and bake for 25 minutes until a golden brown color is achieved and the apples have softened inside.

Bananas & Ice Cream

Prep + Cook Time: 25 minutes | Servings: 2

Ingredients

2 large bananas
1 tbsp. butter
1 tbsp. sugar
2 tbsp. friendly bread crumbs
Vanilla ice cream for serving

Instructions

1. Place the butter in the Air Fryer basket and allow it to melt for 1 minute at 350°F.
2. Combine the sugar and bread crumbs in a bowl.
3. Slice the bananas into 1-inch-round pieces. Drop them into the sugar mixture and coat them well.
4. Place the bananas in the Air Fryer and cook for 10 – 15 minutes.
5. Serve warm, with ice cream on the side if desired.

Raspberry Muffins

Prep + Cook Time: 35 minutes | Servings: 10

Ingredients

1 egg
1 cup frozen raspberries, coated with some flour
1 ½ cups flour
½ cup sugar
⅓ cup vegetable oil
2 tsp. baking powder
Yogurt, as needed
1 tsp. lemon zest
2 tbsp. lemon juice
Pinch of sea salt

Instructions

1. Pre-heat the Air Fryer to 350°F
2. Place all of the dry ingredients in a bowl and combine well.
3. Beat the egg and pour it into a cup. Mix it with the oil and lemon juice. Add in the yogurt, to taste.
4. Mix together the dry and wet ingredients.
5. Add in the lemon zest and raspberries.
6. Coat the insides of 10 muffin tins with a little butter.
7. Spoon an equal amount of the mixture into each muffin tin.
8. Transfer to the fryer, and cook for 10 minutes, in batches if necessary.

Pecan Pie

Prep + Cook Time: 1 hour 10 minutes | Servings: 4

Ingredients

1x 8-inch pie dough
½ tsp. cinnamon
¾ tsp. vanilla extract
2 eggs
¾ cup maple syrup
1/8 tsp. nutmeg
2 tbsp. butter
1 tbsp. butter, melted
2 tbsp. sugar
½ cup chopped pecans

Instructions

1. Pre-heat the Air Fryer to 370°F.
2. In a small bowl, coat the pecans in the melted butter.
3. Transfer the pecans to the Air Fryer and allow them to toast for about 10 minutes.
4. Put the pie dough in a greased pie pan and add the pecans on top.
5. In a bowl, mix together the rest of the ingredients. Pour this over the pecans.
6. Place the pan in the fryer and bake for 25 minutes.

Orange Carrot Cake

Prep + Cook Time: 30 minutes | Servings: 8

Ingredients

2 large carrots, peeled and grated
1 ¾ cup flour
¾ cup sugar
2 eggs
10 tbsp. olive oil
2 cups sugar
1 tsp. mixed spice
2 tbsp. milk
4 tbsp. melted butter
1 small orange, rind and juice

Instructions

1. Set the Air Fryer to 360°F and allow to heat up for 10 minutes.
2. Place a baking sheet inside the tin.
3. Combine the flour, sugar, grated carrots, and mixed spice.
4. Pour the milk, beaten eggs, and olive oil into the middle of the batter and mix well.
5. Pour the mixture in the tin, transfer to the fryer and cook for 5 minutes.
6. Lower the heat to 320°F and allow to cook for an additional 5 minutes.
7. In the meantime, prepare the frosting by combining the melted butter, orange juice, rind, and sugar until a smooth consistency is achieved.
8. Remove the cake from the fryer, allow it to cool for several minutes and add the frosting on top.

Chocolate Cookies

Prep + Cook Time: 30 minutes | Servings: 8

Ingredients

3 oz. sugar
4 oz. butter
1 tbsp. honey
6 oz. flour
1 ½ tbsp. milk
2 oz. chocolate chips

Instructions

1. Pre-heat the Air Fryer to 350°F.
2. Mix together the sugar and butter using an electric mixer, until a fluffy texture is achieved.
3. Stir in the remaining ingredients, minus the chocolate chips.
4. Gradually fold in the chocolate chips.
5. Spoon equal portions of the mixture onto a lined baking sheet and flatten out each one with a spoon. Ensure the cookies are not touching.
6. Place in the fryer and cook for 18 minutes.

Butter Cake

Prep + Cook Time: 25 minutes | Servings: 2

Ingredients

1 egg
1 ½ cup flour
7 tbsp. butter, at room temperature
6 tbsp. milk
6 tbsp. sugar
Pinch of sea salt
Cooking spray
Dusting of sugar to serve

Instructions

1.   Pre-heat the Air Fryer to 360°F.
2.   Spritz the inside of a small ring cake tin with cooking spray.
3.   In a bowl, combine the butter and sugar using a whisk.
4.   Stir in the egg and continue to mix everything until the mixture is smooth and fluffy.
5.   Pour the flour through a sieve into the bowl.
6.   Pour in the milk, before adding a pinch of salt, and combine once again to incorporate everything well.
7.   Pour the batter into the tin and use the back of a spoon to made sure the surface is even.
8.   Place in the fryer and cook for 15 minutes.
9.   Before removing it from the fryer, ensure the cake is cooked through by inserting a toothpick into the center and checking that it comes out clean.
10.   Allow the cake to cool and serve.

Swedish Chocolate Mug Cake

Prep + Cook Time: 15 minutes | Servings: 1

Ingredients

1 tbsp. cocoa powder
3 tbsp. coconut oil
¼ cup flour
3 tbsp. whole milk
5 tbsp. sugar

Instructions

1.   In a bowl, stir together all of the ingredients to combine them completely.
2.   Take a short, stout mug and pour the mixture into it.
3.   Put the mug in your Air Fryer and cook for 10 minutes at 390°F.

Dunky Dough Dippers & Chocolate Sauce

Prep + Cook Time: 45 minutes | Servings: 5

Ingredients

¾ cup sugar
1 lb. friendly bread dough
1 cup heavy cream
12 oz. high quality semi-sweet chocolate chips
½ cup butter, melted
2 tbsp. extract

Instructions

1.   Pre-heat the Air Fryer to 350°F.
2.   Coat the inside of the basket with a little melted butter.
3.   Halve and roll up the dough to create two 15-inch logs. Slice each log into 20 disks.
4.   Halve each disk and twist it 3 or 4 times.
5.   Lay out a cookie sheet and lay the twisted dough pieces on top. Brush the pieces with some more melted butter and sprinkle on the sugar.
6.   Place the sheet in the fryer and air fry for 5 minutes. Flip the dough twists over, and brush the other side with more butter. Cook for an additional 3 minutes. It may be necessary to complete this step in batches.
7.   In the meantime, make the chocolate sauce. Firstly, put the heavy cream into a saucepan over the medium heat and allow it to simmer.
8.   Put the chocolate chips into a large bowl and add the simmering cream on top. Whisk the chocolate chips everything together until a smooth consistency is achieved. Stir in 2 tablespoons of extract.
9.   Transfer the baked cookies in a shallow dish, pour over the rest of the melted butter and sprinkle on the sugar.
10.   Drizzle on the chocolate sauce before serving.

Peach Crumble

Prep + Cook Time: 35 minutes | Servings: 6

Ingredients

1 ½ lb. peaches, peeled and chopped
2 tbsp. lemon juice
1 cup flour
1 tbsp. water
½ cup sugar
5 tbsp. cold butter
Pinch of sea salt

Instructions

1.   Mash the peaches a little with a fork to achieve a lumpy consistency.
2.   Add in two tablespoons of sugar and the lemon juice.
3.   In a bowl, combine the flour, salt, and sugar. Throw in a tablespoon of water before adding in the cold butter, mixing until crumbly.
4.   Grease the inside of a baking dish and arrange the berries at the bottom. Top with the crumbs.
5.   Transfer the dish to the Air Fryer and air fry for 20 minutes at 390°F.

Banana Walnut Cake

Prep + Cook Time: 55 minutes | Servings: 6

Ingredients

16 oz. bananas, mashed
8 oz. flour
6 oz. sugar
3.5 oz. walnuts, chopped
2.5 oz. butter
2 eggs
¼ tsp. baking soda

Instructions

1.   Coat the inside of a baking dish with a little oil.
2.   Pre-heat the Air Fryer at 355°F.
3.   In a bowl combine the sugar, butter, egg, flour and soda using a whisk. Throw in the bananas and walnuts.
4.   Transfer the mixture to the dish. Place the dish in the fryer and cook for 10 minutes.
5.   Reduce the heat to 330°F and cook for another 15 minutes. Serve hot.

Cheesy Lemon Cake

Prep + Cook Time: 60 minutes | Servings: 6

Ingredients

17.5 oz. ricotta cheese
5.4 oz. sugar
3 eggs
3 tbsp. flour
1 lemon, juiced and zested
2 tsp. vanilla extract [optional]

Instructions

1. Pre-heat Air Fryer to 320°F.
2. Combine all of the ingredients until a creamy consistency is achieved.
3. Place the mixture in a cake tin.
4. Transfer the tin to the fryer and cook the cakes for 25 minutes.
5. Remove the cake from the fryer, allow to cool, and serve.

Chocolate Brownies & Caramel Sauce

Prep + Cook Time: 45 minutes | Servings: 4

Ingredients

½ cup butter, plus more for greasing the pan
1 ¾ oz. unsweetened chocolate
1 cup sugar
2 medium eggs, beaten
1 cup flour
2 tsp. vanilla
2 tbsp. water
2/3 cup milk

Instructions

1. In a saucepan over a medium heat, melt the butter and chocolate together.
2. Take the saucepan off the heat and stir in the sugar, eggs, flour, and vanilla, combining everything well.
3. Pre-heat your Air Fryer to 350°F.
4. Coat the inside of a baking dish with a little butter. Transfer the batter to the dish and place inside the fryer.
5. Bake for 15 minutes.
6. In the meantime, prepare the caramel sauce. In a small saucepan, slowly bring the water to a boil. Cook for around 3 minutes, until the mixture turns light brown.
7. Lower the heat and allow to cook for another two minutes. Gradually add in the rest of the butter. Take the saucepan off the heat and allow the caramel to cool.
8. When the brownies are ready, slice them into squares. Pour the caramel sauce on top and add on some sliced banana if desired before serving.

Pumpkin Cinnamon Pudding

Prep + Cook Time: 25 minutes | Servings: 4

Ingredients

3 cups pumpkin puree
3 tbsp. honey
1 tbsp. ginger
1 tbsp. cinnamon
1 tsp. clove
1 tsp. nutmeg
1 cup full-fat cream
2 eggs
1 cup sugar

Instructions

1. Pre-heat your Air Fryer to 390°F.
2. In a bowl, stir all of the ingredients together to combine.
3. Grease the inside of a small baking dish.
4. Pour the mixture into the dish and transfer to the fryer. Cook for 15 minutes. Serve with whipped cream if desired.

Banana Walnut Bread

Prep + Cook Time: 40 minutes | Servings: 1 loaf

Ingredients

7 oz. flour
¼ tsp. baking powder
2.5 oz. butter
5.5 oz. sugar
2 medium eggs
14 oz. bananas, peeled
2.8 oz. chopped walnuts

Instructions

1. Pre-heat the Air Fryer to 350°F.
2. Take a baking tin small enough to fit inside the Air Fryer and grease the inside with butter.
3. Mix together the flour and the baking powder in a bowl.
4. In a separate bowl, beat together the sugar and butter until fluffy and pale. Gradually add in the flour and egg. Stir.
5. Throw in the walnuts and combine again.
6. Mash the bananas using a fork and transfer to the bowl. Mix once more, until everything is incorporated.
7. Pour the mixture into the tin, place inside the fryer and cook for 10 minutes.

Peach Slices

Prep + Cook Time: 40 minutes | Servings: 4

Ingredients

4 cups peaches, sliced
2 – 3 tbsp. sugar
2 tbsp. flour
⅓ cup oats
2 tbsp. unsalted butter
¼ tsp. vanilla extract
1 tsp. cinnamon

Instructions

1. In a large bowl, combine the peach slices, sugar, vanilla extract, and cinnamon. Pour the mixture into a baking tin and place it in the Air Fryer.
2. Cook for 20 minutes on 290°F.
3. In the meantime, combine the oats, flour, and unsalted butter in a separate bowl.
4. Once the peach slices cooked, pour the butter mixture on top of them.
5. Cook for an additional 10 minutes at 300 - 310°F.
6. Remove from the fryer and allow to crisp up for 5 – 10. Serve with ice cream if desired.

Vanilla Souffle

Prep + Cook Time: 50 minutes | Servings: 6

Ingredients

¼ cup flour
¼ cup butter, softened
1 cup whole milk
¼ cup sugar
2 tsp. vanilla extract
1 vanilla bean
5 egg whites
4 egg yolks
1 oz. sugar
1 tsp. cream of tartar

Instructions

1.   Mix together the flour and butter to create a smooth paste.
2.   In a saucepan, heat up the milk. Add the ¼ cup sugar and allow it to dissolve.
3.   Put the vanilla bean in the mixture and bring it to a boil.
4.   Pour in the flour-butter mixture. Beat the contents of the saucepan thoroughly with a wire whisk, removing all the lumps.
5.   Reduce the heat and allow the mixture to simmer and thicken for a number of minutes.
6.   Take the saucepan off the heat. Remove the vanilla bean and let the mixture cool for 10 minutes in an ice bath.
7.   In the meantime, grease six 3-oz. ramekins or soufflé dishes with butter and add a sprinkling of sugar to each one.
8.   In a separate bowl quickly, rigorously stir the egg yolks and vanilla extract together. Combine with the milk mixture.
9.   In another bowl, beat the egg whites, 1 oz. sugar and cream of tartar to form medium stiff peaks.
10.   Fold the egg whites into the soufflé base. Transfer everything to the ramekins, smoothing the surfaces with a knife or the back of a spoon.
11.   Pre-heat the Air Fryer to 330°F.
12.   Put the ramekins in the cooking basket and cook for 14 – 16 minutes. You may need to complete this step in multiple batches.
13.   Serve the soufflés topped with powdered sugar and with a side of chocolate sauce.

Butter Marshmallow Fluff Turnover

Prep + Cook Time: 35 minutes | Servings: 4

Ingredients

4 sheets filo pastry, defrosted
4 tbsp. chunky peanut butter
4 tsp. marshmallow fluff
2 oz. butter, melted
Pinch of sea salt

Instructions

1.   Pre-heat the Air Fryer to 360°F.
2.   Roll out the pastry sheets. Coat one with a light brushing of butter.
3.   Lay a second pastry sheet on top of the first one. Brush once again with butter. Repeat until all 4 sheets have been used.
4.   Slice the filo layers into four strips, measuring roughly 3 inches x 12 inches.
5.   Spread one tablespoon of peanut butter and one teaspoon of marshmallow fluff on the underside of each pastry strip.
6.   Take the tip of each sheet and fold it backwards over the filling, forming a triangle. Repeat this action in a zigzag manner until the filling is completely enclosed.
7.   Seal the ends of each turnover with a light brushing of butter.
8.   Put the turnovers in the fryer basket and cook for 3 – 5 minutes, until they turn golden brown and puffy.
9.   Sprinkle a little sea salt over each turnover before serving.

Chocolate-Covered Maple Bacon

Prep + Cook Time: 25 minutes | Servings: 4

Ingredients

8 slices sugar-free bacon
1 tbsp. granular erythritol
1/3 cup low-carb sugar-free chocolate chips
1 tsp. coconut oil
½ tsp. maple extract

Instructions

1.   Place the bacon in the fryer's basket and add the erythritol on top. Cook for six minutes at 350°F and turn the bacon over. Leave to cook another six minutes or until the bacon is sufficiently crispy.
2.   Take the bacon out of the fryer and leave it to cool.
3.   Microwave the chocolate chips and coconut oil together for half a minute. Remove from the microwave and mix together before stirring in the maple extract.
4.   Set the bacon flat on a piece of parchment paper and pour the mixture over. Allow to harden in the refrigerator for roughly five minutes before serving.

Sugar Pork Rinds

Prep + Cook Time: 10 minutes | Servings: 2

Ingredients

2 oz. pork rinds
2 tsp. unsalted butter, melted
¼ cup powdered erythritol
½ tsp. ground cinnamon

Instructions

1.   Coat the rinds with the melted butter.
2.   In a separate bowl, combine the erythritol and cinnamon and pour over the pork rinds, ensuring the rinds are covered completely and evenly.
3.   Transfer the pork rinds into the fryer and cook at 400°F for five minutes.

Toasted Coconut Flakes

Prep + Cook Time: 5 minutes | Servings: 1

Ingredients

1 cup unsweetened coconut flakes
2 tsp. coconut oil, melted
¼ cup granular erythritol
Salt

Instructions

In a large bowl, combine the coconut flakes, oil, granular erythritol, and a pinch of salt, ensuring that the flakes are coated completely.
Place the coconut flakes in your fryer and cook at 300°F for three minutes, giving the basket a good shake a few times throughout the cooking time. Fry until golden and serve.

Blackberry Crisp

Prep + Cook Time: 18 minutes | Servings: 1

Ingredients

2 tbsp. lemon juice
1/3 cup powdered erythritol
¼ tsp. xantham gum
2 cup blackberries
1 cup crunchy granola

Instructions

1.   In a bowl, combine the lemon juice, erythritol, xantham gum, and blackberries. Transfer to a round baking dish about six inches in diameter and seal with aluminum foil.
2.   Put the dish in the fryer and leave to cook for twelve minutes at 350°F.
3.   Take care when removing the dish from the fryer. Give the blackberries another stir and top with the granola.
4.   Return the dish to the fryer and cook for an additional three minutes, this time at 320°F. Serve once the granola has turned brown and enjoy.

Churros

Prep + Cook Time: 15 minutes | Servings: 1

Ingredients

½ cup water
¼ cup butter
½ cup flour
3 eggs
2 ½ tsp. sugar

Instructions

1.   In a saucepan, bring the water and butter to a boil. Once it is bubbling, add the flour and mix to create a doughy consistency.
2.   Remove from the heat, allow to cool, and crack the eggs into the saucepan. Blend with a hand mixer until the dough turns fluffy.
3.   Transfer the dough into a piping bag.
4.   Pre-heat the fryer at 380°F.
5.   Pipe the dough into the fryer in several three-inch-long segments. Cook for ten minutes before removing from the fryer and coating in the sugar.
6.   Serve with the low-carb chocolate sauce of your choice.

Peanut Butter Cookies

Prep + Cook Time: 15 minutes | Servings: 1

Ingredients

¼ tsp. salt
4 tbsp. erythritol
½ cup peanut butter
1 egg

Instructions

1.   Combine the salt, erythritol, and peanut butter in a bowl, incorporating everything well. Break the egg over the mixture and mix to create a dough.
2.   Flatten the dough using a rolling pin and cut into shapes with a knife or cookie cutter. Make a crisscross on the top of each cookie with a fork.
3.   Pre-heat your fryer at 360°F.
4.   Once the fryer has warmed up, put the cookies inside and leave to cook for ten minutes. Take care when taking them out and allow to cook before enjoying.

Avocado Pudding

Prep + Cook Time: 5 minutes | Servings: 1

Ingredients

Avocado
3 tsp. liquid Sugar
1 tbsp. cocoa powder
4 tsp. unsweetened milk
¼ tsp. vanilla extract

Instructions

1.   Pre-heat your fryer at 360°F.
2.   Halve the avocado, twist to open, and scoop out the pit.
3.   Spoon the flesh into a bowl and mash it with a fork. Throw in the Sugar, cocoa powder, milk, and vanilla extract, and combine everything with a hand mixer.
4.   Transfer this mixture to the basket of your fryer and cook for three minutes.

Chia Pudding

Prep + Cook Time: 10 minutes | Servings: 1

Ingredients

cup chia seeds
1 cup unsweetened coconut milk
1 tsp. liquid Sugar
1 tbsp. coconut oil
1 tsp. butter

Instructions

Pre-heat the fryer at 360°F.
In a bowl, gently combine the chia seeds with the milk and Sugar, before mixing the coconut oil and butter. Spoon seven equal-sized portions into seven ramekins and set these inside the fryer.
Cook for four minutes. Take care when removing the ramekins from the fryer and allow to cool for four minutes before serving.

Bacon Cookies

Prep + Cook Time: 15 minutes | Servings: 2

Ingredients

¼ tsp. ginger
1/5 tsp. baking soda
2/3 cup peanut butter
2 tbsp. Swerve
3 slices bacon, cooked and chopped

Instructions

1.   In a bowl, mix the ginger, baking soda, peanut butter, and Swerve together, making sure to combine everything well.
2.   Stir in the chopped bacon.
3.   With clean hands, shape the mixture into a cylinder and cut in six. Press down each slice into a cookie with your palm.
4.   Pre-heat your fryer at 350°F.
5.   When the fryer is warm, put the cookies inside and cook for seven minutes. Take care when taking them out of the fryer and allow to cool before serving.

App e ndix:R e cip e s Ind e x

Cajun Seasoned Chicken 85
Cajun Shrimp 57
Cajun Spiced Snack 74
Cajun-Mustard Turkey Fingers 82
Calamari 64
Carrot Croquettes 49
Carrots & Cumin 108
Carrots & Rhubarb 66
Cashew & Chicken Manchurian 44
Cast-Iron Cheesy Chicken 30
Catfish 57
Cauliflower 39
Cauliflower Bites 41
Cauliflower Cheese Tater Tots 37
Cauliflower Rice Chicken Curry 30
Cauliflower Steak 41
Cauliflower Tots 48
Charcoal Chicken 90
Cheddar & Bacon Quiche 25
Cheddar Bacon Burst 27
Cheese & Bacon Rolls 45
Cheese & Chicken Sandwich 21
Cheese & Macaroni Balls 45
Cheese Boats 68
Cheese Crust Salmon 61
Cheese Lings 51
Cheese Pizza 45
Cheese Pizza with Broccoli Crust 99
Cheese Sticks 108
Cheese Tilapia 61
Cheeseburger Sliders 46
Cheeseburgers 94
Cheesecake Cups 112
Cheesy Bacon Bread 104
Cheesy Broccoli Balls 74
Cheesy Cauliflower Bites 105
Cheesy Garlic Bread 66
Cheesy Kale 100
Cheesy Lemon Cake 123
Cheesy Lemon Halibut 55
Cheesy Potatoes 109
Cheesy Schnitzel 97
Cherry Pie 120
Chia & Oat Porridge 26
Chia Pudding 125
Chicken & Honey Sauce 79
Chicken & Pepperoni Pizza 77
Chicken & Potatoes 88
Chicken & Veggies 41
Chicken Bites 91
Chicken Breasts & Spiced Tomatoes 78
Chicken Curry 83
Chicken Drumsticks 84
Chicken Escallops 92
Chicken Fillets & Brie 45
Chicken Fillets 85
Chicken in a Blanket 30
Chicken Kebabs 87
Chicken Legs 90
Chicken Meatballs 90

Chicken Nuggets 85
Chicken Pizza Crusts 77
Chicken Quesadillas 44
Chicken Strips 86
Chicken Surprise 85
Chicken Tenderloins 87
Chicken Tenders 88
Chicken Wings & Piri Piri Sauce 81
Chicken Wings 92
Chicken Wrapped in Bacon 91
Chicken, Mushroom & Spinach Pizza 68
Chicken, Rice & Vegetables 91
Chicken-Mushroom Casserole 43
Chickpea & Avocado Mash 38
Chickpeas 37
Chili Potato Wedges 36
Chimichurri Turkey 78
Chinese Chicken Wings 88
Chipotle Jicama Hash 101
Choco Bars 24
Choco Bread 25
Choco-berry Fudge Sauce 113
Choco-Coconut Puddin 113
Chocolate Brownies & Caramel Sauce 123
Chocolate Cheesecake 112
Chocolate Chip Cookies 115
Chocolate Cookies 121
Chocolate Lava Cake 119
Chocolate Molten Lava Cake 120
Chocolate Peanut Butter Cups 113
Chocolate Pudding 113
Chocolate-Covered Maple Bacon 124
Chorizo Risotto 25
Christmas Brussels Sprouts 36
Christmas Flounder 57
Chunky Fish 62
Churros 125
Cilantro Drumsticks 75
Cinnamon Toasts 22
Cocktail Flanks 72
Coconut & Banana Cake 118
Coconut Brownies 116
Coconut Chicken 91
Coconut Pillow 112
Coconut Prawns 57
Coconut Shrimp 70
Cod 61
Cod Nuggets 56
Coffee Donuts 20
Coffee Surprise 112
Colby Potato Patties 50
Colby's Turkey Meatloaf 84
Country Style Chard 102
Crab Croquettes 72
Crab Herb Croquettes 60
Crab Legs 54
Cracked Chicken Tenders 86
Cranberry Cream Surprise 114
Cream Cheese Pancakes 16

Italian Chicken Thighs 77
Italian Lamb Chops 34

J

Jalapeno Chicken Breasts 76
Jalapeño Guacamole 102
Jarlsberg Lunch Omelet 27
Jicama Fries 48
Juicy Mexican Pork Chops 34
Jumbo Shrimp 61

K

Kale Chips 109
Kidney Beans Oatmeal 45

L

Lamb Ribs 34
Lamb Satay 34
Lasagna Spaghetti Squash 28
Lemon & Garlic Chicken 85
Lemon Butter Pound Cake 114
Lemon Butter Scallops 55
Lemon Dill Trout 29
Lemon Fish 61
Lemon Garlic Shrimp 54
Lemon Green Beans 110
Lemon Pepper Chicken Legs 76
Lime & Honey Chicken Wings 87
Lime Dijon Chicken 88
London Broil 93
Low-Carb Pita Chips 47
Low-Carb Pizza Crust 47

M

Mac & Cheese 43
Mac's Chicken Nuggets 84
Macaroon Bites 113
Maple Cinnamon Buns 23
Maple Glazed Beets 67
Marinated Flank Steak 93
Marinated Sardines 59
Marjoram Chicken 83
Marrod's Meatballs 81
Masala Cashew 71
Mashed Garlic Turnips 28
Max's Meatloaf 98
Meatballs 31
Meatballs in Tomato Sauce 71
Meatloaf 94
Mediterranean Salad 65
Mediterranean Vegetables 40
Mexican Pizza 46
Mighty Meatballs 97
Mini Pepper Poppers 103
Mini Strawberry Pies 116
Mix Nuts 109
Mixed Berry Puffed Pastry 119
Monkey Salad 27
Moroccan Chicken 88
Mozzarella Beef 33
Mozzarella Bruschetta 44
Mozzarella Sticks 104
Mozzarella Turkey Rolls 92
Mu Shu Lunch Pork 27

Mushroom Loaf 99
Mushroom Pizza Squares 37

N

Naan Bread Dippers 70
Nearly Pizza 32
New England Pumpkin Cake 119

O

Oatmeal Apple & Plum Crumble 115
Onion Rings 108
Orange Carrot Cake 121
Orange Cauliflower 110
Oriental Spinach Samosa 111

P

Pancakes 16
Paprika Tofu 43
Parmesan & Garlic Cauliflower 102
Parmesan Artichokes 99
Parmesan Crusted Tilapia 62
Parmesan Zucchini Chips 105
Pasta Salad 43
Pea Delight 24
Peach Crumble 122
Peach Slices 123
Peanut Butter Bread 22
Peanut Butter Cookies 125
Pear & Apple Crisp with Walnuts 117
Pecan Pie 121
Penne Chicken Sausage Meatballs 79
Peppered Puff Pastry 49
Pepperoni Pizza 42
Peppery Turkey Sandwiches 81
Pesto Gnocchi 46
Pesto Stuffed Bella Mushrooms 36
Pineapple Cake 120
Pineapple Sticks 118
Pita Bread Pizza 43
Pizza Stuffed Chicken 80
Pop Corn Broccoli 49
Poppin' Pop Corn Chicken 75
Pork Chops 35
Portabella Pizza 45
Posh Soufflé 24
Potato & Kale Nuggets 22
Potato Cakes & Cajun Chicken Wings 80
Potato Chips 106
Potato Croquettes 39
Potato Gratin 53
Potato Side Dish 51
Potato Totes 107
Potato Wedges 107
Prawns 62
Prosciutto & Potato Salad 44
Prosciutto Spinach Salad 28
Provençal Chicken 80
Pulled Pork 35
Pumpkin Cinnamon Pudding 123
Pumpkin Seeds 72
Puppy Poppers 71

R

Radish Chips 104

Ranch Risotto 20
Randy's Roasted Chicken 86
Raspberry Muffins 121
Raspberry Pudding Surprise 112
Ratatouille 35
Red Rolls 26
Ribs 35
Rice Bowl 36
Rice Paper Bacon 24
Riced Cauliflower & Curry Chicken 28
Ricotta Balls 73
Ricotta Wraps & Spring Chicken 82
Risotto 38
Roast Beef Lettuce Wraps 32
Roasted Brussels Sprouts & Bacon 101
Roasted Carrots 110
Roasted Cauliflower 99
Roasted Chicken 79
Roasted Corn 110
Roasted Eggplant 47
Roasted Garlic, Broccoli & Lemon 42
Roasted Parsnip 67
Roasted Peppers 67
Roasted Potatoes & Cheese 51
Roasted Pumpkin Seeds & Cinnamon 118
Roasted Turkey Thighs 82
Roasted Vegetables 53
Rocket Salad 42
Rosemary Chicken 86
Rosemary Cornbread 52
Rosemary Green Beans 49
Rosemary Rib Eye Steaks 33

S

Sage & Onion Stuffing 71
Sage & Onion Turkey Balls 92
Sage Chicken Escallops 40
Sage Potatoes 73
Salmon & Dill Sauce 64
Salmon Croquettes 62
Salmon Mixed Eggs 64
Salmon Omelet 18
Salmon Patties 60
Saltine Fish Fillets 56
Sausage Balls 31
Sausage Egg Muffins 18
Sausage Quiche 18
Sausage-Chicken Casserole 44
Sautéed Green Beans 49
Scallion & Ricotta Potatoes 50
Scotch Eggs 19
Scrambled Eggs 52
Scrambled Mug Eggs 18
Seafood Fritters 63
Sesame Tuna Steak 54
Shortbread Fingers 117
Shrimp Bites 73
Simple Beef 94
Simple Turkey Breasts 91
Smoked BBQ Toasted s 47

Smoked Beef Roast 94
Snack Mix 70
Southern Fried Chicken 75
Spaghetti Squash 100
Spanish Omelet 17
Special Maple-Glazed Chicken 80
Spiced Nuts 73
Spicy Mackerel 55
Spinach Balls 21
Spinach Eggs and Cheese 19
Spinach Quiche 26
Spinach with Bacon & Shallots 101
Sponge Cake 118
Spring Rolls 97
Sriracha Cauliflower 35
Steak Total 95
Strawberry Frozen Dessert 113
Strawberry Rhubarb Parfait 18
Strawberry Shake 112
Strawberry Turkey 78
Stuffed Bell Pepper 96
Stuffed Chicken Rolls 30
Stuffed Eggplant 99
Stuffed Mushrooms 66
Stuffed Tomatoes 109
Stuffed Turkey Roulade 84
Sugar Butter Fritters 117
Sugar Pork Rinds 124
Sugar Snap Bacon 102
Summer Rolls 36
Sunday's Salmon 58
Swedish Chocolate Mug Cake 122
Swedish Meatballs 95
Sweet & Crisp Bananas 117
Sweet & Sour Tofu 40
Sweet Corn Fritters 52
Sweet Onions & Potatoes 37
Sweet Potato Bites 109
Sweet Potato Curry Fries 53
Sweet Potato Fries 68
Sweet Potato Wedges 107
Sweet Potatoes & Salmon 56
Sweet Potatoes 40
Swirled German Cake 115

T

Taco Stuffed Peppers 32
Taco Wraps 20
Taj Tofu 23
Tarragon Chicken 79
Tasty Tofu 67
Teriyaki Chicken 89
Teriyaki Chicken Wings 77
Thai Turkey Wings 83
Thanksgiving Sprouts 42
Thyme Scallops 55
Tilapia Fillets 64
Toasted Cheese 22
Toasted Coconut Flakes 125
Toasted Pumpkin Seeds 69
Toasties 19

CPSIA information can be obtained
at www.ICGtesting.com
Printed in the USA
LVHW101326160621
690358LV00010B/1430

9 781649 845603